As for the future, your task is not to foresee it, but to enable it.

– Antoine St. Exupéry

I just don't want to make the wrong mistake.

–Yogi Berra

Design of Straw Bale Buildings

The State of the Art

By Bruce King

with contributing authors:
Mark Aschheim
René Dalmeijer
Kevin Donahue
Martin Hammer
Kelly Lerner
David Mar
Dan Smith
Nehemiah Stone
John Straube
Matt Summers
Bob Theis

GREEN BUILDING PRESS

Second Edition

Published by Green Building Press, PO Box 6397, San Rafael, CA 94903
www.greenbuildingpress.com
SAN 256-6559

Manufactured in the USA
Printed on recycled paper

Contributing Authors: Mark Aschheim, René Dalmeijer, Kevin Donahue, Martin Hammer, Kelly Lerner,
David Mar, Dan Smith, Nehemiah Stone, John Straube, Matt Summers, Bob Theis
Illustrations and photos by Bruce King unless noted otherwise, except most of chapter 5, and some that are joint efforts, and
some that we're honestly not sure where they came from but are assured by contributing authors that they're OK and unfettered.
To be perfectly honest, it's pretty near impossible to keep track, what with so many contributors, and everyone so busy all the time,
like trying to sweep up the ants. Mainly, we've tried extra hard with text, photos, and illustrations to give credit where it is due, and
beg forgiveness if and where we may have failed.

Cover photo by Bruce King of the Real Goods Solar Living Center in construction (Hopland, California), designed by Van der Ryn Architects
Back Cover photo by J. D. Peterson of the Camp Arroyo Dining Hall (Livermore, California), designed by Siegel & Strain Architects.
Inset photo by Siegel & Strain.
Edited by Jessie Lawson
Design by Debra Turner

Library of Congress Cataloging-in-Publication Data
Bruce King, Mark Aschheim, René Dalmeijer, Kevin Donahue, Martin Hammer, Kelly Lerner,
David Mar, Dan Smith, Nehemiah Stone, John Straube, Matt Summers, Bob Theis

Design of Straw Bale Buildings: The State of the Art
ISBN 978-0-9764911-1-8
1. Straw Bale Buildings 2. Green Building 3. Architecture and Engineering

dedication

In the twenty or so years since the dawn of the "straw bale revival," innumerable people of brilliance and dedication have given freely of their time to promote and understand the use of straw bales in building structures. All deserve mention and thanks, but six in particular stand out for their noteworthy efforts not just to spread a new building technology, but to make this world, in what manner they could, a better place for all of us and our descendants. It is thus with a profound sense of professional respect, a personal affection normally only exhibited by beagle puppies, a simple but immeasurably sincere "Thank you," and one deep Buddhist bow, that this book is dedicated to these six individuals:

David Bainbridge
David Eisenberg
Judy Knox
Matts Myhrman
Bill Steen
Athena Swentzell-Steen

To see friends come from afar – is that not a delight?

To learn, and then put it into practice – is that not a pleasure?

– the Lün Yu

TABLE OF CONTENTS

Caveats

Caveat 1   *Caveat Emptor*

"Let the buyer beware", as that's generally translated, or, as we prefer, let the builder *be aware*. In the text that follows we have made every effort to be factually correct, up-to-date, and sound in our reasoning. We have assembled this text with the intent that it be as useful and accessible as possible to students, teachers, practicing professionals, and just folks who want to build. Still, errors may linger that no one noticed. Even without any errors, however, buildings are very complicated things, and straw bale construction is still very much a developing technology about which we yet have much to learn. In building, as in life, it's unwise to uncritically accept anything you find in writing. Use your own innate (and enormous) intelligence, also known as common sense, and hire a professional if you aren't sure of anything in the design and construction of your own project. We herein offer what assistance we can, but in the end it is your duty, reader, to know what you know, know what you don't know, worry a bit about what you don't know that you don't know, and proceed with unhurried awareness.

Caveat 2   *A foolish consistency is the hobgoblin of little minds,*
adored by little statesmen and philosophers and divines
                    – Ralph Waldo Emerson, *Self-Reliance*

We hear you, Ralph, and take your comment to heart. In the text that follows, we have made an enormous but nonetheless imperfect effort to always say "inches" rather than "in." or " " ", to provide translation from the olde King's wacky system of measures (e.g., "pounds per square foot") to the eminently practical metric system (e.g., "newtons per square meter"), and in general to cleave to the hallowed *Chicago Manual of Style*, the Bible of the written word. Our intent, however, was not to beat our brains out trying to be consistent in such things as to make the entire narrative clear, comprehensive, and, again, accessible. To those who cannot tolerate such irregularities we can only say: Please do get over it, and discern the woods for the trees in finding the value we hope to deliver. (And, let no discredit fall upon our very capable editor, Jessie Lawson, who did her best to correct our wandering verbal ways.)

Caveat 3   *It don't mean a thing if it ain't got that swing*
                 Shoo be doo bah, shoo be doo bah
                 shoo be doo bah, shoo be doo bah

                                              – Ella Fitzgerald

The hallowed tradition in engineering literature is to write in a thorough, deliberate style that dares and challenges the reader to remain awake. Try though we did to honor and maintain that style, levity and even whimsy have seeped in, very much like the way water gets into our buildings despite our many efforts to keep it out. For those who are appalled at the commingling of engineering calculations with Yogi Berra quotes, pictures of hula girls, and Roz Chast cartoons, we can only say, in the hallowed tradition of this page: Please do get over it.

Preface

This book is a collaborative effort in several ways, and would simply not be possible but for the enormous generosity and refreshing ingenuity of innumerable individuals. Particular thanks must go to the State of California's Department of Food and Agriculture, which supplied a large grant to the Ecological Building Network (EBNet) in support of the testing and research that underlies much of this text. Additional underwriting came from the California Straw Building Association (CASBA), the New Mexico Straw Building Association, the Ontario Straw Building Association, the Straw Building Association of Texas, and supportive individuals too many to mention – but let's try:

David Arkin, Anand Arya, Cale Ash, Michael Augustine, David Bainbridge, Laura Bartels, Joy and Maurice Bennett, Bob Bolles, Peter Boyer, Danny Buck, Bill Camp, Bill Christensen, Joyce Coppinger, René Dalmeijer, Darcey Donovan, Bill Druc, Ann Edminster, Doug Eichelberger, David and Pat Eisenberg, Mike Faine, Don Fugler, Pete Fust, Terry Gamble, John "Wolfman" Glassford, Rick Green, Martin Hammer, Marcus Hardwick, Maria Inglesby, Michael Jacob, Bryan Jenkins, Janet Johnston-Armstrong, George Kiskaddon, Judy Knox, Paul Lacinski, Jessie Lawson, Dennis LaGrande, Lori Leyrer, Duncan Lithgow, Dietmar Lorenz, Chris Magwood, Greg McMillan, Frank Meyer, Gernot Minke, Mom, Hugh Morris, Matts Myhrmann, Chris Newton, Graeme North, Ben Obregon, Rick Okawa, Harry Partridge, Mark Piepkorn, Kurt Rhyner, Keith Robertson, Derek Roff, Tim Rudolph, Jeff Ruppert, Mark Schueneman, Siegel & Strain Architects, Turko Semmes, Bill Steen, Athena Swentzell-Steen, Roland Stulz, John Swearingen, Anni Tilt, Daniel Torrealva, Debra Turner, Greg Van Mechelen, Peter Walker, Catherine Wanek, Andrew Webb, Marge Weller, Buddy "Mojo" Williams, Delilah Woods, Tom Woolley, and John Zhang.

Each of the EBNet test program designers gave freely and hugely of time they could hardly spare, over and over again, to make the testing program – and now this text – all that it is. Special mention and thanks thus go heartily and sincerely out to: Mark Aschheim, Kevin Donahue, Kelly Lerner, David Mar, Tim Owen-Kennedy, Dan Smith, Nehemiah Stone, John Straube, Matt Summers, and Bob Theis.

The world of straw bale construction is liberally populated with thoughtful, passionate, knowledgeable, fun and visionary people. Thus, the research and production of this book has been a source of new friendships and pleasure for its authors, even if at times a bit too all-consuming an effort. With that perspective in mind, we want to acknowledge and thank for their forbearance the many spouses, boyfriends, girlfriends, clients, partners, family, children, and pets who didn't see as much of us recently as (we like to think, anyway) they might have preferred.

Bruce King
San Rafael, California

About the Authors

Mark Aschheim

is an associate professor in the Department of Civil Engineering at Santa Clara University. Previously, he was on the faculty of the University of Illinois, after receiving his doctoral, master's, and bachelor's degrees from the University of California, Berkeley. Dr. Aschheim works in the area of earthquake-resistant structural engineering through activities with the Applied Technology Council and participation on building code committees of the Building Seismic Safety Council and the American Concrete Institute. Dr. Aschheim is a registered professional engineer in California.

René Dalmeijer

was born in South Africa and moved to the Netherlands, where he obtained a bachelor's degree in building physics and structural engineering. After working in HVAC (Heating, Ventilating, and Air Conditioning) consulting engineering, information technology, 3D CAD software, and building consulting, he finally became a full-time straw bale/sustainable building contractor in June 2005. Presently he is president of *Strobouw Nederland,* the Dutch SB association.

Kevin Donahue

is a registered structural engineer in private practice in Berkeley, California, and a mathematical wizard. He claims to also play the accordion, and to have done so on stage at the legendary Fillmore Auditorium in San Francisco, but we are not so sure that we want proof.

Martin Hammer

Martin Hammer is an architect in private practice in Berkeley, California. He received a Bachelor of Architecture from New Jersey Institute of Technology in 1980, and has been involved in the design and construction of straw bale buildings since 1995. He is lead author of the currently proposed Strawbale Construction Appendix to the California Building Code, and also, hopefully, the International Building Code.

Bruce King

is a registered professional engineer in private practice in Sausalito, California. He is the author of *Buildings of Earth and Straw/ Structural Design for Straw Bale and Rammed Earth Architecture* (1996) and *Making Better Concrete / Guidelines to Using Fly Ash for Higher Quality, Eco-Friendly Structures* (2005), and is founder and co-owner with his wife, Sarah, of the Green Building Press. He is also the founder and director of the non-profit Ecological Building Network (www.ecobuildnet-work.org). He is the recipient of the Big Head Award for Excellence in Furthering the Understanding of Ecological Building, from the California Straw Building Association, but is not certain that it was intended to be laudatory.

Kelly Lerner

received her Master's Degree in Architecture from the University of Oregon, and is a licensed architect in California and Washington. After graduation, Kelly traveled to China, Mongolia, and Argentina, building homes and public buildings using natural materials. Kelly was presented the 2005 World Habitat Award at the United Nations/UN-HABITAT "World Habitat Day" celebration in Jakarta Indonesia, for her work on the Chinese Straw-Bale Energy Efficient Housing Project. Working with the Adventist Development and Relief Agency (ADRA), she spearheaded the introduction of straw bale construction to China and built over 600 straw bale houses and three straw bale schools in five northeastern provinces in a project funded by Kadoorie Foundation of Hong Kong.

David Mar

is a registered structural engineer and partner in the firm Tipping-Mar + associates in Berkeley, California. He has received numerous awards for his innovative work in seismic design, including the 1999 National Council of Structural Engineers Associations Best Structure Award, 1998 Structural Engineers Association of California Engineering Excellence Award, 1998 Structural Engineers Association of Northern California H.J. Brunnier Award for Excellence in Design, 2002 Excellence in Structural Engineering award from the Structural Engineers Association of Northern California (for a vaulted straw bale structure), 2001 Outstanding Project Award from the National Council of Structural Engineers Associations, a 2001 Structural Engineering Excellence Award from the Structural Engineers Association of California, and a 2001 Excellence in Structural Engineering Award from the Structural Engineers Association of Northern California.

Dan Smith

has over twenty years of experience as principal in the firm DSA Architects in Berkeley, California. Dan was trained at Yale University and the University of California at Berkeley, and it was during this time that he developed a strong interest in sustainable design practices.

Nehemiah Stone

is a Director with the award-winning Heschong Mahone Group in Fair Oaks, California, where he provides energy efficiency related assistance to housing authorities and affordable housing owners. Mr. Stone was a contributor to both the California Energy Commission's and Pacific Gas and Electric Company's efforts to research and develop revisions to Title 24 Building Energy Efficiency Standards for 2005. Immediately after joining HMG, he managed the development of the statewide nonresidential new construction program, Savings By Design. Prior to joining Heschong Mahone Group, he was recruited by the California Energy Commission in 1989 to help rewrite the state's Building Energy Standards. Prior to joining the CEC, he was a home builder, building inspector, plans examiner, chief building inspector for Humboldt County, California, and instructor in energy efficient design at the College of the Redwoods, (Eureka, California). He received his bachelor's in Economics and Environmental Studies from California State University at Sacramento.

John Straube

has an outstanding global reputation for his work in the areas of building enclosure design, moisture physics, and whole building performance as a consultant, researcher, and educator. Dr. Staube is a faculty member in the Department of Civil Engineering and the School of Architecture at the University of Waterloo, where he received his doctor's, master's, and bachelor's degrees, and teaches courses in structural design and building science in both disciplines. He has broad experience in the building industry, having been involved in the design, construction, repair and restoration of buildings in Europe, Asia, the Caribbean, the United States and Canada. As a structural engineer he has designed with wood, hot-rolled and cold-formed steel, concrete, masonry (brick, concrete, aerated autoclaved concrete, natural stone), aluminum, polymer concrete, carbon and glass FRP, fibre-reinforced concrete and structural plastics (PVC, nylon). Dr. Straube also provides expert witness investigations and work on energy efficiency, durability, and indoor air quality. Current interests include the optimal system design of buildings, sustainable buildings, and moisture problem avoidance. Like Bruce King, he is the recipient of the Big Head Award for outstanding contributions to the understanding of natural building and, like Bruce King, is not sure what to make of it.

Matt Summers

earned his doctorate at the University of California at Davis studying the decay rates and mechanisms of rice straw decomposition. He now serves as a consultant on issues related to bio-based renewable energy.

Bob Theis

is a registered architect in private practice in Berkeley, California. Bob came to California from New York City to study architecture with Chris Alexander, and stayed. He designs lots of straw bale buildings, and his focus these days is bringing social spaces to life.

Nature to be controlled must be obeyed.

– Sir Francis Bacon

INTRODUCTION

The oldest known straw bale structure in the world reached the century mark in 2003, an anniversary of both sentimental and technological significance. The historic Burke house in the little town of Alliance, Nebraska (United States) would not necessarily catch your eye as an architectural wonder, or even oddity, yet its presence there is intimately connected to the book in your hands. Had that modest little home and many like it not survived to this day, then straw bale construction might never have caught the skeptical interest of a few builders, this book's authors, or the public at large.

Those first straw bale structures in the Sand Hills of Nebraska were built by European settlers entering the area from the 1800s onwards. Having few other means to shelter themselves, they were driven by necessity to improvise; there was little stone or cement, the sod was often too sandy to cut or too valuable as cropland, and most of the available lumber was what little had come on their wagons. Using the newly invented horse-powered baling machines, they bundled the grasses that surrounded them, stacked the bales to form walls, and applied mud plasters inside and out. Many of those homes still exist in good shape, as do a few more in other parts of the world where baling machines had appeared over the subsequent decades. This was the birth of a promising and completely new building technology, yet with roots in various historic forms of earth and straw-based construction that were widespread in Europe. Nonetheless, as the Industrial Revolution spread in the form of railroads and modern building materials, interest in straw bale construction faded.

In the 1980s the American West witnessed a revival, initially sporadic, generated by some obscure published articles and the scattered efforts of a few architects and owner-builders. In 1989, some of those latter-day pioneers gathered in Oracle, Arizona to play, collaborate, and imagine how best to build with bales; a few newspaper articles followed, interest blossomed, and the straw bale revival suddenly was and still is exploding in size. As more architects, engineers, inventors, and builders began to try this new material, a variety of styles and techniques began to emerge. There are now straw bale health clinics in Mongolia and China, wineries in Australia and California, a prince's palace in Saudi Arabia, a post office in New Mexico, a Buddhist monastery in New York, retail stores, schools, police stations and high-end luxury homes in California, and thousands of houses of every style all over the world. Field experience and laboratory experiments have taught some basic lessons that will be articulated in this book, but straw bale construction remains very much a developing technology. As is the case with any building material, there is no "right way" to build independent of climate and rainfall, soils and earthquake hazard, building usage, and architectural style. There are many right ways to build with straw bales – and many wrong ways. Many bale building techniques, first rediscovered almost entirely from a short article by Roger Welsch published in the book *Shelter*[1], were inherited from the first Nebraska settlers. Steel or wood pins driven down through the bales to stabilize them, for example, were codified in the first modern straw bale guidelines. But "pinning" is no longer thought to contribute strength or be worth the trouble, and has been largely abandoned. In any event, publicity fueled popularity, and to this day public interest worldwide has stayed well ahead of engineering knowledge about straw bale structures.

The explosive rise in interest has resulted in thousands of built straw bale structures throughout the globe, and a small and increasing number of books on the subject. (For more general discussions of straw bale construction, and access to a wealth of photographic images, see the *Resources* section at the end of the book.) To date, however, there have been relatively few resources to help architects and engineers design straw bale structures to endure the driving rain, humidity, extremes of hot and cold, fire, wind, and earthquakes that routinely cause the early demise of buildings of all types around the world. In responding to the question "How will this building perform?" we have relied mostly on intuition and anecdotal evidence.

Now, with the completion of many tests in recent years, we have a much clearer picture of how straw bale buildings behave under the normal range of stresses that affect structures. This book is a review of all those tests and of the anecdotal knowledge gained over a hundred years (particularly the last fifteen). It is also a studied effort to digest and present that knowledge in a way that can be of practical use. This is architecture and construction at its most elemental: we try things out, we make mistakes, we learn, we adapt, and we thus build our knowledge of how to build. It may be that an architectural straw bale vocabulary will emerge as our understanding of the material evolves – just as it did with stone, wood, structural steel, and reinforced concrete – and the intent of this book is to lay down a rational foundation on which to develop the architecture of straw bales.

Context

The re-emergence of straw bale construction over the past fifteen years has occurred within a particularly hospitable environment, in the United States and around the world. *Green building* in general has become a commonplace term, referring to the design, construction, and maintenance of buildings that are careful in the use of material, human, and energy resources to create shelter, with great regard given to protecting not only the building occupants but also the local and global system of life from which those resources are drawn. Green building means building with the welfare of future generations, not just this one, and not just human, in mind. Straw bale construction, by virtue of being unusual and photogenic – and thus the star of innumerable media pieces – has been the introduction for quite a few people to the wider concerns of green building for healthy interior environments, energy efficiency, and waste reduction. It is also a classic example of what has been dubbed *Industrial Ecology,* i.e., the idea that one industry's waste can be another's feedstock. What the farmer throws away, the builder turns into warm, durable houses.

The Internet has also been key to the growth of straw bale construction, as the sudden ubiquity of Web access has made it astonishingly easy for the nascent straw bale community – for lack of a better word for a very loose-knit worldwide group

IMPORTANT
DISTINCTION

Top image: little grass shack in Hawai'i

Bottom image: straw bale house

Bottom image courtesy of
David Bainbridge

of inventors, builders, scientists, architects, and engineers – to communicate, collaborate, and learn from mistakes. And, as straw bale construction remains almost completely in the public domain, there is little protection of secrets or glossing-over of mistakes. Quite in contrast with other building technologies that are jealously guarded, the non-proprietary nature of straw bale building – with a few exceptions – has kept innovation, refinement, and failures out in the open for all to learn from.

Finally, it bears mentioning that straw bale construction is perhaps the most visible part of a revival of interest in "natural" building, generally understood to mean use of minimally-processed materials with roots in historic or indigenous (i.e., pre-Industrial Revolution) ways of building. Before fossil-fueled engines enabled us to move any material anywhere in the world, and to make building materials themselves from oil, we had to build with what was at hand. The extraordinary range of styles and material uses that evolved over the centuries is being rediscovered for the ingenuity and experience that went into them. (See, for example, *Built by Hand*[2].) What are routinely derided as "mud huts" and "grass shacks" often, if not always, turn out to be very effective means of shelter (as architectural conservators the world over already know). The adobe buildings of the American Southwest, the lime-plastered timber-frame houses of medieval Europe, and the Roman concrete monuments, to choose just three examples, have all proven themselves to be in many ways superior to the "modern" structures that now surround them. Thus, building professionals who have taken an interest in straw bale construction have been startled to discover that there is so much to be learned from the old ways – that we have very nearly thrown out the baby with the bathwater in abandoning everything old in favor of anything new. Perhaps the preeminent example is what we've learned about the interrelationship of moisture and buildings. We invented plastic sheeting and then figured we could shrink-wrap our buildings to keep all the water out – and ended up trapping it in and getting great mounds of mold. Ditto with cement plaster, which has been applied to ill effect over historic earthen buildings around the world, and which can cause – and hide – moisture degradation in wood-framed walls. Slowly we're re-learning what our ancestors had always understood: buildings get wet no matter what you do, so in your design and construction, always provide a means for them to dry out. In the case of straw bale construction, for example, this knowledge of the old ways has led to favoring vapor-permeable earthen and lime plasters over more brittle cement-based plasters, while utilizing modern steel or plastic reinforcing meshes and fasteners to deal with earthquake forces.

This is not to suggest an anti-technology or neo-Luddite view of building so much as to point out that, as with all other domains of life, it's worth knowing a bit of history. The most effective way of building any particular project employs not so much primitive or modern, but *appropriate* technology. (John F.C. Turner best defined this by saying, "Truly appropriate technology is technology that ordinary people can use for their own benefit and the benefit of their community that doesn't make them dependent on systems over which they have no control.") As the easy availability of fossil fuels decreases with the attendant rise in fuel costs, there will inevitably be a trend towards building with what is near at hand. We won't return to "mud huts" and "grass shacks"; we'll simply learn to be smarter in the way we build, and we'll eliminate the very concept of waste.

Systems thinking – no material is an island

This book may be unusual just for advancing our engineering perspective on a hitherto obscure building material: straw bales. It is also somewhat unusual for addressing several engineering properties under one cover, i.e., structure, moisture, durability, fire, and thermal insulation. This is reflective of the fact that a plastered straw bale assembly *is* structure, insulation, air barrier, finish, and fire resistance all in one – as opposed to most building materials, which typically perform only one or two of the requisite functions of a building enclosure.

The book is also organized to reflect an emerging development in the way buildings are thought about and designed. The past several decades have seen increasing specialization in the architecture and engineering professions, spawned in large part by rapidly increasing proliferation of and knowledge about building methods and materials. A moderately large or complex project may have design architects, project architects, landscape architects, construction administrators, disability access specialists, lighting and energy consultants, interior designers, and engineers of every stripe: structural, mechanical, electrical, civil, acoustical, etc. Each specialist addresses his or her own aspect of the design, theoretically under the watchful, knowledgeable, capable, and all-seeing eye of the project architect. Sometimes the system works; sometimes it doesn't. This is not said as a criticism of architects so much as to point out that without some form of capable and holistic overview, the designed building may not function as intended, or even fail outright. Those who design with straw bales are generally aware of this, and thus have discovered and embraced both *collaborative design* – working and communicating as a team from start to finish – as well as the emerging body of knowledge known as *building science,* which comprehensively considers the effects of temperature, moisture, vapor, air flow, and structural stresses – along with aesthetics – in designing a building enclosure or detail. You get the big picture, or you get problems: good design is important, yes, but a pretty house that cracks, leaks and rots is no longer pretty.

This is intended to serve as an engineering guidebook. It has been written as much as possible to be accessible to any building professional, or even layman, but will inevitably have sections that are obscure without an engineering background. Nevertheless, in contrast with many other engineering texts, no problem-and-answer sections are provided. More importantly, the book offers few cookbook formulas that might delude the reader into a false sense of design confidence. It is simply not yet possible to comprehensively delineate a prescriptive way of designing or building with straw bales, if in fact it really is with any building material. The technology, as mentioned, is still rapidly developing, so we have focused on identifying rules where they have become clear ("Keep those bales dry!"). Otherwise our aim is to present underlying principles by which the reader can work out site-specific building challenges. Common sense, and a knowledge of local culture and climate, have always been and will continue to be the overarching guidelines for any building designer.

ENDNOTES

1
Welsch, Roger 1973.
Shelter Shelter
Publications, Inc,
Bolinas, California

2
Steen, Bill and Athena,
and Eiko and Yoshio
Komatsu, 2003.
Built by Hand
Gibbs-Smith Publishers,
Layton, Utah

In the hundred years since straw bale building was first pioneered, the basic technique has remained as straightforward as stacking the bales and plastering both sides. Our knowledge of the material properties of these walls has blossomed in tandem with the extraordinary revival of the past fifteen years, and we now are now equipped, at least roughly, to design for any conditions. That there are enormous environmental and energy-conserving benefits to straw bale construction is now without question, so any strategy to move the construction industry towards a sustainable course must allow for and encourage this intriguing new building technology. This text offers to designers and builders a sound scientific and common-sense basis for exploring and contributing to the development of plastered straw bale architecture.

THE FIRST PERMITTED
EARTH-PLASTERED HOUSE
IN CALIFORNIA (WITH
LIME PLASTER FINISH)

*Design by Kelly Lerner
and Pete Gang*

photo courtesy of Kelly Lerner

He had driven half the night from far down San Joaquin
Through Mariposa, up the dangerous mountain roads,
and pulled in at eight a.m. with his big truckload of hay behind the barn
with winch and ropes and hooks we stacked the bales up clean
to splintery redwood rafters high in the dark, flecks of alfalfa
whirling through shingle-cracks of light, itch of haydust in the sweaty shirt and shoes.

At lunchtime under Black oak out in the hot corral,
— The old mare nosing lunchpails, grasshoppers crackling in the weeds —

"I'm sixty-eight" he said, "I first bucked hay when I was seventeen.
I thought, that day I started, I sure would hate to do this all my life.
And dammit, that's just what I've gone and done."

—Gary Snyder, *Hay for the Horses*
from *Riprap and Cold Mountain Poems*

STRAW AND BALES

COMMON STRAW BALES

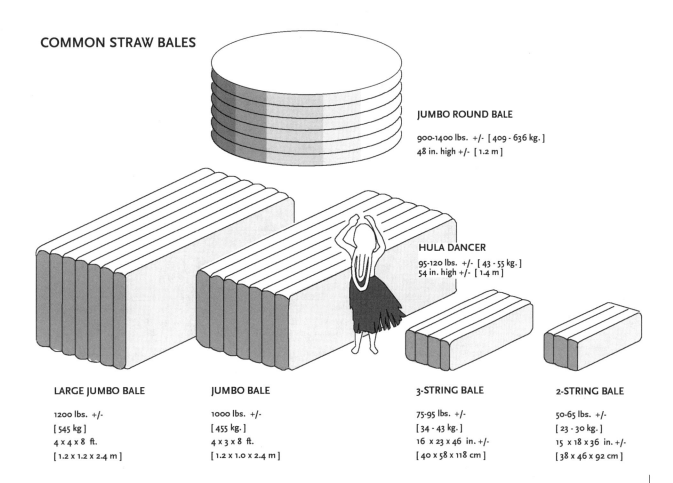

JUMBO ROUND BALE

900-1400 lbs. +/- [409 - 636 kg.]
48 in. high +/- [1.2 m]

HULA DANCER
95-120 lbs. +/- [43 - 55 kg.]
54 in. high +/- [1.4 m]

LARGE JUMBO BALE

1200 lbs. +/-
[545 kg]
4 x 4 x 8 ft.
[1.2 x 1.2 x 2.4 m]

JUMBO BALE

1000 lbs. +/-
[455 kg.]
4 x 3 x 8 ft.
[1.2 x 1.0 x 2.4 m]

3-STRING BALE

75-95 lbs. +/-
[34 - 43 kg.]
16 x 23 x 46 in. +/-
[40 x 58 x 118 cm]

2-STRING BALE

50-65 lbs. +/-
[23 - 30 kg.]
15 x 18 x 36 in. +/-
[38 x 46 x 92 cm]

1.1 Straw

Farmers know what the rest of us generally don't: straw is the tubular plant structure between the roots and the grain head, whereas hay is straw that includes the grain — the protein and carbohydrate-rich fruit of the plant. Hay is for horses; straw is for buildings. Many kinds of straw can be baled and used for building, such as the meadow hay used by the first known bale builders in Nebraska. But by far the most prevalent are those produced from the harvesting of cereal grains. Most straw bales, in other words, are the byproduct of our food production.

The small-scale properties of straw — such as the fact that most straw has a much higher tensile strength than softwood — are generally not as important to straw bale construction as are the properties of bales themselves. Still, it is worth reviewing some basics of plant structure and chemistry, pointing out those properties of particular interest or concern.

Straw, like wood, is a lignocellulosic plant, composed by volume of the following constituents in descending order. The actual proportions and chemistry of the components varies greatly with the type and weather exposure of the plant; the proportions below are averaged values for rice straw:

Cellulose (about 40% of volume) Very long cellulose microfibrils consisting of crystalline regions and less well-ordered regions provide the tensile strength and "structure" of the plant.

Hemicellulose (about 25% of volume) Shorter and less crystalline hemicellulose molecules act as a structural adhesive to bind the long cellulose fibers.

Ash and other minor constituents, mainly silicon dioxide (about 20% of volume, generally less in non-rice species) The more of this silica ash present in the plant, the better the resistance to fire and decay.

Lignin (about 15% of volume) Lignin is the glue that binds the whole thing together, akin to the way concrete surrounds rebar to create a composite structure. Photochemical degradation caused by ultraviolet radiation takes place mainly in the lignin component (visible to us as color change, that is, fading and weathering). In contrast to the carbohydrates, lignin is the most stable element of the straw — oil and coal deposits are sources of prehistoric lignin. Modern pulp and paper plants extract the lignin from wood pulp and then use its high caloric value as fuel.

Two particular qualities of straw affect bales, and thus bear discussion.

1. Type of grain From a building perspective, there seems to be little difference among the qualities of most of the different cereal grains such as wheat, barley, oats, and rye. There are, however, two factors that make rice straw bales better than all others: the higher silica content makes the straw more resistant to decay, and the slightly barbed surface of the straw makes the strands tend to "grab" each other, resulting in bales that remain coherent even when cut or untied (see figure 1.1A). How much superiority there really is depends on which strains of grain you are talking about, and it has not been methodically studied, but builders in California will often import rice bales from hundreds of miles away even when other bales are locally available.

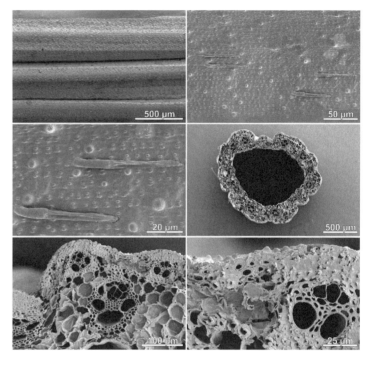

1.1A

RICE STRAW UNDER SCANNING ELECTRON MICROSCOPE.

The surface fibers seen in the upper right and center left pictures probably contribute to the ability of individual stalks to interlock, giving the bale more coherence.

photos courtesy of Delilah F. Wood, USDA-ARS-WRRC, Albany, CA

2. Fertilizers Many people have argued for the use of organically grown straw for building bales, on the logic that agricultural pesticides shouldn't, for health reasons, be buried within the structure of a building. There may or may not be merit to that argument, depending on which exact pesticide is in question. Some pesticides degrade into inert matter long before the straw is even baled, while others might remain pernicious for years. Evaluation of pesticides and their importance must be left to each individual case, considering both the batch of bales and the sensitivities of builders and occupants.

More generally relevant to bale building is the distinction between *fertilized,* whether organic or petrochemically based, and *non-fertilized* straw. We add nitrogen, phosphorus, and other substances to the soil in the form of manure or processed pellets to hasten plant growth and/or increase yield, and then pay a price (from the perspective of bale building) by getting straw much more susceptible to rot. The higher nitrogen content of straw from fertilized plants is widely known to farmers to hasten the rate at which the straw will decompose back into soil. That's great for the farmer, bad for the builder. Given the nature of modern large-scale agriculture, this is a distinction of mere footnote importance to people in the industrialized countries; the bales you can readily buy are from fertilized plants.

1.2A

BALE STACK AND A SELF-PROPELLED BALING MACHINE

photograph courtesy of Bryan Jenkins, University of California, Davis

1.2B FUZZY BRICKS

The typical rectangular bale usually has a lot of surface irregularities – loose straw pieces on the verge of falling out, and bulges reflecting variations in the binding pressure of the tie strings. Good building practice is to (sometimes) trim each bale with a weed-whacker or a chainsaw prior to installation in the wall, and always to trim the wall surface prior to plastering. The dark discoloration in the center of the pictured bale indicates decay – possibly enough to reject it for building.

1.2 Bales

Bales are masses of straw compressed and bound into rectangular blocks. Polypropylene twine is the most common tie, but wire, hemp, and other types of baling line are sometimes used. Building bales might be the smaller *two-string* or slightly larger *three-string,* and like most masonry blocks are most stable and strong when stacked in a running bond. Much larger bales, both rectangular and circular, are increasingly common in industrialized countries, and have been used in some building structures. Their sheer size, however, requires machinery such as forklifts just to move and place them.

Bales are usually stacked *flat,* i.e., with the longest dimension parallel to the wall, and the shortest dimension vertical. In other applications, the bales can be stacked *on edge,* i.e., with the shortest dimension horizontal.

In the mechanized bale production typical of the industrialized countries, bales are made by stuffing masses of straw into chambers whose cross-sections define the bale's two smaller dimensions. The straw is stuffed in pulses that become *flakes*—semi-discrete masses of straw about 3 to 4 inches (75 - 100 mm) thick which stack like books on a shelf to comprise the bale. After the stack reaches a minimum length, the machine cuts along one side or face and ties off the bales. The cutting process leaves a face consisting mostly of exposed straw ends – the *cut* face as it's known – leaving the opposite face to be called, somewhat misleadingly, the *folded* face. When cut and folded faces are left exposed in the stacked wall, common practice is to alternate back and forth, with equal numbers of cut and folded faces showing on each side of the wall. The length of the bale will often vary by +/-10% due to irregularities in the moisture and stiffness of the straw and flakes.

The typical straw bale is bound with two or three strings of polypropylene twine, and is relatively easy for one man or woman to handle. In other words, bales as farmers have always made them are, generally, just fine for construction. Nevertheless, experience and some laboratory testing strongly show that five qualities determine the utility of a bale for building:

1. Moisture content The drier the better — very generally, a moisture content hovering for an extended period of days above 30% and 40° F is considered cause for worry about decay. (See section 5.3.)

2. Density Dry density (i.e., with moisture content accounted for and subtract-

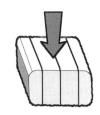

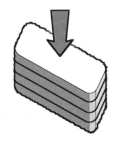

1.2C

FLAT (ABOVE) VS. *ON EDGE* BALE (BELOW) STACKING AND LOADING

ed) should generally be at least six pounds per cubic foot (96 kg/m³) if the bales are intended for load-bearing or shear walls, and should be bound tightly enough that lifting a bale by one string will leave no more than about a fist-sized gap between bale and string.

3. History Bales that have been moistened once or repeatedly will show grey or black

KNOW THY BALES!

Whether you are buying bales or making your own, identify and obtain the bales to be used before designing any structure. Their dimensions are logically the modules by which the overall building is sized, and by which doors and windows are, ideally, sized and located. Why? Because cutting and retying partial size bales to fit odd spaces is time-consuming and therefore expensive. Just as production homebuilders in the United States will design buildings to fit carefully to the 16 and 24 inch modules of modern lumber, plywood, and other materials, a bale builder should know and work with the building module given by the bales' average dimensions— especially the vertical dimension, and especially for load-bearing structures.

Example: As this text was being drafted, new baling machines were appearing in California that produced three-string bales 14 1/2 inches x 22 1/2 inches in cross-section, where formerly they had been 15 inches x 23 inches. That half-inch difference may not seem like much—and often just isn't—but can also make for problems with wall dimensioning or foundation bolt layout. For example, six-course walls based on 15 inch high bales become 3 inches (8 cm) shorter, requiring modifications to other building dimensions.

areas where mold spores have begun proliferating. Such bales should always be discarded, even if very dry at the time of construction, as they are especially prone to experience problems if the wall is ever wetted.

4. Fiber length A concern to bale builders is the type of combine used to harvest the straw – conventional combines leave long straw fibers (which are good for building), while rotary combines chop the straw into short fibers (which makes for unstable, "crumbly" bales). Experienced builders look for average fiber lengths of at least 10 inches (25 cm).

5. *Straw, not hay* The original straw bale buildings in Nebraska used meadow hay, seeds and all, and many have lasted well. That said, it bears repeating that *hay* (i.e., bales containing a significant amount of seed or grain) is for horses, because the grain is carbohydrate that attracts insects and other animals, and is more inclined to rot. *Straw* (i.e., bales with minimal or no grain) is best for building.

1.2D

BALES TRANSPORTED BY FLATBED TRUCK

photograph courtesy of Bryan Jenkins, University of California, Davis

Remember:
Amateurs built the Ark,
Professionals built the Titanic
                          − Anonymous

2

THE STRAW BALE FAMILY TREE

2.1A

A classic timber frame home from medieval Europe, framed with heavy timbers treated with pine tar or other natural protection. The walls were infilled with a packed straw-clay mix that was then plastered with lime. In addition to its high vapor permeability, this building type is very durable because it sheds water away from itself everywhere it can − at the roof, at windowsills, and even by building the floors to overhang the wall below with drip edges.

photo courtesy of John Straube

With the invention of the horse-powered baling machine about 140 years ago, the invention of straw bale construction was soon to follow. That development in the Sand Hills of Nebraska occurred within the far older context of European straw-clay construction − of which those early settlers were likely aware − and has of late spawned a number of new developments. This is a cursory look both back into history and forward to present and imminent developments in the marketplace.

2.1 Historic Precursors to Straw Bale Construction

Straw-clay construction

Various traditions date back as much as thousands of years, in areas all over the world, of building walls by packing straw mixed with clay into or onto wood frames. Some, generally known as *wattle and daub*, involved packing the straw-clay mixture around a basketlike weaving of reeds, canes, bamboo, or wood. Another, more local to northern European and some Asian countries, involves densely packing straw soaked in light clay slip between the timbers of a stout wooden frame. Typically the straw-clay was then coated with lime plaster, producing the classic effect of white panels surrounded by exposed timber frames − mythologized in children's fairy tales, and horribly imitated in American housing tracts.

Cob construction

Cob could be thought of as heavy straw-clay − much more clay and sand than straw − that doesn't require a wood frame nor any formwork; lumps (cobs) of material are packed and sculpted by hand into walls and vaults. As with straw-clay, cob construction has a long history in many parts of the world (in some cases continuing through to the present), most famously in southwest England and Arabia. It is also enjoying a modest revival in various parts of the world where it had previously been unknown or had fallen into disfavor.

2.1B

Adobe church in Abiquiu, New Mexico, United States.

Adobe

Mud brick, sun-dried brick, or *adobe* (from the Arabic *a-daube*) are the oldest known, and still the most common, building elements on earth (rendering somewhat ironic their brief mention in modern building codes as "alternative" or "archaic"). Easy and cheap to produce, they can be thought of as cob bricks, occupying the far end of a spectrum of straw-clay building blocks: on one end, pure blocks of straw, aka straw bales, and on the other, pure, or nearly pure, blocks of clay and sand – adobes. In between those two extremes, as many are discovering, are innumerable variations in terms of size, composition (varying types and proportions of clay, sand, straw, and other additives and stabilizers), and density. Quite a lot of research has been done in the past decade on the properties of adobe structures, particularly under moisture and seismic loads. In addition, the traditional adobe has been updated to include both compressed adobe and stabilized adobe (typically with asphalt bitumen or cement), and a fair amount of research is available about those as well.

2.2 Some New Offshoots of Straw Bale Construction

2.2.1 Other kinds of straw bales

With the increased mechanization of farms, and the need to be able to move straw around more efficiently, other types of bales are beginning to predominate in the industrialized world:

1. **Jumbo bales** Rectangular blocks bound with six or ten strings, of a typical size like 3 x 4 x 8 feet (1 M x 1.3 M x 2.2 M), which can only be handled with mechanized equipment. Compressive strengths of jumbo barley bales well within the elastic range have been measured (Schmidt, 2003) at +/- 20 psi (138 kPa), with Elastic Moduli of +/- 55 psi (380 kPa).

2. **Circular bales** Thick disks bound with twine, of typical dimension 3 feet thick x 6 feet in diameter [1 M x 2 M] – also only handled with machinery.

3. Supercompressed bales Ordinary bales (or straw) compressed to roughly twice the normal density, making for bales weighing 120 to 150 pounds (+/- 18 pcf). Compressive strengths of on-edge bluegrass bales were measured (Stephens, 2000) up to the elastic limit of 17 psi [117 kPa], with an Elastic Modulus – substantially higher than ordinary bales – of 992 psi [6840 kPa].

According to emails and journal articles over the past few years, each of these has been tried in building structures in (at least) North America and Australia. So far as this author knows, they work very well, and though comparatively little testing as been done, would presumably have load-carrying capacities even better than ordinary bales simply because they are so massive or dense. The disadvantage, of course, is that they require machinery to move around and place in walls. (See beginning of chapter 1, *Straw and Bales,* for illustration.)

2.2.2 Plastic and other baled materials
Jean Nielsen built an experimental load-bearing structure of paper bales at the University of Arizona some years ago, and others have experimented with baled paper, cardboard, and many types of plant fiber, but there have been no reports as yet of promising developments.

2.2A
PLASTIC BALES

photographs courtesy of
Doug Eichelberger and George Nez

Architect/builder Doug Eichelberger is experimenting with baled plastic water bottles, and collaborating students at the University of Colorado conducted a cursory battery of tests[1] from which the following comments are drawn.

Advances in technology or changes in economic conditions can affect a building material's viability, availability, and usage. As an example, plastic is a petroleum product; thus its price follows the price of oil. Today [2005] in the United States discarded water bottles have a recycled value of as much as $0.30 per pound, partly due to material value and partly due to labor and transportation costs. These costs have risen exponentially in the past ten years, and in some cases this kind of plastic used for a foundation may cost as much as concrete. However, agencies such as the World Health Organization have noted the growing problem of plastic waste in developing countries. This problem is hugely exacerbated after a war or natural catastrophe ravages an area, triggering an influx of food, water, and other aid in plastic bottles and packaging. Could baled waste plastic be a shelter solution for developing countries? Plastic as a raw material has an extremely long life, is mois-ture- and decay-resistant, and is lightweight and strong. The building technology is both simple and ancient: stacking blocks or bales of materials on top of each other to create walls.

Building a test structure is the best means of trying out a new material, both for its inherent properties and as a system. In the 1990s Doug Eichelberger built the first permitted prototype, a 36 x 48 foot [11 x 14.6 M] barn, followed by two bale homes in the mountains of Colorado. All of the structures were constructed with plastic bale foundations and difficult-to-recycle paper bale walls.

His current project, described here, uses bales of household plastic to create both foundation and wall systems. The project starts with collecting the plastic bottles and baling them into building blocks. Previous projects had used large, heavy bales (1800 lbs. [816 kg.] each), requiring machines to move and stack. This new process involves much smaller bales that can be moved and stacked by hand, much like straw bales.

Baling

In Eichelberger's current project, the large bales were broken down and rebaled on site. The baler is small by industry standards (used balers like this are available all over North America for between 500 and 2000 USD), was loaded manually, and the three-wire tie-off was also done by hand. The resulting bales weighed about 40-45 lbs. [18 to 20 kg.], their dimensions were approximately 30 x 24 x 16 inches [76 x 61 x 41 cm], and they took about 15 minutes to make.

Despite the simplicity of the machine and process there were numerous variables. The baler ram force is a constant, but the actual material amount varied, so, like straw bales, the bales could expand in length from 24 to as much as 30 inches. The wires were hand-tied when the ram had the material in maximum compres-sion; when the ram was released, the bales then expanded to the wire tension. That tension varied from person to person, and according to the time of day and an individual's fatigue level. Eventually the project team devised a crude tool that maximized tension at a somewhat consistent rate. Although this improved process still resulted in a range of bale strengths, weights, and sizes, the variations were manageable.

Stacking/stabilization

Since plastic bales are unaffected by moisture they were used for the foundation, though the long-term durability of the wire ties is unknown. The bales were simply placed in a rough trench and pushed as close together as possible. The site slopes slightly, so the foundation varied from one to two bales deep. Colored plastic bales were used for the foundation, as they were rougher in shape. Above grade, two different wall types were constructed: load-bearing (bales flat, 16 inches high) and infill or post-and-beam (bales vertical, 24 inches high).

Due to the strength of the plastic and the confused orientation of the material in the bales, it was impossible to drive spikes through the assembly to gain stability. Also, the slick, slightly convex surface of the bales and the stiffness and memory of the bottles made tight stacking difficult.

Bale proportion also became a stacking complication. A typical straw bale or adobe brick has a 2:1 dimensional ratio, making a running bond easy to accommodate. The running bond creates a sort of lock to the bale courses. The baler used created a more square bale which made a running bond and its locking qualities impossible.

The solution for all this was a panelization process using vertical stabilizers and a simple form of post-tensioning. Since internal spikes proved so difficult to install, #3 external vertical reinforcing bars were sunk into the ground on the outside of the bales and tied together at each bale course, creating a series of quasi-columns. Next, poles were placed vertically at the end of each run of bales. Wires were run horizontally and tied tight, pulling the panels of bales together to create a unified wall. The next form of post-tensioning used a wood plate laid on top of the wall with wires tied over the plate from side to side and fastened at the bottom (as is often done with straw bale walls). Through this process the walls were compressed vertically as much as 4 inches. This system also allowed the top plate to be leveled. These stabilization methods were used in both wall types, and appeared to greatly strengthen the walls prior to roof loading.

Roof

A simple roof structure was installed and finished to load the walls prior to finishing. The above-mentioned top plate became the bearing point for 2x wood rafters on the load-bearing wall. External wood columns and a wood beam carry the load on the opposing wall. Corrugated metal is the roofing material. The structure was left open so that added load could be applied to test differential loading and settlement.

Stucco

One-inch stucco netting was fastened directly to the bale wires and tie-down wires using cage clips and hog rings. Gaps between bales were filled with loose plastic bottles to reduce stucco thickness. A cement stucco base coat was mixed using $1/3$ inch pea gravel as filler for the first/ filler coat. A typical one-coat topping was applied as a finish.

Lab testing

Testing on plastic bales was completed in the spring of 2005 at the University of Colorado[1]; results can be viewed and/or downloaded at http://www.edc-cu.org/ppt/PlasticBales.pdf. The bales showed a range of strengths as follows:

- Compressive strength up to 5 psi [35 kN/m^2] at strains between 0.15 and 0.28
- Modulus of elasticity of 30 psi [207 kN/m^2] +/-
- Density of 4 to 10 pcf [64 to 160 kg/m^3]

Since the wall system required a panelization/post tension approach, further lab tests will be completed on bales configured in those conditions. From those results structural design criteria can be established. Further tests could evaluate a plastered bale wall's insulative qualities.

Collection

In urban areas of the industrialized world, large amounts of plastic are typically available from local recycle centers. Depending on local collection processes, recycled plastic comes in three basic categories: PET (Polyethylene Terephthalate; water and soda bottles, which have the most value), HDPE (High Density Polyethylene milk jugs of lesser value), and finally colored plastics which include detergent, juice, and some food product containers. They typically are available in large bales, allowing transport of a greater amount of material in a small volume. (PVC, or Polyvinylchloride, is at once among the most useful, ubiquitous, toxic, and nearly impossible-to-recycle plastics in the marketplace.)

Potential problems

Baled, recycled plastic poses several problems that limit its utility as a construction material:

- Variability in bottle sizes and strengths — Sizes ranging from two liter soda bottles to tiny prescription drug bottles make for highly heterogeneous bales;
- Lids — Some bottles still have their lids while others don't; bottles with lids are harder to compress, and the lids make the bottles want to return to their original shape;
- Some bottles still contain some of their contents, making for potential insect or mold problems;
- Once plastic catches fire it is difficult to extinguish, and fumes emitted from plastics can be toxic. Furthermore, some bottles contain volatile materials like oil or lighter fluid;
- The reliance on metal wire ties, particularly below grade, requires long-term protection from corrosion.

2.2B
PLASTIC BALE BUILDINGS

*photographs courtesy of
Doug Eichelberger and George Nez*

Conclusion

The test structure appears to be a success, as it is carrying load without distress. The passage of a few years will reveal any freeze/thaw problems, differential movement, or other problems should they occur.

What is the appropriate use of waste plastic? The high cost of plastic in the industrialized world may make baled plastic construction impractical there. On the other hand, areas of war, poverty, tropical climate, or natural disaster that already have a surplus plastic problem are also places where the availability of material and labor, coupled with the need for simple shelter, creates an opportunity — or even need — for baled plastic construction.

2.3 Straw Panels, Blocks, and Lumber

It seems that you can mix just about anything with water and lime or cement and get relatively strong blocks: e.g., papercrete, lime-hemp blocks, and so on. But, as is all too often the case, little money has been found to conduct the thermal, structural and other tests by which we might know how valuable these new materials might be.

There are also efforts underway to develop commercial building products with straw, such as blocks that will be denser, stronger, and of smaller and more consistent dimension than bales, or may have better insulating properties.

In the past decade straw panel companies have been appearing and disappearing at a bewildering rate. That's a whole story in itself, but there's no question that, as the dust settles, straw panels – be they nonstructural, (as for cabinetry), structural, and/or insulating – will become a fixture in the mainstream construction market. As of this publication, one company, AboveBoard™, should have a structural panel on the market (akin to OSB or plywood), and AgriBoard™ in Texas is back up and running with new owners, making straw-core structural insulated panels. For that matter, by the time of this publication there may be others available, and the reader must look about for himself or herself to see what's out there.

Structural straw panels, for now, anyway, will generally rely on MDI[A] binders for their strength and durability; the same technology, by extension, will lead to straw lumber to replace traditional sawn lumber and fabricated lumber products. In other words, we are seeing the dawn of a time when straw fiber – sronger than softwoods – will begin to replace wood fiber as the structure in our homes and other buildings. It's a wide open field out there.

2.4 Retrofit: the bale wrap

The ongoing and worldwide proliferation of concrete and concrete block buildings, especially housing, is rapidly adding to the stock of buildings that are strong, durable, and thermally terrible. Hot in summer, cold in winter, they are nonetheless becoming the material of choice for many people, for whatever reasons, in just about every culture and climate. That trend shows no signs of abating – concrete is, worldwide, by far the most commonly used building material by volume – so a very large opportunity exists to take what people are building and improve on it with an insulating straw bale jacket.

Generally, the thermal performance of a building is improved with insulation, and is further improved if the greater mass of the building is contained inside the insulating layer. This is due to the thermal mass effect that evens out diurnal temperature swings in a building by storing heat (or, in summer, "coolth," as it has

2.2.3A
THE NEW BUILDING FIBER – STRAW REPLACING WOOD

Blocks, panels, and lumber made with straw and a variety of binders are beginning to enter the marketplace, with many others in development. Soon lumber, particle-board, plywood, and oriented-strand board (OSB) will be available – with equal or greater strength and durability – using straw fibers instead of wood.

FOOTNOTE

A
methylene diphenylisocyante; MDI is highly toxic to manufacture, but does not emit formaldehyde or other VOC's (Volatile Organic Compounds) in use.

been dubbed; see chapter 7, *Insulation*). Thus, wrapping the exterior of an existing concrete or concrete block building with an insulating coat of plastered straw bales is a fairly easy way to vastly improve both comfort and appearance.

In figure 2.2.4A, bales were stacked on a slab foundation around the outside of an existing concrete block shed, and the exposed surfaces were plastered with earth and lime.

In another application, a police substation in Visalia, California is under construction at this writing, with the same basic arrangement: concrete block walls comprise the structure, and plastered straw bales provide insulation against the intense summer heat at that location.

There are two main considerations in constructing a bale wrap. One, the bales must be held securely against the concrete (or concrete block) surface, for both fire protection and structural integrity. If the wall is particularly large or tall (and thus subject to large wind suction), and/or in a zone of high seismic risk (and thus subject to shaking), the fastenings must be that much closer or stronger so as to keep the bales in place under any forseeable conditions.

Second, the bales must be protected from weather; roof eaves must be extended or created in such a way as to protect the wall. The taller the wall, or the stronger the local wind-driven rains, the wider the eaves must be. (See chapter 5, *Moisture*.)

2.2.4A
MATTS MYHRMAN AND JUDY KNOX'S GUEST HOUSE, TUCSON, ARIZONA

An older concrete block house was wrapped with straw bales, plastered with earthen plaster, and finished with lime plaster at openings and exposed walls

photo courtesy of David Eisenberg

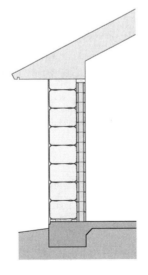

2.2.4B

Protect a bale wrap with a roof overhang, and secure the bales to the structural wall with wire or poly twine tied to the plaster mesh, and to fasteners installed in the structural wall.

2.5 Proprietary Straw Bale Building Systems

Efforts are underway in various countries, with patents in effect or pending, to improve the efficiency of straw bale construction by various engineered methods. Prefabricated straw bale panels in a wide range of systems are in development in Australia, the United States, Canada, the United Kingdom, Austria, and probably other places as well that we just haven't heard of yet. As with other construction materials, the general idea is to radically decrease jobsite labor requirements by bringing to the site completed wall panels that need only a minor bit of assembly. And, also like other building materials, the difficulties lie in working out all the connections and making a panel that can be easily transported and erected without damage. As of this writing, no significant breakthroughs have been announced on that front.

Other proprietary systems involve unique ways of assembling and plastering the bales. One, generally only in northern New Mexico, involves stacking the 2-string bales, then drilling 4 inch [102 mm] holes vertically at a spacing to match the bale length, then filling the holes with a piece of reinforcing bar and concrete grout. There is a lot of labor and little structural logic to this system, as the plaster skins can carry substantial load (see section 4.2) without help, but the system does get around New Mexico's outdated (but still in force as of this writing) disallowance of load-bearing straw bale structures.

Another concrete-based system, developed by a California engineer and in limited use, consists of inserting rebar cross-braces between the bale head joints in order to develop the firmer, quantifiable shear connection upon which a true stress-skin panel depends. The bales – here considered expendable temporary formwork – are then sprayed with three inches or so of lightly reinforced shotcrete or gunite, making for a very sturdy and ductile structure. The two main flaws with such a system, by no means minor, are:

1) The bales are trapped in vapor-impermeable containers (the three inches of concrete), and thus are more likely to experience moisture degradation. Indeed, reports of such problems have already surfaced in at least one case. If the bales decay appreciably, then there is a lot of mold trapped in the wall cavity, with the attendant potential health risks.

2) In the extreme case, i.e., if the bales decay partially or fully, then the insulation value of the wall assembly plummets; there is then only a convective air chamber between the exterior and interior surfaces. Furthermore, the system by its nature requires the concrete to wrap around all door and window openings, making for sizeable "thermal bridges" – places where heat can and will conduct easily through the concrete.

Other proprietary methods may also exist that have escaped general attention to date, and we don't mean to discourage or denigrate innovation by pointing out the flaws evident in existing systems. Undoubtedly, one or several viable and less labor-intensive systems will emerge that are appropriate to their place. For the time being, however, straw bale construction technology remains predominantly in the public domain, in a form very much like that conceived on the plains of Nebraska a century ago.

BURKE HOMESTEAD, ALLIANCE, NEBRASKA *(Built in 1903)*

photo courtesy of David Eisenberg

ENDNOTES

1
Camann, R,
Chamberlin, B,
Eggers, J, and
Whittlesey, J (2005),
Plastic Bale Construction
University of Colorado,
Boulder, Colorado

*If this were easy
it wouldn't be so hard.*

— Yogi Berra

PLASTER AND REINFORCING

with Mark Aschheim, Kevin Donahue, David Mar and, especially, Kelly Lerner

3.1 What is Plaster?

Plaster is a wet-applied, mineral-based coating used to protect and finish interior and exterior walls. It can be made of a variety of raw materials, from minimally processed elements like earth, sand, and straw to materials that must be mined and fired like gypsum, lime, or cement. Plaster can be and has been used on many substrates – gypsum board, metal lath, wood lath, concrete block, brick, stone, adobe and, of most interest to us, straw bale walls.

Nearly all straw bale walls are – or should be – finished with plaster skins of some variety, typically one to three inches (25-75mm) thick. During renovations to the Pilgrim Holiness Church in Arthur, Nebraska, preservationists uncovered the Church's original 1925 plaster – gumbo mud from the local river.

Plaster is uniquely suited as a finish for straw bales because it can fill and seal the irregular surface of straw bales and protect them

---

Plaster, Stucco, or Render?
Generally in North America the word **plaster** refers to any coating with binders of cement, lime, gypsum, or earth used on the exterior or interior of a building. **Stucco** usually refers to exterior plasters with cement binder. **Synthetic stuccos** are cement-based plasters with an added acrylic latex binder; these should not be used on straw bale buildings because of their low vapor permeance (see chapter 5, *Moisture*). The term **Render** is used in the United Kingdom, Ireland, New Zealand, and Australia to describe exterior plasters (regardless of their ingredients). In this text we will use "plaster" to refer generically to any of these materials.

3.1A
THE PILGRIM HOLINESS
CHURCH, ARTHUR,
NEBRASKA, 1927 (ABOVE)
AND 1995 (BELOW)

modern photo courtesy of
David Eisenberg

from a host of threats. When most people imagine a beautiful straw bale wall, they are usually responding to the beauty of the plaster "skin" – its depth, texture, and color. But the plaster skins are more than what meets the eye; they have multiple, complex and overlapping functions.

3.2 The Functions of Plaster Skins

Plaster skins play an integral role in the overall performance and longevity of straw bale wall systems, protecting them from damage, rain, air infiltration, fire, pests, and the occasional wandering hungry heifer. And, whether desired or not, because plaster skins are the stiffest components in the straw bale wall assembly they also serve a structural role, bearing both vertical and horizontal loads. A better understanding of the primary functions required of plaster skins can help you decide on the best plaster mixture for a particular straw bale wall system.

3.2.1 Moisture Control

Straw, like wood, decomposes when exposed to enough moisture for enough time at a warm enough temperature – see section 5.3 for more about that. This moisture can be in the form of liquid (generally precipitation from the exterior – rain or snow) or in the form of vapor (from both the interior or the exterior depending on climatic conditions). Plaster skins keep exterior liquid moisture (rain and snow) at bay, slowing it at the surface of the wall, and often storing it safely until conditions change and it can dry out of the wall. Plaster skins also stop air movement into and through straw bale walls, preventing moisture vapor-laden air from entering the wall system. Be very aware, however, that plaster serves neither of these functions – keeping out liquid water or vapor-laden air – if the plaster is cracked or not well-sealed at all joints and penetrations. Often, exterior plasters are coated with a water-repellent coating to improve their weathering performance. For more on the moisture properties of various plaster types and recommendations, see chapter 5, *Moisture*.

3.2.2 Thermal Resistance and Thermal Storage

Plaster skins play a critical role in the thermal resistance of straw bale walls by preventing air movement into and through walls. Just visit an unplastered straw bale house in windy winter weather and you'll see that without their plastered skins, straw bale walls lose much of their thermal performance – a strong, cold wind can blow right through. The skins also add thermal mass to the exterior and the interior faces of the wall, slowing the movement of heat through the wall and modulating temperature swings. Interior thermal mass serves as a "heat sink," which is ideal for direct-gain solar heating strategies and also for night ventilation cooling strategies. (See chapter 7, *Insulation*.)

3.2.3 Fire Control

Plaster skins protect bales from fire by both restricting the flow of oxygen and acting as a non-flammable physical barrier which is a relatively poor conductor of heat. (See chapter 6, *Fire*.)

3.2.4 Protection from Pests: Insects, Rodents and Ruminants

Straw, by definition, isn't a good food source for insects or other animals; the grain is mostly removed, and there is little carbohydrate (food) to attract hungry creatures. Even so, if they are hungry enough, cows, goats, and horses may tear bales apart looking for grain, and have done so on a few straw bale projects left too long without plaster. Plaster skins provide a physical barrier to all those who may eat straw and those who are looking for a warm home in the interior of the wall. (See chapter 9, *Insects*.)

3.2.5 Structural Behavior

Plaster "skins" are typically the stiffest elements in straw bale wall assemblies, and for that reason end up (intentionally or not) carrying most of the vertical and lateral loads imposed on the walls. The relatively thin skins, in turn, are reinforced and buttressed against buckling by the straw bale core, resulting in composite structural performance. Plaster skins also resist in-plane and out-of-plane loads, though their capacity to do so is limited both by their strength and by the connections to the foundation and roof. Neither the straw bale walls nor the plaster skins could perform in the same structural fashion individually; the sum is greater than its parts. The structural performance of a straw bale wall is also affected by the wide range of reinforcing and connection techniques for plaster skins. (See chapter 4, *Structure*.) When compared to the structural models in standard construction, the structural models for plastered straw bale walls are most closely akin to stress-skin panel models for vertical and out-of-plane loads, and to reinforced concrete models for in-plane lateral loads.

3.2.6 Finishes and Aesthetics

Like human skin, plaster is the part we all see. A well-finished plaster job can hide a host of flaws, while a poor plaster job can make even the best-built wall look bad (not to mention perform poorly for all the functions described above). While some plaster finishes *are* more resistant to rain and physical damage than others, preferences for plaster finishes are highly personal. Some people prefer their plaster skins undulating and rounded, while others like them flat with square corners. Some like plaster finishes smooth with a glint of mica, and some like them rough with sand. Some like integrally colored plaster, while others like an overlay of different stains and pigments.

3.3 The Components of Plaster

All plasters have at least three basic components:
- **a binding agent,** which usually gives the plaster its name: gypsum, lime, cement, and clay (or *earth*, meaning clay is the binder).
- **a structural filler:** non-organic components like sand, chipped rock, or other aggregates.
- **water** as needed for mixing, activating binders, and application. In the case of lime- and/or cement-based plasters, keeping the plaster moist for at least a few weeks after application – allowing it to properly cure – is crucial to developing the best plaster strength and durability.

Plasters also often contain:
- **fiber,** such as chopped straw, hair, hemp, fiberglass fibers, plastic fibers or mesh, and steel fibers or mesh for tensile reinforcement and ductility (the ability to remain coherent even when stretched, compressed, or deformed).
- **additives or admixtures,** to improve plasticity, workability, durability, or curing time.

3.3.1 Binders, when mixed with water, become adhesive and hold the components of the plaster together in a workable material that will stick to and spread on a substrate. Binders continue to hold the plaster mixture together after curing or drying and are primarily responsible for the plaster's strength and moisture permeability. Some binders, such as cement, lime and gypsum, are highly processed from their natural state and change chemically during the curing process. These

binders cannot easily return to a pre-cured state. Clay is the only binder that can return directly to a pre-cured state (by combining with water) and be re-used. Generally speaking, plasters should contain just enough binder to hold the components together and provide workability. Too much binder in a mix usually leads to cracking, weakness, or extreme brittleness.

3.3.2 Sand is the most typical structural filler in plasters. It often accounts for most of a plaster's volume and is the strongest component. In plasters that bear compressive structural loads, it's best if the sand is sharp (not round river or beach sand) and well-graded (including a range of sizes from very small to larger). Like reinforced concrete, a sharp, well-graded sand locks everything together well. Very fine particles smaller than sand but bigger than clay (technically, between 0.76 mm and 0.002 mm) are called silt. Silt will weaken the plaster by preventing good adhesion with the binder; that is, the enormous surface area of a given volume of silt will greatly dilute the binder's ability to coat every particle and therefore bind them together. Generally, the less silt, the better the plaster will be by every measure.

3.3.3 Fiber in a plaster provides tensile reinforcement and improves elastic performance, preventing cracking and increasing material ductility. Fiber can also add bulk to a plaster and allow it to be applied in a thicker coat.

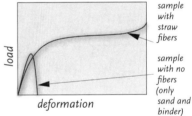

sample with straw fibers

sample with no fibers (only sand and binder)

load

deformation

3.3A

A two-inch plaster cube in a compression testing machine, and a generic load-deformation graph showing the difference between a sample with no fiber (brittle) and one with fibers (ductile)

A good balance among binder, sand, and fiber is critical to both workability and ultimate performance of plaster skins. The properties of plaster are determined by the type of binder used, the additives, the overall proportions of binder, filler, fiber, and water, and the quality of the curing. If there's not enough binder in a mix, it won't hold together. If there's too much sand, the plaster may be too heavy to stick to the wall and may sag during application. If there's too much fiber, the plaster will be unworkable and not spread easily. A plaster with too much binder may stick to the substrate well, but it will tend to crack (shrink) as it cures. Any plaster that is poorly cured through being immediately exposed to sun, wind, or freezing temperatures and/or through premature drying after application, will crack more and be weaker.

Different application systems may require different mixes as well. For example, a plaster that is blown on (as opposed to one applied by hand) typically requires a mix with less fiber because the fiber can clog the spray nozzle.

Sand and fiber also play controlling roles in the thickness of the plaster coat during application. The size of the largest pieces of sand or fiber in a plaster mix will determine how thin a plaster can be applied. For example, a plaster with pieces of fiber ⅛ inch in diameter will need to be applied thicker than ⅛ inch or the fiber will catch and drag on the trowel. Thick plasters (¾ inch thick and greater) generally require a higher percentage of fiber in the mix; the weight of a thick application of plaster with just binder and sand will pull it off the wall. Fiber reduces the weight of the plaster while also reinforcing it both while wet and after curing.

3.4 Types of Plasters

Plasters can be categorized in many ways: by type of binder, by weather resistance, by application method, by moisture properties, or by structural properties. Again, the primary binder (cement, lime, gypsum, or clay) determines the structural and the moisture properties of the overall plaster. Since this book, like straw bale building design, is much more concerned with the moisture and structural properties of plaster than is usual in construction, let's begin with categories grouped by structural properties:

- **"hard-skin" plasters:** plasters with, roughly, compressive strengths above 1000 psi [6895 kPa], modulus of elasticity (MOE)[A] of more than 100,000 psi [690 MPa], and modulus of rupture (MOR)[A] of more than 250 psi [1724 kPa]. The binder for hard-skin plasters is generally cement (sometimes mixed with lime or with clay soil in a high-strength soil-cement), and such plasters are generally the least vapor-permeable.

FOOTNOTE

A
Very generally, MOE is a measure of how stiff a material is, and MOR one of several measures of tensile strength – more on this in chapter 4, *Structure*.

- **"semi-soft-skin" plasters:** plasters with compressive strengths roughly between 300 and 1000 psi, MOE between 1000 and 10,000 psi, and MOR between 100 and 250 psi. The binders for semi-soft-skin plasters include non-hydraulic lime, hydraulic lime, and low-strength soil-cement mixtures. These plasters are moderately to very vapor-permeable.

- **"soft-skin" plasters:** plasters with compressive strengths generally less than 300 psi, MOE less than 3000 psi, and MOR less than 100 psi. The binders for soft-skin plasters include clay, clay-lime, or gypsum. These plasters are highly vapor-permeable.

3.4.1 Cement Plasters

Portland cement is made primarily from calcium carbonate (usually limestone) and lesser amounts of silica and alumina, typically from clay or sand. The raw materials are finely ground and mixed, then fired at about 2700°F [1480°C] in a kiln that rotates slowly to mix the contents moving through it. In the kiln, the raw materials undergo complex chemical and physical changes to become *lime* (calcium oxide) and carbon dioxide gas, which is emitted into the air – about half of the carbon emissions associated with cement production. Secondary reactions form dicalcium and tricalcium silicates, tricalcium aluminate, and tetracalcium aluminoferrite. The relative proportions of these four principal compounds determine the key properties of the resultant Portland cement. As the new material cools, it solidifies into solid pellets called *clinker*. The clinker is then ground to a fine powder, a small amount of gypsum is added, and now you have Portland cement.

Since Portland cement – a very specific type of hydraulic lime – is a mass produced, standardized, commercial product, the performance of cement-based plasters is relatively predictable and consistent (though curing conditions hugely affect the final product). Typical mixes and their structural properties are generally well-known and documented. Mixes are described generally as a ratio of volumetric parts, cement:lime:sand, and often contain some proprietary cement mixes and/or additives.

Special Considerations for Cement Plasters over Straw Bale Walls

While cement plasters have been used on straw bale walls for many years, not all cement-based mixes are appropriate for straw bale walls because of their low vapor permeability (for a more in-depth discussion of the importance of vapor permeability in plasters over straw bale walls, see chapter 5, *Moisture*). To allow for the passage of water vapor (permeability), which allows the straw bale wall to dry, a cement-based plaster must contain at least enough lime to increase its vapor permeance above two or three U.S. Perms. Some appropriate cement-lime mixes currently in use in the field include 1:1:6 and 1:2:9 (cement:lime:sand by volume, as stipulated in many building codes) and generally are of strength comparable to plain cement plasters. Elastomeric plaster mixes (usually proprietary) are not advisable because their vapor permeability is too low to allow for adequate drying.

While cement plasters are very strong, they are also the most brittle of the plasters. This can be problematic when cement plasters are used over more flexible substrates like straw bales and wood. To avoid cracking from differential movement, cement plasters must always be reinforced with expanded metal mesh (often called

A Glossary of Lime Terminology

Agricultural Lime
Ground raw limestone used as a soil amendment. Not suitable for plasters as it has no binding abilities.

Non-Hydraulic Lime
Non-hydraulic lime requires exposure to air to carbonate and will not set under water. It is the most permeable of all the building limes, and takes longest to set.

Hydraulic Lime
Hydraulic lime is produced from limestone containing clay. It sets partly by a chemical reaction with water, without exposure to air, but also by carbonation. Hydraulic limes set up more quickly than non-hydraulic limes, and they are slightly less vapor-permeable and slightly more weather resistant. Portland cement is a special type of hydraulic lime.

Quicklime
Quicklime is a mixture of calcium oxide and magnesium oxide made by firing limestone (calcium carbonate).

Lime Putty
Lime putty is calcium hydroxide and magnesium hydroxide made by combining quicklime with water (called *slaking*). Lime putty is combined with sand to make lime plaster.

Hydrated Lime
Hydrated lime is a preslaked, dried, and ground lime powder available in bags.

Type S Hydrated Lime
Type S lime, or "Special" hydrated lime, is fully hydrated under pressure and requires less time for slaking than type N lime.

Type N Lime
Type N lime, or "Normal" hydrated lime, is only partially hydrated and requires longer slaking times for good workability.

Carbide Lime
Carbide lime is a byproduct of the production of acetylene gas from calcium carbide and water. It has the same chemical composition as quicklime, and carbide lime putty can be substituted for lime putty one to one.

"blood lath" by those who install it) around window and door openings, at inside and outside corners, and wherever the substrate changes, as at a wood post in a straw bale wall. Although it's not strictly necessary under non-seismic conditions, cement plasters are generally reinforced with some type of mesh over the whole straw bale wall surface. In seismic areas, mesh is required and may be used as part of structural system to resist shear forces (see chapter 4, *Structure)*.

3.4.2 Lime Plasters

Lime plasters – there are many kinds – have been used in building construction for over six thousand years, the first recorded use being around 4000 BC in what is now Turkey. They have been used typically to protect (and render more beautiful) the substrate below, usually stone masonry or earthen construction. Lime plaster has a long history of use throughout the world and is still used in many areas. In the United States, the use of lime plaster (except in historic restoration) has been mostly superseded by the widespread use and popularity of gypsum board and cement-based plasters. As designers and builders of straw bale buildings learned more about the importance of vapor-permeable plasters over straw bale walls, they have become increasingly interested in lime plasters.

Lime itself is derived, much like Portland cement, from heating and calcining limestone – calcium carbonate, $CaCO_3$. Limestone is rock formed from the accumulated skeletons of small marine animals that settled and compressed in thick layers on the ocean floor long ago, eventually consolidating into rock. Limestone deposits also contain varying amounts of magnesium carbonate ($MgCO_3$) which precipitated out of the sea water. High calcium/low magnesium limes (less than 5% magnesium carbonate) are considered the best material for lime plasters.

Limestone is mined in open quarries and fired in a lime kiln at 2000 degrees F, which drives off water (H_2O) and carbon dioxide (CO_2). The result is combination of calcium oxide (CaO) and magnesium oxide (MgO), commonly known as *quicklime*. In order to be made into a plaster or mortar, the quicklime is combined with water (called *hydrating* or *slaking*) and reacts quickly – hence the name quicklime – to form calcium hydroxide ($Ca(OH)_2$) and magnesium hydroxide ($Mg(OH)_2$), a thick, creamy paste, commonly known as *hydrated lime* (not to be confused with *hydraulic lime)* or *lime putty*. This exogenic chemical reaction releases energy in the form of heat – lots of heat. Historically, the best quality lime puttys

3.4A

(TOP) FIRED LIME
BEING SIFTED
(BOTTOM) A LIME KILN.

*Even a relatively simple
kiln as shown in rural
China is similar in
operation to a cement
plant: limestone is
heated and then
sifted and ground.*

photos courtesy of Kelly Lerner

were stored moist (covered by a little water) for many years before use. A long slaking period allows for complete hydration of all the chunks of calcium oxide and magnesium oxide, yielding a smoother, finer, and more plastic lime putty. To make lime plaster, lime putty is combined with sand and often a fiber such as hair. When exposed to air, lime plaster, like concrete, *carbonates,* reabsorbing the carbon dioxide that was driven off during the firing process to become limestone ($CaCO_3$) once more.

Hydrated Lime

Hydrated lime, also known as *bagged* lime, is partially hydrated quicklime. The process takes place in a hydrator, which combines the dry, pebbly quicklime with a carefully controlled amount of water (generally 23 to 24 percent for high calcium lime). All of the water is chemically combined with the quicklime, so the product remains a dry, free-flowing powder. If more water is added, the result is lime putty. Really, the only difference between hydrated lime and lime putty is the amount of water that has been added to them. Many plasterers advise that lime plasters made with hydrated lime should be mixed with water at least 24 hours in advance to improve hydration of the lime.

Unique Characteristics of Lime Plasters

Somewhat unlike the one-way process used to make gypsum and cement, the production and use of lime for buildings creates a closed loop, starting and ending with calcium carbonate. Though the production of lime for plaster releases carbon dioxide, a similar amount of carbon dioxide is reabsorbed over a long period of time as the plaster returns to limestone on the wall.

Lime plasters are less rigid and brittle than cement plasters and tend to crack less when used over flexible substrates like earth or straw bales. Hairline cracks in lime plasters are self-healing – the carbonation of calcium hydroxide fills the cracks. Larger cracks can be filled with several coats of limewash (a thin mixture of lime putty with water at a consistency like skim milk).

The very open microstructure of lime plaster makes it highly vapor-permeable (19-30 ng/Pa s m) and slightly more absorbent than cement or earthen plasters. While this open structure means that lime plasters can store large amounts of water safely and dry out easily, they can also wick moisture easily (via capillary action) through the plaster to the substrate. Although lime can hold a lot of moisture, it is very alkaline and inhibits the growth of mold and mildew.

Compared to cement and earthen plasters, lime plaster is quite sensitive to environmental factors. Lime plaster must be kept moist and out of direct sun for a long time (weeks and even months) in order to cure well. Because lime strengthens by carbonation, not hydration, it sets up slowly and must have ongoing access to carbon dioxide and moisture. In order to carbonate, lime plaster must be applied in thin coats (no more than $^3/_8$ inch [9.5 mm]) and kept moist for at least 7 to 14 days. Each coat must cure at least 5 to 7 days (more is better) before the next coat is applied. Lime plaster will not carbonate at temperatures below 45° F, and exposure to freezing temperatures before the lime has set up sufficiently will ruin the plaster.

Hydraulic limes set up more quickly than non-hydraulic limes, but they are not at present (2006) available in the United States except via importation from abroad. Pozzolanic[A] materials can be added to non-hydraulic limes to speed up set time and strength. There are no standardized formulas for mixes, but a decent rule of thumb is to replace half the sand with pozzolanic material.

Because lime plaster sets up slowly, slow-working, inexperienced owner-builders may find it easier to use, but this ease can be offset by the great care which must be taken during the curing process. Lime is also very alkaline and caustic, so it must be mixed and applied with protective gloves and clothing.

Lime plasters must be mixed with clean, washed sand. Clay or contaminants in the sand can interfere with the curing process.

3.4B

Lime plaster delaminating from poorly-prepared earthen plaster base, i.e. one without fibers or mechanical scoring to receive the lime coat.

photo courtesy of Chris Newton

3.4C

Lime plaster being applied over well-prepared earthen plaster base, with mechanical scoring to receive the lime coat.

photo courtesy of Matts Myhrman

FOOTNOTE

A

Pozzolans *are a range of materials that, when combined with cement or lime in the presence of water, will yield more "glue" to harden and strengthen the cured material. There are all sorts of pozzolans currently available in the marketplace, some mined directly from the earth, such as diatomaceous earth and some volcanic tuffs; some manufactured, such as calcined clay (metakaolin); some (most) retrieved as industrial by-products, such as slag, fly ash, and silica fume; and others, such as rice hull ash (the burned and ground hulls from rice kernels).*

Lime plasters are generally "sealed" with 4 or 5 coats of limewash and must be resealed periodically depending on weathering, from every 4 or 5 years on an exposed façade to once per generation on a very protected face.

In lime plasters, gains in strength are made by carbonation and take place slowly. ASTM standards stipulate that strength testing take place at 28, 56, and 128 days, but in lime plasters the strength at one year can be over 40% greater than the 28-day strength, and the strength at two years can be 50% greater.

The largest barrier to the use of lime plasters in the United States is a lack of skilled contractors and building designers familiar with the material.

Special Considerations for Lime Plasters over Straw Bale Walls

The use of lime plasters on straw bale walls is, at the current time (2005), limited and without an extensive field history, but more and more designers and owners are considering lime plaster because of its high vapor permeability. Lime plasters can be applied directly on straw bale walls, or as a finish coat over an earth plaster. Each approach has advantages and drawbacks.

Lime plasters have a long and successful history when applied over solid substrates like stone, brick, cob, and adobe, or straw-clay compressed between timber frames. All these substrates can carry a heavy moisture load without damage because they are readily able to release the water back to the air, i.e., dry out. Lime plaster prevents erosion of the substrate and can act as a durable sacrificial coat protecting the mortar in brick or stone walls.

To apply lime plaster as a finish coat over a thick earth plaster base coat is to mimic its historical use, and the finish will work well if certain precautions are followed. There is some risk in using dissimilar materials, as the layers may expand and contract differently in response to temperature and moisture and thus delaminate over time. This risk can be minimized by creating a strong mechanical bond between the two materials by scoring or scratching the base coat deeply — hence the term *scratch coat* — and consolidating the finish coat well. The earth plaster base coat should be well-consolidated, with no loose particles. A coat of limewash before the lime plaster will improve the adhesion, though the surface must be thoroughly rewetted before applying the lime plaster coat.

Lime plasters can also be applied directly over straw bale walls. While their high vapor permeability suits the drying requirements of straw bale walls, the active capillary action and high absorption rates of these plasters may allow a lot of water into the wall. Where this is of concern, such as on walls that are exposed to large amounts of rain, extended overhangs or other protections should be considered.

3.4.3 Earthen Plasters (clay binder)

Earthen plasters are the primordial plasters, having been used since humans first started building. They can be found all over the world both in historical and modern buildings, in almost every climate, wherever clay soil can be found, in beautiful and wonderful variety.

The binder in earth plaster is clay. Unlike cement and lime, clay does not change chemically during its curing process. It does not require firing like cement or lime, and its embodied energy is minimal. Because clay is a minimally processed and (usually) locally sourced material, it varies widely in its chemical composition, structural properties, and performance. Excellent earth plasters can be formulated with a host of different clays, but it takes experimentation or local experience with the local material to get a high-quality plaster.

What is clay?

Soils are classified based on their *Atterberg Limits* (see below) and on particle size as determined by sieving:

> *gravel* > 4.7mm
> *sand* > 0.76mm
> *silt* > 0.002mm − usually
> *clay* < 0.002mm − usually

Clay refers to a family of hydrous alumino-silicates that are microscopic, with particle sizes generally though not always less than 0.002 mm. Unlike gravel, sand, and silt, which are products of erosion, clay is a product of leaching. Some clay mineral grains are larger than 0.002mm and some soils finer than 0.002mm have no clay minerals. There are many, many types and colors of clays with widely-ranging properties in terms of shrinkage/expansion and binding strength. Just because you've found a source of clay doesn't mean you have a good building material; we'll discuss how to measure the properties of importance for plasters.

Atterberg Limits are used to describe the *Shrinkage Limit*, *Plastic Limit*, and *Liquid Limit* of a soil. As water is added to a dry soil, the soil changes from solid to semi-solid to plastic to liquid. The moisture content in the soil at the threshold between semi-solid and plastic is called the *Plastic Limit*. The moisture content in the soil at the threshold between plastic and liquid is called the *Liquid Limit*. Subtracting the Plastic Limit from the Liquid Limit yields the *Plasticity Index*. Clay-rich soils are characterized by a large Liquid Limit (LL > 40) with high compressibility and high shrink-swell tendencies, and a large Plasticity Index (PI > 20) with low shear strength. The Plasticity Index can be lowered by adding sand and raised by adding clay.

Clay minerals, like mica, are phyllosilicates: silicate minerals made up of layers or sheets of SiO_4 tetrahedra. Clay derives its distinctive adhesive characteristics from its physical, electrochemical makeup: the chemical bonds within the silicate sheets are strong ionic bonds, but the bonds between the silicate sheets are weak Van der Waals forces (these forces occur when unbalanced electrical charges around molecules attract each other). This weak bonding permits other ions and chemicals (typically water) to occupy sites between the silicate layers, letting the silicate sheets "slide" by each other. When dried out, the sheets grab each other and won't slide, accounting for the slippery-when-wet and adhesive-when-dry nature of clay.

In clay minerals, the chemical composition of the silicate layer and the number and type of cations/chemicals which fit between the silicate layers determine the type of clay and its physical performance (more or less expansive, more or less compressive strength, more or less adhesion, etc). Water is the most common chemical found between layers in clay minerals, and clays can absorb and release substantial amounts of water. This absorption and release of water accounts for the expansive nature of clays.

Unique Characteristics of Earth Plasters

Because of its chemical structure, clay is very *hydrophilic*, literally attracting and adsorbing water between its silicate sheets. As these spaces fill with water molecules, the clay expands and forms a water-resistant barrier. In fact, highly expansive clays like bentonite are used as waterproof membranes to line ponds and waterproof below-grade retaining walls. (Highly expansive clays, however, are not appropriate for earth plasters.)

Both cement and lime plasters wick water by capillary action. The actual structure of the material does not change when wet, so the rate is the same whether lime and cement plasters are wet or dry. Because clay expands when wet (as the spaces between the silicate sheets fill with water molecules), earth plasters act like "smart membranes" – the wetter they are, the more they resist the passage of liquid moisture. Because of the electrical charges between silicate plates, earth plasters tend to store moisture rather than just wicking it through. This is important in keeping moisture away from straw bale walls, be it rain from the outside or the intense humidity of a hot shower room inside.

As a rule, both cement and lime plasters must be separated from wood with a membrane or capillary break because they are *capillary-active* – they wick water. Since wood is also capillary-active, it will absorb water from the plaster, and with enough time, warmth, and moisture, eventually rot. Though straw bales are much less dense than wood (and thus less likely to absorb water through capillary action), a plaster that continually wicks moisture to a straw bale wall is less than ideal.

Because clay is hydrophilic, earth plaster actually protects straw and wood from moisture both by absorbing any moisture already present (drawing it out of the wood or straw) and by preventing moisture from reaching the wood or straw. This effect can be seen in old timberframe buildings where the wood frame in direct contact with the straw–clay infill is sound after hundreds of years of weather exposure.

Because the clay binder does not change chemically during curing, earth plasters can be rewetted and reworked indefinitely (as long as they don't have an additive that prevents reworking). Earth plasters return to the earth easily at the end of a building's useful life. Without proper weather protection, however, they will do so faster than one might wish.

This erosion varies depending on exposure and climate. Unplastered cob walls in England have been estimated to erode at a rate of no more one inch per century, while adobe walls in New Mexico may lose up to an inch in twenty years. This large difference is probably due to the wide eaves on the English buildings, versus few eaves, freeze-thaw conditions, and strong seasonal rainstorms in New Mexico. Traditionally, earth-plastered walls were recoated every 2 to 10 years depending

3.4D

A classic timberframe house dating from medieval Germany, with straw-clay packed between timbers, and lime plaster applied as protective cover, now at least 400 years old.

photo courtesy of John Straube

3.4E

The straw-rich earth plaster block held its shape for six hours under the slow-drip impact of over 6 gallons [23 liters] of water from a height of 54 inches [137 cm].

3.4F

The earth plaster block without straw reinforcement melted away in less than an hour after only 0.63 gallons [2.4 liters] of slowly dripping water.

on the climate and the wall exposure. Erosion can be eliminated completely by sheltering earth-plastered walls with deep overhangs or a rain screen (see chapter 10: *Design and Detailing* for further discussion of rain screens).

In vernacular building traditions, erosion is often controlled by embedding small, flat rocks in the surface of the plaster to break up the water flows and act as mini-overhangs. In a similar approach in Korea, earth plasters on exposed gable ends are protected by embedding layers of thatch or rice straw.

Erosion can be limited by introducing large amounts of chopped straw or other fiber into the plaster mix. As the plaster erodes and the straw is exposed, it protects the earth plaster below by dispersing the water and keeping it at the surface. In recent erosion testing[1], an earth plaster block with a high percentage of straw lasted six times as long as one with no straw when exposed to a steady drip at a rate of approximately one gallon per hour.

A top coat of lime plaster can protect earth plasters from erosion (see discussion above in the lime plaster section), but care must be taken to create a good mechanical bond between the dissimilar materials.

Special Considerations for Earth Plasters over Straw Bale Walls

The use of earth plasters over straw bale walls is growing because they are beautiful, easy for owner-builders to apply, and have very low environmental impacts. From a more technical standpoint, earth plaster is a good match for straw bale walls because of its elasticity, high vapor permeability, and ability to absorb and store relatively large amounts of moisture safely without transferring it to the bales. Earth plasters set up slowly and are especially friendly and forgiving to people who are just learning to plaster. They are not alkaline or caustic and can be applied directly by hand. They also can be quite durable, but successful formulations require experimentation with locally available clays and other ingredients. Processed, bagged clays from known sources will give more predictable and consistent results but are usually more expensive.

Although earth is everywhere, skilled earth plasterers are not. A great deal of knowledge and training goes into mastering how to gather, transport, screen, store, apply, and cure an earth- (i.e., clay-) based plaster. You can just "throw some mud on the wall," but you wouldn't very likely then get the kind of elegant, durable finish for which earth plasters are becoming popular.

> **If you don't know how yourself, make sure you can find someone who does before deciding to use earth – or lime, for the same reasons – plaster on your walls.**

3.5 Key Structural Properties of Plasters

Because all plasters are more rigid than straw bales, they carry nearly all of the structural loads on straw bale walls, intentionally or not. Even a very soft earth plaster is at least five times stiffer than the bales themselves (unless the plaster is wet – see chapter 5 and protect it). In many cases, such as for a post-and-beam house in a non-seismic zone, this hardly matters. In cases where the bale wall will be part of the building's structure, however, the plaster must be selected and applied with an eye to strength and durability.

3.5.1 Plaster Bonding

For structural effectiveness, plasters must be well-bonded to the straw bale substrate. Any barrier (a membrane or a very fine mesh, for example) that prevents or interferes with this bond should be avoided. To achieve good bonds, plasters should be well-embedded into the rough surface of straw bale walls. For this reason, some practitioners believe that blown-on plaster achieves a stronger bond than hand-applied material, but others believe that a good plasterer can achieve the same results by firm hand application. Depending on how conscientiously the job is done, either can be right. Plaster bond strength is also affected by bale quality; a loosely compressed bale or one with very short straw will yield a poor bond strength. The plaster may bond to the straw, but under loading, the loose or short straws just pull away from the bale. In other words, good bond between plaster and straw depends on the type of plaster, the quality of bales, and especially the quality of plaster application.

3.5.2 Compressive Strength

Compressive strength is the most important measure of whether a plaster is suited to use with bale walls subjected to structural loading, and, as with concrete, can be

3.5A
COMPRESSION
CONFIGURATION

Two inch cube sample placed on a steel support between two inch pipes. The load is applied to the sample directly from the bottom flange of the lever arm beam at the top. The sample is placed and supported so that the beam is level and the load is evenly applied.

3.5B
MOR CONFIGURATION

Two inch square by six inch long sample spans between two inch pipes. The load is applied to the sample directly from the bottom flange of the lever arm beam at the top. The sample is placed and supported so that the beam is level and the load is evenly applied.

used as a key indicator of the plaster's other properties. The most common ways of measuring compressive strength are by making two inch [5 cm] cubes for testing in a laboratory by standard test procedures (e.g., ASTM C109), or by testing in the field with a leverage device such as that shown in figure 3.5A. As simple as it may be in concept, there is a surprising amount of knowledge, art, and care required to accurately measure the compressive strength of a material, be it in the lab or the field. (Detailed descriptions of field testing devices and procedures can be found in many sources, such as *Building with Earth* by John Norton, or *Adobe and Rammed Earth Buildings* by Paul McHenry.) See 3.5.6 for strength test results.

3.5.3 Modulus of Rupture (MOR), roughly the tensile strength

True tensile strength is remarkably difficult to measure for plaster materials, so common practice is to measure the breaking, or snapping, strength of a small plaster "beam". Common ways of measuring MOR are by making two inch [5 cm] square by six inch [15 cm] long "beams" for testing in a laboratory by standard test procedures (eg, ASTM C293), or by testing in the field with a leverage device (figure 3.5B). As with compression testing, there is a surprising amount of knowledge, art and care required to accurately measure the compressive strength of a material, be it in the lab or the field.

3.5.4 Modulus of Elasticity (MOE), or stiffness

The Modulus of Elasticity is the slope of the linear portion of the stress-strain curve, or the ratio of stress to strain in the *elastic region*, i.e., before any permanent deformation has occurred. In EBNet testing[1], the average MOE for cement-lime plasters (at 57 days) was 1,140,000 psi, which is very close to the value predicted by the formula typically used for concrete (MOE = $57,000\sqrt{f'_c}$ = 1,342,000 psi, with f'_c being the ultimate breaking compressive strength of the material). The average MOE values for earth plasters (1811 psi for higher straw samples and 3103 psi for lower straw samples) were about 200 times smaller than the values predicted by the concrete formula, indicating (as we might expect) far more flexible behavior of earth plasters for a given compressive strength than that of cement-based plasters.

3.5.5 General conclusions about structural qualities of plasters[1]
Compressive strength

Whereas earth plaster mixes with more sand and less straw exhibited brittle failure, the high-straw mixes were quite ductile, with average strengths ranging from 105 to 150 psi [724 to 1034 kPa]. Again, the general tendency is that higher straw yields greater strength (and erosion resistance). Portland cement-lime plasters ranged from 280 psi [1930 kPa] (using poorly-hydrated lime) to about 500–600 psi [3447 to 4136 kPa] for common stucco plaster with type S lime. These were values taken at ages one and two months, and would be expected to increase with time as the lime component carbonates.

Modulus of Elasticity (MOE)

Portland cement-lime plasters showed an MOE with the same ultimate strength relationship to breaking strength, $57,000\sqrt{f'_c}$, as do concrete mixes. Earth plaster MOE values were about 200 times smaller than the values predicted by the same formula.

Modulus of Rupture (MOR)

Earth plasters adhere well to the ultimate strength concrete formula for MOR, $7.5\sqrt{f'_c}$. Cement-lime plasters appear to have significantly more MOR strength, and by extension shear strength, than would be predicted by the concrete formula. (In an idealized cube of material subjected to uniaxial tension, there exists shear stress of equal magnitude on a plane rotated 45° from the load axis – and vice versa; shear stress = tension stress. In design formulas, however, be they strength or allowable stress methods, allowable shear is much less than the calculated MOR due to variations in geometry, brittleness, importance to collapse prevention, and other factors.

The number of samples tested in the EBNet test program was too small either to establish a reasonable statistical spread or to compute a meaningful standard deviation to use as the basis for exploring values for capacity reduction factors (φ) for ultimate strength design, or factors of safety (FS) for allowable stress design. In the absence of a project-specific testing program, if a small sample of tests such as these is used as the basis of design, a very large factor of safety (in the order of 8 to 10) should be used to account for the uncertainty of statistical spread. This comment would apply to both MOE and MOR/allowable shear values.

3.5C
THE SHRINKAGE TEST

This one is relatively simple and easy. Build an open box (typically about 18 inches [48 cm] long and two inches [5 cm] in cross-section) with smooth, greased sides. Fill it with the plaster material, being sure to use the same water content as will be used on the building; then let it dry.

It can take a week or more to fully dry, depending on conditions, but when it does, the width of the crack that has appeared (c) divided by the length inside the box (l) gives the percentage shrinkage (shrk.) of the dried vs. wet plaster. Shrk. = c/l. Now you can figure out how much cracking to expect – or if the plaster is just too expansive to use.

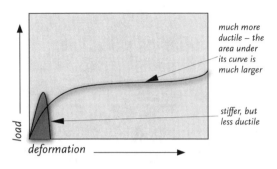

much more ductile – the area under its curve is much larger

stiffer, but less ductile

load

deformation

**3.5D
BRITTLENESS VS.
DUCTILITY**

*When measuring
the load–deformation
curve of a material
or assembly (in
compression or
bending, typically),
a curve is generated
as shown here and
previously. The area
under that curve is
one measure of ductility,
or the amount of energy
absorbed as the material
deforms, and the smaller
the area, the more brittle
or non-ductile the
material or assembly
is. In earthquakes, you
want ductility – if not
in the material itself,
then certainly in the
system. That, to a
great extent, is what
keeps the roof from
falling on your head.*

Even strong plasters cannot carry loads, however, if the whole assembly is detailed poorly, or, in the case of unstabilized earth plaster, subjected to soaking. In order for plasters to carry loads from the top of the wall to the bottom, they must be able to receive the load at the top of the wall and transmit it to the foundation or floor at the bottom of the wall. Detailing at the top of the wall should also bear the top plate or roof-bearing assembly (as it sometimes called) directly on the plaster. The plaster skin acts like a thin, hard bearing wall continuously braced by the softer straw core, so the strength of the assembly depends on many things besides just the plaster's compressive strength; see chapter 4, *Structure,* for a detailed discussion of load paths.

3.6 Reinforcing for plasters

Plasters can be reinforced internally by adding various fibers to the mix or by embedding woven or welded mesh in the plaster. Plaster reinforcement serves many functions. It can prevent micro and macro cracking at openings and in the field of the wall, help a plaster span over two dissimilar materials, and hugely improve the structural performance of a wall system. The less ductile a plaster, the more its shear-resisting performance will be improved with reinforcing.

3.6.1 Fiber reinforcements

Typical fiber reinforcement for cement plaster includes fiberglass, polypropylene, and fine steel fibers. Lime plaster is traditionally reinforced with animal hair (at least ¾ inch long) from the bodies of cows, goats, horses or dogs (mane or tail hair is not used, as it is too glossy). Earth plasters are generally reinforced with some type of plant fibers: chopped straw, chaff, or manure (straw or grass pre-processed by ruminants). Generally speaking, the more fiber in the mix, the tougher it will be (less brittle, with a higher modulus of rupture), but the percentage of fiber in a mix is generally limited by workability needs or by the application method. Too much fiber in a mix leaves it unworkable – it cannot be spread on a wall by hand. Blown-on mixes are generally lower in fiber because fiber clogs the blower nozzle.

3.6.2 Mesh reinforcements

Unlike short fibers mixed with the plaster, mesh alone is effective in transferring shear loads between plasters and structural elements like the roof or foundation.

Meshes with welded intersections are much stronger than woven varieties that allow individual strands to slide by each other. Connections between the mesh and other structural elements (like the roof or foundation) deserve attention during both design and construction because they are often the weakest link in the system. To be most effective, mesh should be well embedded in the center of the plaster. Some engineers, architects, and builders have taken great pains to create systems that hold the mesh off the face of bales slightly (so it will be completely embedded in the plaster). However, given the uneven surface of the bale wall itself, this usually just amounts to inserting non-corrosive spacers between the mesh and the more prominent points on the straw surface. Mesh needs to be open enough (roughly 1½ inch [40 mm] square holes or larger) to readily allow plaster through; mesh with too tight a weave will prevent plaster from developing the crucial bond with the straw.

3.6A

Hemp mesh modelled by world famous architect Carol Venolia

While mesh is not required in all circumstances, cement plasters and lime plasters are usually reinforced with galvanized metal mesh. In non-seismic areas, builders typically use (if anything) a 16 or 17 gauge, hexagonal woven wire mesh (aka "stucco mesh"). Though this may help prevent small cracks, it is not suitable to carry significant structural loads because it can stretch under tension. In California, the use of 14 gauge, 2 inch [50 mm] x 2 inch, welded, galvanized mesh has become common because it has a structural capacity well matched to the strength of the cement plasters and it can be adequately stapled to sill plates and roof bearing assemblies.

There is a strong argument against the use of galvanized metal mesh in earth plasters. As discussed before, earth plasters are hydrophilic and tend to store water, perhaps more than cement or lime plasters. They are also highly vapor-permeable, and the presence of adequate oxygen and moisture in earth plasters together may speed the rusting of metal. This effect is most certainly highly dependent on the moisture load of the wall. To be on the safe side, use welded plastic mesh (high density polypropylene or HD polyethylene). Fiber meshes such as hemp, jute, or coconut fiber also work well in earth plasters but will decay if exposed to repeated wetting. On the other hand, the presence of intact natural fiber reinforcing in centuries-old earthen structures tells us that natural fibers can and do last a very long time if protected from wetting. In summary: if the mesh matters a lot structurally, and will get wet often, use some sort of plastic. If not, almost anything – including no mesh – will do.

3.6B

A WELL-DESIGNED MIX OF MODERN AND TRADITIONAL MATERIALS — A WALL READY FOR PLASTERING.

The steel X-brace over the straw bales is there to carry the very high seismic loads of coastal California, and is bolted to the foundation and floor framing above.

The reed matting is stapled to the window bucks so as to locally reinforce the earthen plaster against cracking.

photo courtesy of Kelly Lerner

If designed to resist structural loads, meshes should be firmly attached to structural elements. If mesh is used solely to prevent cracking, it can be embedded between coats of plaster. Woven reed mats make an effective lath directly over wood members. Meshes especially designed for long-lasting earth contact are commercially available as a variety of geo-textiles used for soil and stream bank reinforcing.

Though plasters do bond well to straw, wall systems that must carry high loads require that the mesh on either side of the wall be connected with through-ties (galvanized or polypropylene). This reinforces the plaster skins against buckling and traps the ductile straw bale core in a fully enclosed cage. For a more in-depth discussion of mesh reinforcement of plastered straw bale walls for seismic resistance see chapter 4, *Structure.*

Special Reinforcement Around Openings – Window and Doors

Regardless of the plaster, the area around windows and doors should always be reinforced against cracking caused by differential movement from use and temperature. For cement and lime plasters, builders typically use 16 gauge expanded metal mesh (also known as *diamond mesh* or "blood lath" by those working with it without gloves). For earth plasters, woven reed matting and burlap work well.

3.6.3 Summary of recent mesh and anchorage tests[2]

Two important components of the structural load path in a plastered straw bale wall are the mesh reinforcement and its anchorage to the mud sill and roof-bearing assembly. The selection of suitable meshes and anchorage has been complicated by issues related to the recent introduction of wood preservatives that are highly corrosive to steel fasteners. Recent tests[2] investigated the strengths of several meshes: 14 and 16 gauge steel wire mesh, Cintoflex® C polypropylene, and hemp twine, and anchorage by means of pneumatically or manually driven electro-galvanized and stainless steel staples. Based on the data reported there, we can make recommendations for the anchorage of meshes in straw bale walls.

3.6.3.1 Materials

The following materials were used in the experimental tests:

Meshes

- 14 gauge 2 inch x 2 inch [51 x 51 mm], manufactured by the Vataert Corporation in Van Buren, Arizona. The mesh is galvanized before welding and comes in a 4 x 100 ft [1.22 x 30.5 m] roll. This mesh is from the same batch that was used in the construction of the corresponding large-scale wall tests[3].

- 16 gauge 2 inch x 2 inch [51 x 51 mm] welded wire fabric used in plaster finishing, bright in appearance. Manufactured by Davis Wire, Type 1, Grade D, with Double D paper.
- Hemp netting, hand knitted from hemp twine, with an 80 x 80 mm mesh, produced in a 6.71 x 22.86 m panel, product QHK001-080 Net. Obtained from Trade Marker International, http://www.trademarker1.com/Contact_TMI.htm
- Cintoflex C 1.73 x 1.92 x 0.047 inch [44 x 49 mm] plastic polypropylene mesh. See www.tenaxus.com/agriculture/product%20specs/deer.html.

The mesh materials are not manufactured for structural use and thus do not have to satisfy minimum strength requirements. Consequently, there is no assurance that nominally identical materials will have strengths comparable to those of the samples tested therein. No previous strength tests are known to have been conducted for these mesh types.

Staples
- Stainless steel: 16 gauge x 1.75 inch [45 mm] medium crown chisel point (SENCO N19BGBN)
- Electro-galvanized: 16 gauge x 1.75 inch [45 mm] medium crown (SENCO N19BAB).
- Electro-galvanized: 16 gauge x 1.25 inch [32 mm] medium crown (SENCO N15BAB).
- Manually driven staples: 1/2 inch crown, 1 inch length with chisel point. Note: the medium crown staples have a $7/16$ inch [11 mm] crown.

Sill Plates
- 4x4 (nominal 4 x 4 inch, actual 3½ x 3½ inch) [89 x 89 mm] No. 2 grade Douglas fir, pressure-treated with copper azole.
- 4x4 [89 x 89 mm] No. 2 grade Douglas fir, without pressure treatment.
- 1x2 (nominal 1x2 inch, actual ¾ x 1½ inch) [19 x 38 mm] pine, used along the side of a pressure-treated 4x4. These materials were obtained at a local building supply store.

Building Paper

- Fortified Flashing SK-10, Type 1, Grade A, Style 4 building paper was used to provide a physical barrier between the mesh and pressure-treated wood in some configurations.

3.6.3.2 Wire Tests

Tension tests were performed on the individual wires of each mesh (here a *wire* may refer to a wire of the steel mesh, hemp twine, or polypropylene strand). Longitudinal wires (extending in the direction of the roll) were selected for the tests, recognizing that the mesh typically is placed vertically along the height of a wall, and that the vertical wires in a wall are the ones subject to axial tensile stresses through the uplift/holdown action of a wall subject to in-plane or out-of-plane lateral loads. Each wire sample was subjected to a monotonic tension test in a Universal Testing Machine. The wire sample was positioned so that the weld to the transverse wire (or strand junction in the case of Cintoflex C mesh) and a short length of that wire were located in the test region, between the grips on either end. For the hemp mesh, a straight length of twine (without knots) was positioned in the grips.

TABLE 1A: INDIVIDUAL WIRE TEST RESULTS

SAMPLE (Run) Number	14-GAUGE MESH Strength lbs	Failure Location	16-GAUGE MESH Strength lbs	Failure Location	HEMP Strength lbs	Failure Location	CINTROFLEX C Strength lbs	Failure Location
1	408.5	Wire	327.6	Wire	55.2	Twine	76.2	Junction
2	326.7	Weld	340.9	Wire	55.9	Twine	77.1	Junction
3	386.9	Wire	338.5	Wire	66.3	Twine	75.6	Junction
4	404.1	Weld	353.2	Wire	61.8	Twine	75.2	Strand
5	391.3	Wire	299.4	Wire	53.9	Twine	76.6	Junction
6	363.3	Weld	297.1	Wire	54.8	Twine	76.9	Strand
7	414.4	Wire	306.2	Wire	54.8	Twine	69.7	Strand
8	412.7	Wire	292.2	Wire	--	--	72.4	Strand
9	365.7	Wire	320.2	Wire	--	--	73.7	Strand
10	366.4	Wire	324.2	Wire	--	--	76.8	Strand

Ultimate strengths and failure modes are reported in Table 1A for the four materials; sample statistics are reported in Table 1B. While the steel wires generally yielded over their lengths, the hemp mesh failed through an unraveling and sliding of individual fibers of the twine relative to one another. The strand of the Cintoflex often failed somewhere along its length between the grips, but in four instances the failure occurred at the junction of longitudinal and transverse strands, with the transverse strand splitting along its length and through the junction with the longitudinal strand.

TABLE 1B: WIRE TEST SUMMARY STATISTICS*

MATERIAL	MEAN STRENGTH, LBS	COEFFICIENT OF VARIATION	DIAMETER, IN.	AREA, IN²	MEAN STRENGTH, KSI
14-Gauge	384.2	7.34%	0.07961	0.00498	77.2
16-Gauge	330.0	6.27%	0.06361	0.00318	103.8
hemp	57.9	8.12%	0.10	0.0079	7.3
Cintoflex C	75.2	3.19%	0.047	0.00173	43.5

* Mean of 10 measurements, consisting of two measurements offset by approximately 90 degrees per wire for five wires.

Monotonic tension test results are plotted for a few representative wires in Figures 1 and 2. Total load is plotted as a function of the displacement of the test machine's loading head. The data were recorded manually. It is apparent that even the failure at the weld in Run 4 of the 14-gauge wires occurred after considerable yielding over the length of wire between the grips.

3.6.3.3 Mesh Anchorage Tests

Anchorage of the mesh to a mud sill and roof-bearing assembly is an essential element of a complete load path for resisting lateral forces. The widespread use of new chemical preservatives in pressure-treated wood members such as ACQ[A] that are more corrosive to steel has given impetus to develop practical corrosion-resistant details capable of fully mobilizing the strength of the mesh. The wood industry recommends the use of hot-dipped galvanized fasteners (with thicker coatings than for CCA[B] treated lumber) or the use of stainless steel fasteners in wood treated with ACQ. However, hot-dipped galvanized staples are not manufactured for use with pneumatic staple guns. Stainless steel staples are available, although they cost approximately eight to ten times more than ordinary electro-galvanized staples.

The medium- and large-scale tests done as part of the EBNet Straw Bale Test Program demonstrated that a 4x4 mud sill with anchor bolts at 2 foot [61 cm] centers was sufficient to anchor the mesh to the foundation, while a conventional

FOOTNOTES

A
Ammoniacal Copper Quaternary
B
Chromated Copper Arsenate

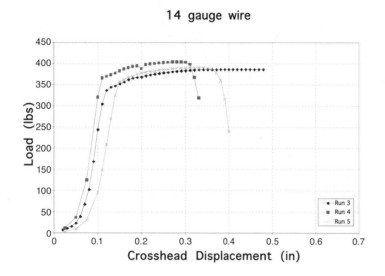

14 gauge wire

▲ **3.6C** LOAD-DISPLACEMENT RESPONSE FOR REPRESENTATIVE **14**-GAUGE WIRES

▼ **3.6D** LOAD-DISPLACEMENT RESPONSE FOR REPRESENTATIVE **16**-GAUGE WIRES

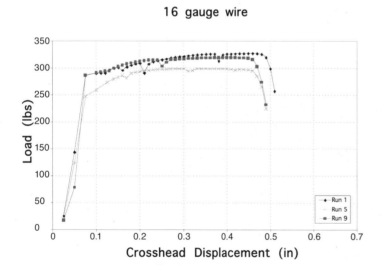

16 gauge wire

2x4 mud sill was inadequate for developing the strength of 14 gauge mesh. These tests also determined that the strength of the 16 gauge mesh could not be developed because premature failures occurred at the welds between longitudinal and transverse wires. In contrast, the strength of the 14 gauge mesh could be developed, without having failures induced at the weld locations. However, in the present tests of individual wires, three of the ten 14 gauge wires failed at the weld, while none of the ten 16 gauge wire tests failed at the weld. Whether similar results would occur under more realistic test scenarios that included the 4x4 and anchor bolts in a concrete foundation is not clear.

The objective of the mesh anchorage tests was to establish the combinations of staple type, staple orientation, and mesh that are adequate to develop the strength of the mesh anchored into a 4x4 mud sill. The configurations investigated are summarized in Table 2. Electro-galvanized staples were used with untreated mud sills, while stainless steel staples were used with treated mud sills. Building paper was used to prevent direct contact between the steel meshes and a treated mud sill. The shorter staples were used with the Cintoflex C and hemp meshes. The staple anchorage was believed to be weakest when the staples were driven parallel to grain, and thus the 4x4 was rotated to select the face that most closely duplicated this orientation. The staples were driven to avoid crimping the wire and varied from a loose to a snug fit.

Many designers are using an untreated 4x4 placed directly on top of a 1x4 redwood or plastic mud sill, thus providing the necessary capillary break from a foundation without having to use a corrosive-treated structural sill plate. This is most closely represented by Configuration A. The large scale tests indicated that the steel mesh is severely worked under reversed cyclic loading in the vicinity of the staple – in effect, where it passes from the plaster's inside face to the interior plaster where it is well protected. Configuration D aims to keep the mesh aligned in a vertical plane by using a 1x2 furring strip to anchor the mesh in the interior of the plaster rather than at the inside face (Figure 3.6E).

3.6E

1x2 furring strip to anchor the mesh in a vertical plane (Configuration D)

For the steel and Cintoflex meshes, a segment of mesh containing nine longitudinal wires was stapled at its base to the 4x4 mud sill. The staples were placed in an alternating pattern over the lowest two transverse wires, which were centered (approximately) over the face of the 4x4 (see Figure 3.6F). Longitudinal wires were isolated from one another by cutting the transverse wires on either side above the rows of staples. The two longitudinal wires at either end of the sample were considered to provide a boundary at the periphery of the test region, which consisted of the innermost five wires. Again, giving consideration to anchorage provided by staples on either side of the wire being tested, the wires were pulled individually in the sequence identified in Figure 3.6E. Note that for Configuration D, the staples were placed along a single transverse wire, with three additional staples placed at seven inches on o.c. (on center) to anchor the 1x2 to the 4x4.

The large spacing of the hemp wires required that the staples be placed in a single row. In these cases a horizontally-oriented staple was placed just above a knot. Three or four wires were tested, and the boundary consisted of a single wire on either side of the test region.

3.6F

Detail showing alternating staples and sequence of individual wire tests; (below) test set up

The adequacy of the staple anchorage was determined by testing the individual wires monotonically. While the monotonic tests are relatively simple and reliable, the tests do not replicate dynamic seismic effects wherein the wires can be expected to be loaded more uniformly and under repeated cycles. The testing of wires individually may place more severe demands on the weld at the transverse wire nearest the staple, but, on the other hand, monotonic demands are generally not as severe as reversed cyclic demands. Thus, some judgment (as always) is required for interpretation of the results.

TABLE 2   MESH ANCHORAGE CONFIGURATIONS

CONFIGURATION	MESH	MUD SILL	STAPLE TYPE	STAPLE ORIENTATION
A	14 gauge	Untreated 4x4	Electro-galvanized 1.75 inch legs	Diagonal at weld intersection
B	14 gauge	Pressure-treated 4x4 with building paper	Stainless steel 1.75 inch legs	Diagonal at weld intersection
C	14 gauge	Pressure-treated 4x4 with building paper	Stainless steel 1.75 inch legs	Horizontal above weld intersection
D	14 gauge	Pressure-treated 4x4 with untreated 1x2	Stainless steel 1.75 inch legs	Diagonal at weld intersection
E	16 gauge	Pressure-treated 4x4 with building paper	Stainless steel 1.75 inch legs	Diagonal at weld intersection
F	Cintoflex C	Untreated 4x4	Electro-galvanized 1.25 inch legs	Horizontal above junction
G	Cintoflex C	Untreated 4x4	Manually-driven 1 inch legs	Horizontal above junction
H	Hemp	Untreated 4x4	Electro-galvanized 1.25 inch legs	Horizontal above knot
I	Hemp	Untreated 4x4	Manually-driven 1 inch legs	Horizontal above knot

TABLE 3   MESH ANCHORAGE TEST RESULTS

TEST	CONFIGURATION A Strength, pounds	Failure Description	CONFIGURATION B Strength, pounds	Failure Description	CONFIGURATION C Strength, pounds	Failure Description
1	358.4	Transverse wire failed at weld	267.8	Weld failure	251.0	Staple pulled out
2	321.3	Wire failure	363.4	Weld failure	368.2	Staple pulled out
3	293.5	Staple leg snapped	201.4	Weld failure	270.9	Staple pulled out
4	334.2	Weld failure at staple	281.7	Weld failure	244.9	Staple pulled out
5	248.6	Weld failure at staple	286.6	Weld failure	311.4	Staple pulled out

TEST	CONFIGURATION D Strength, pounds	Failure Description	CONFIGURATION E Strength, pounds	Failure Description	CONFIGURATION F Strength, pounds	Failure Description
1	311.5	Weld failure at staple	97.4	Separation of wires from one another at weld	76.2	Failure of junction at staple
2	260.4	Weld failure at staple	118.2	Separation of wires from one another at weld	77.1	Strand failure at top junction
3	260.9	Weld failure at staple	108.3	Separation of wires from one another at weld	75.2	Strand failure top junction
4	wires not tested		101.9	Separation of wires from one another at weld	76.6	Wire failure at top weld
5	wires not tested		70.2	Horizontal weld failure	75.7	Strand failure at top junction

TEST	CONFIGURATION G Strength, pounds	Failure Description	CONFIGURATION H Strength, pounds	Failure Description	CONFIGURATION I Strength, pounds	Failure Description
1	78.4	Failure of upper junction	55.2	Twine failure by unraveling	53.9	Twine failure by unraveling
2	69.8	Failure of upper junction	55.9	Twine failure by unraveling	54.8	Twine failure by unraveling
3	73.5	Failure of upper junction	66.3	Twine failure by unraveling	54.8	Twine failure by unraveling
4	75.2	Failure of upper junction	61.8	Twine failure by unraveling	wires not tested	
5	76.9	Failure of upper junction	wires not tested		wires not tested	

3.6G *Failure of transverse wire at weld (Configuration A)*

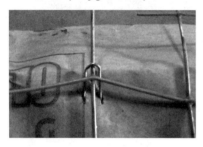

3.6H *Pullout of staple (Configuration C)*

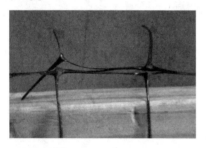

3.6J *Lengthwise split of transverse wire and junction (Configuration G)*

3.6K *Unraveling of twine – note the elongation of other wires, which have not yet been loaded (Configuration H)*

Figures 3.6G through 3.6K show photographs of some of the failures observed in the mesh anchorage tests.

Figure 3.6L compares the strengths measured in the mesh anchorage tests with the mean individual wire strengths of Table 1b. It is apparent that the test procedure was not able to mobilize the strengths of the individual wires for Configurations A through E. The failures for Configuration C were characterized by the staple pulling out from the 4x4. The failures for Configurations A, B, D, and E often involved wire fracture or wire separation at the welds. Yet the 14 gauge wire used in Configurations A-D was fully developed in the large-scale tests. This suggests that the test procedure used places more severe demands on the welds than are encountered in practical applications as wall reinforcement. The staples used in configurations A-D were able to support the loads delivered by the wire; the highest strengths observed in Configurations A, B, and D were able to support the loads transmitted prior to failure of the weld, with the exception of one instance in which an electro-galvanized staple leg failed. The highest tested strengths approached the mean strength of the 14 gauge wire, suggesting that these staples may well be adequate for the 14 gauge mesh, just as was observed in the large-scale tests. Configuration C demonstrates that the staples should be oriented diagonally over the weld rather than horizontally above the weld. The increased likelihood of failure of the welds of the 16 gauge mesh, first observed in the medium scale tests, is also evident in the low strengths obtained for Configuration E. The lower-strength Cintoflex C and hemp meshes were adequately anchored by the staples used in Configurations F, G, H, and I. There appears to be no obvious pattern of the strengths obtained relative to the test number, which might have occurred if the integrity of the adjacent wires or welds along the two transverse wires had been essential for resisting the applied load.

3.6.3.4 Recommended Stapled Mesh Details

Based on the test results described[2], and those obtained in earlier medium- and large-scale tests[3], we recommend the following for seismic load-resisting walls:

1. 14 gauge mesh should be anchored using 16 gauge medium crown (7/16 inch or 11 mm) staples having 1¾inch [44.5 mm] legs oriented diagonally over the welds and installed at a depth that does not crimp the mesh against the 4x4. If the mud sill is pressure-treated, the mesh should not be in contact with it, and a stainless steel staple is required. Building paper may be used to provide a physical barrier between the mesh and pressure-treated lumber, or a 1x2 [18 x 38 mm] furring strip may be used with adequate fastening to the 4x4 (Configuration D) to separate the mesh from the treated 4x4 and keep the mesh in the center of the plaster. An alternative is to use electro-galvanized staples with an untreated 4x4 over a 1x4 plastic or treated mud sill. The 14 gauge mesh should be used with a cement or lime-cement plaster.

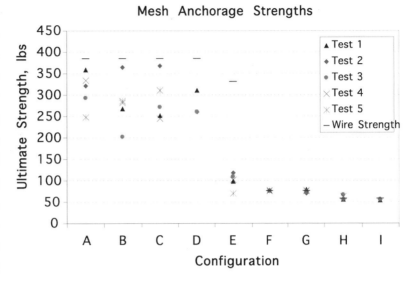

3.6L
COMPARISON OF MESH ANCHORAGE STRENGTH RESULTS AND WIRE STRENGTHS

2. Cintoflex C (or equivalent polypropylene or polyethylene) and hemp meshes may be anchored using 16 gauge medium crown staples having 1¼ in. [32 mm] legs or using heavier gauge manually-driven staples having 1 inch [25 mm] or longer legs. The staples should be oriented horizontally and located just above the strand junction or twine knot. The Cintoflex C and hemp meshes should be used with an earth or lime plaster, not a strong and brittle lime-cement plaster.

3.7 The Role of Plasters in Moisture Control

With increasingly (and appropriately) airtight building enclosures and higher levels of insulation, moisture performance is among the most important issues in construction today. *"Won't straw walls rot?"* is the most common question asked about straw bale construction. Straw, like any other organic material, *will* rot, but only under conditions rarely encountered in a well-built wall (see section 5.3). In fact, field testing and a large body of anecdotal evidence has shown that straw bale walls don't rot unless they are subjected to large moisture loads from sources such as:

- roof leaks (including and especially parapet walls)
- improper flashing at window sills or heads that lead to leaks
- direct contact with soil
- direct contact with concrete foundations
  (that wick water from the soil into the bales)
- cracks in plaster
- condensation on barrier membranes such as plastic

A well-detailed and skillfully-applied plaster is both an important defense against and a solution for moisture problems. The continuous nature of plaster helps prevent air leaks, keeping vapor-laden air from transporting tremendous amounts of moisture into a wall (as long as the joints between plaster and other materials are well detailed and sealed). Plasters also play a major role in keeping straw bales dry by intercepting and repelling liquid moisture (mainly precipitation). Finally, the vapor permeability of a plaster will govern how easily a moisture-laden wall can dry out.

Moisture can get into straw bale walls in several ways (in descending order of magnitude):
- via water leaks – cracks in plaster, poor flashing details, roof leaks, leaks at window sills, etc.
- via air leaks – vapor-laden air can carry large amounts of moisture into the wall
- via capillary action (wicking) through the plaster or concrete foundation
- via vapor diffusion through the plaster or concrete foundation

Assuming that a wall system is detailed and built well enough to avoid major air and water leaks, the two important measures of a plaster's moisture performance are:
capillary absorption (the rate at which plaster will absorb liquid water – wetting capacity) and
vapor permeance (the rate at which vapor diffuses through the plaster – drying capacity)

The imaginary ideal plaster for a straw bale wall would be a one-way membrane that prevents water from entering the wall (low wetting capacity) but still allows the wall to dry out (high drying capacity). In their "natural" state, without coatings, the ideal plasters do not exist. Fortunately, however, an inexpensive, clear, non-toxic surficial treatment is available that can be brushed or sprayed on porous surfaces without altering their appearance. That product is known generically as *silane* or more often *siloxane* ("Any of a class of organic or inorganic chemical compounds of silicon, oxygen, and usually carbon and hydrogen, based on the structural unit R2SiO, where R is an alkyl group, usually methyl", according to the *American Heritage Dictionary)*; various siloxane products are readily available from concrete supply houses. Here is how siloxane treatment affects the moisture properties of common plasters:

TABLE 4   MOISTURE PERFORMANCE OF PLASTERS WITH AND WITHOUT
SILOXANE COATING[4]

PLASTER	CAPILLARY ABSORPTION SUCTION (KG/M²S^{1/2})	VAPOR PERMEABILITY (NG/PA S M)	PERMEANCE (US PERMS)
Cement 1:3 cement:sand	0.378 (without siloxane) 0.0004 (with siloxane)	1.7 (without siloxane) 1.7 (with siloxane)	0.68 (without siloxane) 0.7 (with siloxane)
Cement-Lime 1:1:6 cement:lime:sand	0.0917 (without siloxane) 0.0006 (with siloxane)	10.3 (without siloxane) 8.3 (with siloxane)	5.13 (without siloxane) 3.54 (with siloxane)
Cement-Lime 1:2:9 cement:lime:sand	0.1100 (without siloxane)	14.9 (without siloxane)	5.13 (without siloxane)
Lime 1:3 lime:sand	0.1273 (without siloxane)	18.9 (without siloxane)	9.85 (without siloxane)
Earth plaster	0.152 (without siloxane) 0.0117 (with limewash) 0.0017 (with siloxane)	23.3 (without siloxane) 40.8 (with lime wash)	16-19 (without siloxane) 19.2 (with lime wash)

Clearly siloxane is an excellent coating for plasters over straw bale walls because it almost eliminates water absorption (wetting capacity) without reducing vapor permeability (drying capacity). In fact, siloxane compounds were long ago developed and well-researched by the concrete and masonry industries, which share with straw bale builders a concern for durability in ultraviolet, moist, and sea air environments. It has been found to be generally stable, with ultraviolet light only affecting the outer few hundred nanometers (less than a thousandth of a millimeter). In the case of porous materials like the surface of a plastered wall, most of the applied siloxane would never be exposed to ultraviolet light, so there is presumably a long life to a well-applied coating.

Note also that while earth plasters are significantly more vapor-permeable than cement and lime plasters, they are not appreciably more absorbent. Anecdotal reports from the field indicate that the most noteworthy difference between the moisture performance of cement and lime-based plaster and earth plasters is that while cement and lime plasters will wick moisture into wood and bale walls (when liquid moisture is present), earth plaster will draw moisture out of wood and bale walls and also help prevent moisture from reaching those walls unless the earth plaster is totally saturated. More research is needed in this area to fully understand and model this effect.

In short – pay close attention here – **moisture will get into walls,** but there are strategies to keep the moisture in walls from reaching dangerous levels. In general terms, you want to minimize the moisture that gets into walls and also make sure that they have a safe way to dry out:

1. Reduce moisture loads by creating a continuous coating of plaster to prevent air leaks. Take special precautions to caulk around edges and openings: sill plates, top plates, electrical boxes, doors, and windows.
2. Reduce moisture loads from plaster absorption
   - by protecting walls with overhangs, porches, or rainscreens
   - by coating walls with water repellant coatings that reduce absorption without reducing vapor permeance (Silane, Siloxane, etc)
   - by fine-tuning the protection level for a given wall to its climate and weather exposure
3. Avoid using sheet moisture barriers like plastic or house wrap. They provide surfaces for condensation and prevent drying – in other words, they usually end up trapping water *in,* not keeping it out.
4. Use plasters with a high drying capacity (high vapor permeability) to give moisture that does get into the wall a way to escape. This is especially true in wetter climates because the drying capacity is already limited by high humidity.

For a more detailed discussion about protecting straw bale walls from moisture damage see chapter 5, *Moisture.*

3.8 Durability and Maintenance: Erosion, Coatings, and Repairability

Durability and the ongoing expense of maintenance are considerations with any building material, but are especially important with plasters given their structural and moisture control responsibilities. On walls exposed to precipitation or mechanical damage, cement and lime plasters are more durable than earth plasters. Since earth plasters begin to erode most drastically when they reach saturation, any measure that slows saturation will protect the earth plaster – including macro solutions like overhangs, porches, and rain screens (see chapters 5 and 10), and micro solutions like mixes with a high percentage of straw, straw thatch embedded in the plaster, or a rough surface (see section 3.4.3 on earth plasters).

Cement-based plasters, well applied on a stable substrate and well cured, are very durable. However because of their rigidity (brittleness) they are more apt to crack when faced with differential movement, structural loading, or thermal expansion. This is of special concern because cracks in cement plasters are difficult to repair. Both lime and earth plasters are both more ductile (flexible) than cement plaster and are more easily repaired. Small cracks in lime plaster are self-healing, and larger cracks can be filled with several coats of limewash. Cracks in earth plasters can be repaired easily by moistening the plaster in situ and reworking it.

3.9 Environmental Considerations

As our world awakens to the harsh reality of limited fossil fuel energy and natural resources, the environmental performance of materials is quickly (but maybe not quickly enough) becoming as important as their other performance measurements. The production of Portland cement requires huge energy inputs, to say nothing of the environmental destruction of mining, the release of CO_2 and other pollutants during firing, or transportation costs. The production of lime requires somewhat less energy than that of cement, but both reabsorb CO_2 as they carbonate over the years. Earth plasters, which are typically locally sourced, take little energy to process and can return gracefully to the earth at the end of a building's useful life.

3.10 Methods of Application

Plasters can be applied in a variety of manners:

- Troweled on by hand (in the case of earth plasters, without any tools)
- Harled on by hand (a traditional way of throwing the final coat of lime plaster onto the wall with a shovel-like trowel and a flick of the wrist)
- Sprayed on (wet plaster mixture pumped from a hopper)
- Shot on (water and dry material mixed at the spray nozzle)

Some practitioners argue that because sprayed-on and shot-on plasters are applied with more pressure, they penetrate further into the face of the bales and create a better bond with the straw. In practice, however, both hand-applied and machine-applied plasters show good bonding with straw bales if they are well consolidated (worked into the face of the bale).

The overspray from sprayed-on applications can be quite messy and requires full masking of windows, doors, and trim. There is sometimes quite a bit of waste material left around the building that must be cleaned up at the end of the day. But spraying a plaster is relatively fast and does not require as much skilled hand labor. Successfully troweling on plaster requires some skill, but can be done quite neatly with little waste and little cleanup. In general, spray-on applications are more suitable for projects with larger expanses of unbroken wall surface or in areas without skilled plasterers. Troweled-on finishes are most appropriate for projects with a lot of architectural detail and/or in areas with a large supply of skilled plasterers.

3.11 Preparation and Curing

Common practice is to give the straw bale wall a "haircut" before plastering – trimming the bulges, loose straw, and other surface irregularities, typically with a weed whacker, chainsaw, and/or stiff broom. Depending on the quality of the bales, some builders will trim each bale before placing it in the wall to get a better, tighter assembly.

All plasters are better by every measure if they dry out slowly and evenly, and cement or lime-based plasters depend heavily on proper curing (meaning: being kept moist and above freezing) for at least a few weeks after application. A light spray of water on the wall just prior to plastering helps that cure – contrary though that may seem to all the admonitions throughout this book to fear and avoid water. Then, after each coat is applied, plasters should be protected from the sun and wind to prevent premature drying, and kept moist for as long as possible. This is especially true if there's cement in the mix, and doubly so if it's a lime plaster – this just can't be emphasized enough. The plaster is going to do so many things for you, and it will be what people see of your walls, so take the time to do it right.

References

Holmes, Stafford and Wingate, Michael. *Building with Lime, A Practical Introduction,* Intermediate Technology Publications, 2000.

Guelberth, Cedar Rose and Chiras, Dan. *The Natural Plaster Book,* New Society Publishers, 2003.

Lacinski, Paul and Bergeron, Michel. *Serious Straw Bale*, Chelsea Green, 2000.

Schofield, Jane. *Lime in Building, A Practical Guide,* Black Dog Press, Great Britian, 2001.

Steen, Bill and Athena. Personal conversations and Canelo Project workshops, 2000 through present.

Straube, J.F. *Moisture Properites of Plaster and Stucco for Strawbale Buildings,* Report for Ecological Building Network, 2003.

ENDNOTES

1
Lerner, Kelly, and Donahue, Kevin (2003) *Structural Testing of Plasters for Straw Bale Construction* Ecological Building Network, Sausalito, California

2
Parker, A, Aschheim, M, Mar, D, Hammer, M, and King, B. (2005) *Recommended Mesh Anchorage Details for Straw Bale Walls* Ecological Building Network, Sausalito, California

3
Ash, C, Aschheim, M, Mar, D, and King, B. (2004) *Reversed Cyclic In-Plane Tests of Load-Bearing Plastered Straw Bale Walls* 13th World Conference on Earthquake Engineering, Vancouver, B.C., Canada

4
Straube, J. F. (2000) *Moisture Properties of Plaster and Stucco for Strawbale Buildings* Report for Canada Mortgage and Housing Corporation

4

STRUCTURE

4.1 Introduction to Structural Behavior

4.1.1 A first look

Imagine a hard-boiled egg: a thin, hard shell protects the interior from moisture, insects, wind, and, to a limited extent, impact. The shell is backed up by a thin, tough membrane; both are attached to and braced by the soft interior, which in turn consists of two parts of similar density and stiffness but only lightly attached – if pushed very hard, the yolk and the white can separate. None of the components of a hard-boiled egg is particularly strong, but the assembly is very efficient at resisting structural loading in the elastic range (up to the point where the shell cracks) and is surprisingly *ductile* – able to hold its shape far into the inelastic load range after the cracks first appear. You probably don't think of a hard-boiled egg as being very strong, but if you were two inches [51 mm] high, you would, and our analogy would then start to give you a proper sense of the subject of this chapter – that the strength of the whole is far greater than the sum of its parts.

It is very much the same with a plastered straw bale wall, on which the shell is the plaster and the membrane is whatever tensile reinforcing is placed in the plaster,

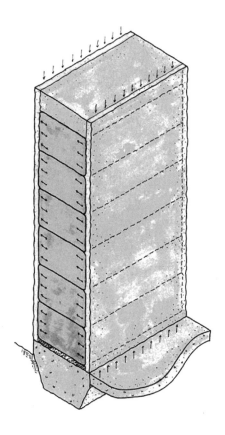

4.1A

The stacked straw bales and plastered skins of a bale structure interact with and reinforce each other

illustration by David Mar

be it chopped straw, fibrous mesh, or welded wire fabric. The egg white and yolk behave like stacked bales in being relatively soft and deformable, yet able to provide a reasonably firm substrate to support and brace the thin plaster skin. Again, the strength of the whole is far greater than the sum of its parts.

In the brief twelve or so years since structural engineers first began examining and testing straw bale wall assemblies, they have reached a good understanding of how these assemblies behave. Plastered straw bale walls are like masonry, but only to an extent; they are big, soft, fuzzy bricks coated by and relying on thin, hard "skins" that tend to absorb all types of loading due to their much greater stiffness. "So," the engineers typically reason, "they are really more like thin-shell concrete structures, or like a certain breed of stress-skin panel insulating concrete form." And indeed they are, but, again, only to an extent. Unlike engineered stress-skin panels, or "sandwich structures" in which the material properties of the core are known, uniform, and consistent, a finished wall of stacked straw bales is a relatively complex and irregular assembly of heterogeneous materials. Add to that plaster skins of widely-varying qualities that may or may not be reinforced with any of a number of materials whose properties may not be well known, and you have an assembly that is demonstrably robust, but maddening to try and mathematically quantify.

> *This is a new type of structural assembly, and it is essential for structural engineers and builders to recognize this.*

The structural materials and systems we are accustomed to, be they steel, concrete, masonry, wood, or stress-skin panels, provide only partial insights into the behavior of a plastered straw bale system. There are plenty of similarities, as will be seen in the pages to come, but it bears emphasizing that we are talking here about a unique material combination and a unique structural system. Furthermore, as with any structural assembly, the behavior of an element will often be governed – as is the case here – as much or more by the boundary conditions than by the assembly itself. A plastered straw bale wall, or a reinforced concrete wall, or a steel column, or a plywood-sheathed wood stud wall, will succeed easily or fail spectacularly at serving its intended purpose depending on how well and artfully it is connected to the building surrounding it. The design of boundary connections for plastered straw bale walls, as needed to carry the various kinds of structural loads, will also be covered in the sections to follow.

Connecting the dots . . . a word about our thinking

Early in the writing of this chapter, one of the authors rightly expressed concern that we were obscuring the woods for the trees – presenting too much raw testing information without providing a clear narrative of behavior and design methodology. To the extent we were able, we have rectified that, but also leave in a great bulk of the testing information generated to date, and for good reason.

Structural engineers around the world are trained to design and work with steel and concrete, sometimes also with masonry and wood. That's it! Unless you engineers have gone on to learn, formally or informally, how to work with other materials, you may be inclined to think that there exist no other viable structural materials. If so, you will be quite mistaken. There are all sorts of indigenous building materials such as adobe, rammed earth, and Roman (pozzolanic) concrete whose 2,000+ year-old representatives around the globe testify to their durability, while new materials such as fiber composites, structural insulated panels (SIPs), and plastics are rapidly and justifiably entering the everyday construction world.

We here introduce a semi-new structural system – plastered straw bales – with a hundred years of usage but precious little testing background. The constituent materials are straw bales, many kinds of plasters and reinforcements, and (usually) wood with staple fasteners. We know a lot about some of these, less about others, and even less about how the assembly, in its many forms, behaves under various structural loads. We now *do* know enough to sketch out structural behavior in a way never before possible, and herein do so, but don't yet have a data base anything like that now accumulated for concrete, steel, and wood.

This is cause for caution, of course, but not cause for decrying the whole package as untested and unknown. We who have conducted many tests and authored this structural section (four structural engineers with a fair collection of registrations, grey hair, advanced degrees, decades of experience, awards for seismic design, and membership on mainstream seismic design committees) here present to you our thoughts and conclusions, but also the bulk of the information upon which our thinking is based. We think that only appropriate, and invite readers to send feedback, as well as new findings from lab or field, that will refine and develop everybody's understanding. With time, we will know enough to confidently assign load reduction factors or safety factors appropriate to engineering design as we know it, and to fully welcome straw bale construction into mainstream building.

As straw bale construction continues to grow in popularity around the world, we need more engineers, architects, and builders to contribute toward our understanding of how to make the best use of this truly ecological building system.

4.1.2 Types of Wall Assemblies

Many details and wall systems are now in use, and dozens have been tried and discarded for one reason or another. In other words, straw bale construction is still very much a developing technology. It is nonetheless true that, as with every other building material, the ideal wall assembly for a particular project depends very much on area climate and seismicity, on building function, and on aesthetic and cultural preferences.

Until recently there were thought to be two basic styles of straw bale construction: *load-bearing* – or the eponymously named *Nebraska-style* in which the bale wall carries vertical load – and *non-load-bearing*, or *post-and-beam*, in which bales are used as infill panels between or around a structural frame. Post-and-beam style predominates in most areas for several compelling reasons:

1) It is generally more adaptable to varying architectural styles, to the inclusion of lots of doors and windows as for passive solar design, and to changes during or after construction.

2) The inherent conservatism of the construction industry resists anything "new"; building officials, mortgage lenders, insurors, and others all have to be convinced of the efficacy of anything unusual or different, and many building owners simply opt to use a structural frame to avoid the attendant, extended arguments that might hold them back. It is substantially easier to get a building permit, mortgage, and insurance for a "post-and-beam building with thick cellulose insulation" than for a "load-bearing straw bale structure" in highly regulated areas such as coastal California.

3) In the event of water or fire damage, it sometimes makes repair or replacement of portions of the bale wall easier because they carry no weight.

4) It allows the construction of a protecting roof prior to bale delivery and placement. This particular reason is huge, as an untimely rainstorm during construction has been the downfall of, or at least a major problem for, many load-bearing projects. Good bale builders wisely obsess about avoiding water problems anywhere in the lifetime of the bale, from the field to the completed wall. (See chapter 5, *Moisture*.)

With all of that said one may wonder why choose to build a load-bearing straw bale wall system at all. Again, there are several reasons:

1) Many who build with straw bales are seeking, more broadly, to build "green," that is, in as environmentally-friendly a way as possible. This often means minimizing the use of wood, in response to the worldwide devastation of old-growth forests over the past century. As has been pointed out, there are no old-growth fields of straw, so many seek to replace wood fiber with straw fiber wherever possible in the building. (See chapter 2, *The Straw Bale Family Tree*.)

2) A load-bearing structure is often simpler and faster to erect. If the project is in a location like western Nebraska of the late 1800s, where other building materials were scarce or just unavailable, then the appeal becomes that much stronger. The smaller the building, the easier it is to quickly erect the bale walls and put up a roof, even prior to any plastering. For exactly the same reasons, load-bearing structures make enormous sense for emergency post-disaster housing in areas that have the bales, or at least straw, available. (At this writing, several noble souls are developing and importing a simple straw bale house design for the mountainous region of Pakistan recently devastated by an earthquake.)

4.1B

Setting the box beam, or roof-bearing assembly, on a load-bearing straw bale wall

photo courtesy of David Eisenberg

3) A load-bearing structure will generally perform more effectively, i.e., with greater ductility and energy absorbtion, than its post-and-beam counterpart under dynamic seismic loading (see section 4.4). This is typical for all structural walls: up to a point, vertical load on the wall stabilizes it against overturning and generally increases the shear strength of the assembly.

With all of that said, the more important distinction is really between *structural* straw bale construction, in which bale assemblies are designed to carry vertical and/or lateral load, and *non-structural*, in which the only structural demand on a wall assembly is to remain intact and in place under out-of-plane load. As will be seen, a plastered straw bale wall can carry substantial vertical and lateral loads, and is more than adequate to the demands of almost any one- and two-story residential-scale building. Thus, using a post-and-beam frame is usually redundant and even counterproductive, but at this still-early stage in the evolution of straw bale construction technology, no one has yet developed a load-bearing system meeting all the requirements of economy, durability, and freedom from construction-phase rain anxiety. (This is not for lack of trying – again, see chapter 2, *The Straw Bale Family Tree.*)

4.1.C

Top: an electrical junction box screwed to a wood stake driven into the face of straw, and Lower: setting corner plumb posts to guide bale erection

photos courtesy of Bruce King and David Eisenberg

4.1.3 Common Practice with All Straw Bale Building

Despite the many variations, there are several qualities common to all straw bale buildings:

4.1.3a Voids All straw bale buildings have dozens of oddly-shaped spaces among the bales as well as between bales and surrounding framing, windows, doors, etc. The convention is to fill those spaces, prior to plastering, with a straw-clay mix that dries and then acts as a substrate for the plaster. Alternatively, some use a sprayed insulation like cellulose or polyurethane foam to fill cavities. The material chosen may vary, but this "chinking" of all the various voids is no minor matter; besides providing continuity for the plaster's support, the fill material is crucial to insuring thermal and acoustical insulation, and to blocking the potential passage of fire.

4.1.3b Pinning The bales must often be braced during stacking for stability and alignment in a manner akin to the temporary bracing of a wood studwall. Internal or external pinning of the walls with rebar or bamboo dowels was prescribed in early straw-bale codes, but is no longer considered to provide much structural value and is generally unnecessary. If used, however, external pins – typically, matched, parallel vertical rebar or bamboo on opposite sides of the wall, tied through the bales with twine – are far easier to build and have been shown[1] to contribute measurably to the wall stiffness.

4.1.3c Fear of Water Yes, straw will rot, and moisture problems – even more than is generally the case in construction – are ever on the minds of designers and builders (or should be; see chapter 5, *Moisture*). The foundation must keep the bales well above grade, and the roof should provide a wide overhang – the proverbial "good hat and good pair of shoes." Roofs are conventional, or at least need not be anything special, connecting to the walls for shear and uplift via some manner of *roof-bearing assembly* (RBA) or bond beam (most commonly a wood assembly). The bottom of the bale wall must be well separated from the foundation by a waterproof barrier over the supporting surface, and by a layer of pea gravel (capillary break) between wood sill plates along the inside and outside faces, thereby ensuring that the bales will never be sitting in water.

4.1.3d Basic Details (See chapter 10, *Details and Design*.) Windows and doors are typically framed wood bucks that either sit on the foundation or "float" in the bale wall. Cabinetry and fixtures are screwed to wooden stakes pounded into the straw, and conduit can be let into grooves carved by chainsaws or weed whackers into the straw surface.

4.1.3e Flat or On Edge? The designer/builder must decide whether to stack the bales *flat* or *on edge*. There is some debate as to which is better for load-carrying capacity, and testing evidence to support both sides, but flat bales are more stable during stacking and thus generally more common. Flat bales are also more easily bent for curving walls and allow the builder to let in posts – typically by carving a notch with a chainsaw or rotary saw – for a post-and-beam structure. By contrast, bales on edge have their ties exposed on the inside and outside face, making let-in posts difficult, and rendering them somewhat more vulnerable to fire damage (see chapter 6, *Fire*). In general, a post-and-beam structure performs more efficiently if the posts are set within the bale wall core, as the plaster can then brace the posts and rely on them as edge elements under lateral loading.

4.1.3f Precompression The rice straw bales commonly used in California are well-known for being very stiff, that is, not very compressible (the reasons why are uncertain, but probably have a lot to do with the "hairiness" of the rice straws, making them stick together somewhat like velcro; see figure 1.1A). This is the exception, however; most bales in locations around the world are relatively compressible. For example, an eight foot high [2.4 M] stack of ordinary wheat straw bales in Canada or Australia or Germany might settle two or three inches [50-70 mm] with time under its own weight, or, as is now commonly done, under mechanical precompression after stacking; a stack of the same height of rice bales might not settle at all. This settling phenomenon is attributable to the compression of the space between bales and to the initial "set" within the bale itself, and is only partially related to the measured Modulus of Elasticity of the bales. Many builders of walls, especially ones intended to be load-bearing, routinely precompress the walls before applying plaster so as to avoid the otherwise inevitable settling cracks.

4.1D

NOMENCLATURE OF FLAT VS. ON EDGE BALE STACKING

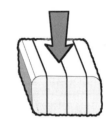

*Bales stacked and loaded **flat** are loaded perpendicular to their largest face – parallel to the plane of the tie hoops, and generally perpendicular to the straw fibers.*

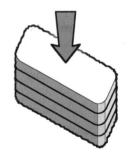

*Bales stacked and loaded **on edge** are loaded parallel to their largest face – perpendicular to the plane of the tie hoops, and generally parallel to the straw fibers.*

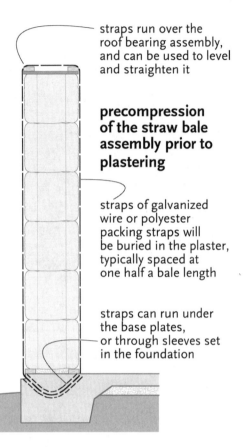

straps run over the roof bearing assembly, and can be used to level and straighten it

precompression of the straw bale assembly prior to plastering

straps of galvanized wire or polyester packing straps will be buried in the plaster, typically spaced at one half a bale length

straps can run under the base plates, or through sleeves set in the foundation

Precompression also stiffens the bale wall as a structural plaster substrate (even with stiff rice bales), and is therefore a good way to improve the wall's structural performance by providing that much better support for the plaster – which does most of the structural work.

Your decision on the need for precompression, and the means of achieving it, will vary from project to project. There are many ways to precompress a stacked wall of bales: let them simply settle with a few month's time; force them under a roof-bearing assembly deliberately framed slightly low; or wrap them with galvanized fencing wire at (typically) two- to four-foot intervals, then cinch the wire ends together with levered devices such as the "Grippler"™. All of these methods have disadvantages, however. Who can wait two months? How do you build and attach a roof plate strong enough to hold the bales down? What happens when the wire rusts through? The emerging favorite is to use polyethylene or nylon packing straps instead of fencing wire, wrapping it around the wall (through or under the foundation and over the top plate) and cinching it down. These straps can adjust around corners (such as the corner of the roof-bearing assembly), are very strong, and won't rust away unseen.

4.1E

Pre-tensioning the straw bale wall assembly using polyester packing straps (one among several systems in use for pre-tensioning)

photo courtesy of David Eisenberg

4.1.3g Plaster Virtually all straw bale wall systems are plastered straw bale, where *plastered* is being used generically to include traditional earthen plasters, lime and gypsum plasters, shotcrete or gunite, common cement or lime-cement stucco, and various combinations of these (See chapter 3, *Plaster and Reinforcing.*)

As noted, it is essential to understand that once plaster is applied directly to the straw bale surfaces, the completed wall assembly is now a hybrid of straw and plaster – a quasi-sandwich panel. In contrast to a pure concrete structure, however, where failure of the structural panel's skins could be both sudden and catastrophic, the failure of the plaster skin is greatly slowed and resisted by the straw-bale assembly. Like a hard-boiled egg, it's far more ductile with the attached core.

4.1.4 General Loading Considerations

In the sections to follow we will review testing and analysis of plastered bale walls as affected by forces in each of the three principal directions: vertical, in-plane, and out-of-plane. Recall that the important distinction between different wall systems is really between *structural* straw bale construction, in which bale assemblies are designed to carry vertical and/or lateral load, and *non-structural*, in which the only structural demand on a wall assembly is to remain intact and in place under out-of-plane load. If your project uses non-structural walls as defined, then your only structural concern is out-of-plane strength and stability.

It bears emphasizing that, regardless of what loads any particular straw bale wall must resist, and as with many other structural systems, there are two phases of behavior: *elastic* and *inelastic*. In layman's terms, the elastic phase is the first range of loading up to the point where anything starts to crack or permanently change shape (that is, it will bounce back when the load is removed.) The inelastic phase is after that point, when it won't bounce back, at least not fully. Plastered straw bale walls, again like other structural systems, should be designed to resist most loads without leaving the elastic range; to return to the hard-boiled egg analogy, the shell (plaster skins) should be able to carry every day and every year loads like wind, snow, dance parties on the roof, and huffing, puffing wolves.

In many parts of the world, buildings are never subjected to the rare and extreme loads that will push a structural system into the inelastic zone. If your project is in an area where the wind never blows hard enough (hurricanes, "Santa Ana"-type thermal canyon winds, and tornadoes) to toss large objects at your walls, and is also in an area without any appreciable seismic liveliness, then be happy, you've got it easy. Otherwise, read the rest of this chapter very carefully.

Buildings in the proximity of known earthquake faults will probably get shaken up a few times during their lifetimes. "Probably" is the key term here: earthquake engineering is founded on a combination of statistical probabilities, and on incomplete and imperfect understandings of both the materials we build with and the frequency and severity of future earthquakes at any particular point on the earth. You may live right beside a major fault line, known to be active (i.e., it's not a question of *if* but *when*), but you cannot know if a major shaker will happen in twenty seconds or three hundred years. Your site *will*, however, almost certainly experience lots of small earthquakes and a few medium ones in its lifetime. At the very least, you must allow for that in design and construction, as all that shaking can loosen or break important (life safety) connections and also will degrade waterproofing details. Earthquakes collapse roofs and take lives all over the world, with all kinds of buildings, all the time, but it need not be so. Pay attention to detail, and design and build for violent shaking; nature to be controlled must be obeyed.

4.1.5 Structural Model of a Plastered Straw Bale Wall

As stated, a plastered straw bale wall resembles, more than anything else we know, a stress-skin panel. Because of their widespread usage in aviation, industry, and even construction, stress-skin panels are fairly well understood, and we can draw some benefit from extensive research done to date in order to try and model and predict behavior under any kind of load. In 1996 a first attempt to model behavior[2] simply suggested the pure bending model for a stress-skin panel under out-of-plane load (and by extension against buckling under axial load)

$$I = b(d^3 - d_1^3)/12$$

where "I" is the gross Moment of Inertia of the wall section

$$\triangle_{bending} = 5wl^4/384E_s I_g$$

where "E_s" is the Modulus of Elasticity – stiffness – of the skin (plaster), "l" is the span, and "w" is the load per unit length

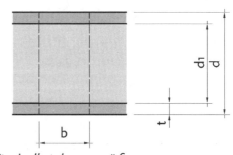

(typically taken as 12" for a representative section of the wall)

This model did not fit well, even with what little data – a single test on a plastered wall under out-of-plane load – was available. Since then, a fair amount of testing has provided much more understanding of the material properties and behavior of plastered straw bale walls and their components. Even if it's less information than we engineers might prefer, it nonetheless enables us to begin to lay out a more exact structural model and design methodology.

4.1.5a The Transformed Section To simplify calculations, engineers can consider the plastered bale wall to be a *transformed section*, very much like a steel wide flange beam:

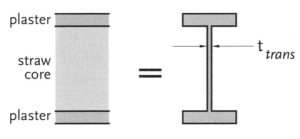

plaster

straw core

plaster

t_{trans}

A vertical or horizontal section of a plastered straw bale wall can be thought of, for the purpose of structural modeling, as a *transformed section*

A stress-skin panel is equivalent to an "I-section" made entirely of the same material as the skins (plaster), and whose web thickness is proportional to the relative stiffnesses of the core (straw bales) and the skin (plaster)

$$t_{trans} = b\left(\frac{E_{CORE}}{E_{SKIN}}\right)$$

For walls with earthen plasters only five to ten times stiffer than the bales, that gives a fairly substantial t_{trans}, on the order of an inch or two thick for a 12-inch width of wall – by no means negligible. For walls with cement or lime-cement plasters, however, for which E is about 15,000 times as big as E for the bales, t_{trans} is only wafer-thin – a hundredth of an inch or less thick. This begins to explain what tests to date have intimated: that the behavior of a plastered straw bale wall, at least under out-of-plane load, is overwhelmingly dominated by shear distortion – not bending. (More on this in section 4.3.)

4.1.5b The Sliced Transformed Section The structural model is further complicated by the fact that the core is very heterogeneous; besides the obvious discontinuity between bales, the material properties within any bale vary widely and, for the most part, unpredictably along different axes. Other than having tested many bales in compression, we know little about the properties of bales (e.g., internal tensile strength, which is undoubtedly both low and widely varying depending on grain, orientation to bale axes, and moisture content). We know a lot about the material properties of *straw*, courtesy of innumerable agricultural engineering studies over the decades, such as that a typical cereal straw such as rice, wheat, or oats has a higher tensile strength than most softwoods. However, at the macroscopic scale within the bale, the length of the straw fibers and their frictional "bond" to each other are of substantially more importance – and are largely unknown.

With that caveat aside, the more refined model of the wall is the *sliced transformed section*, equivalent to a steel wide flange beam with regular vertical slices cut through its web:

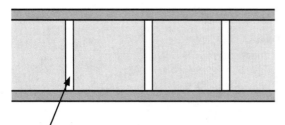

*Slices (slots) in the web of the transformed section represent the joints between bales – either vertical head joints or horizontal coursing. This model will prove to be conservative in section 4.3, as there clearly **is** some frictional shear transfer between bales, but that will vary within the wall, with load conditions, and with types of bales*

At this point we pause, for this model is of only limited use in understanding the behavior of the wall under vertical or in-plane load. We will develop this further in section 4.3, *Out-of-plane loading*. With that said, it bears repeating: Plastered straw bale walls are a new type of structural assembly, similar to but different from the various systems already known to structural engineers. Big, soft, fuzzy bricks are encased in a shell of plaster, somewhat analogous to a big hard-boiled egg, and the boundary conditions for that ungainly assembly play a huge role in determining how well or poorly it will function structurally. In light of all that uncertainty, and the relative paucity of testing information on bales, plasters, meshes, and assemblies of all those materials, design methodologies to follow will generally use the more conservative Allowable Stress Design (ASD), as opposed to the more sophisticated and increasingly popular Ultimate Strength (or "Limit States") Design.

It also bears mentioning, however, that by their sheer width the walls are very sturdy; in the twenty years of the straw bale "revival", marked by a plethora of owner-built structures, fire and moisture problems (as discussed in those respective chapters), and more than a few outright dumb ideas, we have yet to hear, thankfully, of any structural failures. We're only just beginning to understand this subject, but at the same time appear to not yet have really pushed the limits of what is possible.

ENDNOTES

1
Gay, Robert, Ebeltoft, Richard, and Bolles, Robert, 1998, *Straw Bale Exterior Pinning Report* (for the Pima County Building Department) Tucson, Arizona

2
King, Bruce, 1996, *Buildings of Earth and Straw,* Ecological Design Press, Sausalito, California

CAMP ARROYO DINING HALL IN CONSTRUCTION, LIVERMORE, CALIFORNIA

photo courtesy of David Eisenberg

4.2 Vertical Load

4.2.1 Wall Behavior and Failure Modes

Unplastered straw bale walls can only carry a very modest amount of load before compressing beyond acceptable limits or outright buckling. Once plastered, however, their load-bearing capacity increases dramatically – all the more so if a load path is detailed and built to carry load from the floor or roof above to the supporting floor or foundation via the plaster skins.

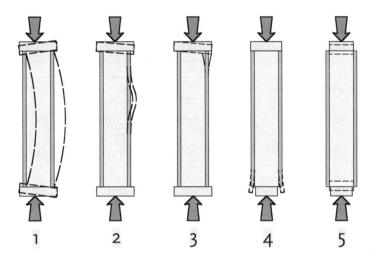

4.2A

FAILURE MODES FOR A LOAD-BEARING STRAW BALE WALL

Under vertical load, axial load on arch structures, and in-plane lateral load, there are five basic types of failure modes. Tests conducted to date have resulted in all of these, either singly or in combination:

1. Global buckling The whole wall bends and breaks – typically when the wall is well-built but eccentrically applied load induces bending; a rare mode of failure.

2. Local buckling Part of the skin delaminates and pulls off the core, or one coat of plaster delaminates and separates from the coat beneath – the result of poor plaster application causing an insufficient bond, failure to tie the mesh through the bales, and/or surface irregularity causing local bending; a common mode of failure.

3. Bearing The skin crushes under the top or bottom plate, and/or the top or bottom plate crushes under the edge of the skin – the wall components have not been designed or built to sustain the focused stress at the joint; also a common mode of failure.

4. Slippage Unsupported skin slips past the top or bottom plate – typically, a failure of fasteners attaching mesh to the sides of plates or beams.

5. Core crushing If load is applied and resisted only at the straw bale core, there will be a crushing deformation – a failure to provide a clear load path through the plaster skins.

The next section is a detailed survey and synopsis of test results, conducted over the past ten years around the world, on vertically-loaded bales and walls using

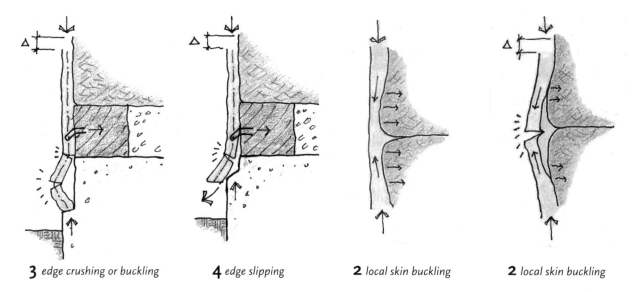

3 *edge crushing or buckling*   **4** *edge slipping*   **2** *local skin buckling*   **2** *local skin buckling*

4.2B
DETAIL OF
FAILURE MODES
FOR A LOAD-BEARING
STRAW BALE WALL

illustrations by David Mar

earth, lime, and lime-cement plasters. These show a range of ultimate compressive strengths and failure modes – and may also be more than the reader may care to know (in which case skip ahead to section 4.2.3). These numbers all compare favorably with California's current "straw bale code," HS18944, which allows an 800 plf [11.7 kN/m] vertical load on a wall with cement or lime-cement plaster. A methodology for design, modeling the plaster skins as thin but well-braced bearing walls, is then presented.

4.2.2 Summary of Test Results

Following is an incomplete survey of vertical load tests done to date. (We know it to be incomplete because a number of good tests have been run in Denmark, Germany, Holland, and Austria for which English translations were not available.) Full height wall tests will be reviewed to point out the height-to-width (h/t, or aspect) ratios at failure loads. By way of comparison, various prescriptive building codes and standards from around the world for unreinforced masonry and adobe allow aspect ratios of 5 to 8 in high seismic risk areas and up to 10 or 12 in low-risk areas. Tests have been conducted on single bales, single plastered bales, unplastered bale walls, and plastered bale walls. First, recall the nomenclature of bale stacking:

4.2.2a Tests on Unplastered Bales

A1 Bou-Ali, 1993

Bou-Ali, Ghailene, 1993. *Straw Bales and Straw-Bale Wall Systems*
University of Arizona, Tucson

A variety of tests on single three-string wheat bales and unplastered wall assemblies were conducted; see section 1B for wall test results.

Single flat bales were loaded up to 84 psi [579 kPa], deflecting to as much as half of the original height without permanent distortion. The elastic modulus was measured to be 78 to 211 psi [538 to 1455 kPa] (stiffening under load), and Poisson's ratio was measured to be 0.30.

Single bales on edge were loaded up to 21 psi [145 kPa] and typically failed suddenly when the strings burst. The elastic modulus was measured to be 60 to 260 psi [414 to 1792 kPa]; Poisson's ratio was not measured in this direction.

The authors commented that bale-bearing capacity increased with bale density, and that, at least with bales flat, there was a strain-hardening phenomenon – stiffening under increased load. Also of note was the fact that fully loaded flat bales, which had compressed to half their height, had fully rebounded by the next day.

A2 Thompson et. al, 1995

Watts, K., K. Wilkie, K. Thompson, and J. Corson 1995. *Thermal and Mechanical Properties of Straw Bales As They Relate to a Straw House*
Canadian Society of Agricultural Engineering Paper No 95-209, Ottawa, Ontario

Wheat, oat, and barley bales with moisture contents averaging 9% were loaded flat, with at least six specimens of each. Maximum applied compressive loads were 6 to 10 psi [41 – 69 kPa] and were all in the elastic range. Modulus of Elasticity ranged from 18 to 26 psi [124 – 179 kPa], the relatively low values probably being due to measuring the value from zero, i.e., not discarding the initial set portion of the stress-strain curve, and not testing up to and beyond the proportional limit. Poisson's ratio was measured both longitudinally and laterally, averaging .37 and .11 respectively. The authors commented (p. 6):

a. *There is considerable variation in the Modulus of Elasticity between bales of the same type* [i.e., of plant grain] *and bales of a different type.*

b. *Bale density has a greater effect on bale strength than bale type.*

c. *Continuous exposure to high moisture contents decreases the Modulus of Elasticity*

d. *Poisson's ratio in the longitudinal direction is much greater than the lateral in unconfined tests.*

A3 Stephens, Budinger, 2000

Stephens, Don, and Budinger & Associates, Inc. 2000. laboratory test
Spokane, Washington

This is the only test this author has found of the "supercompressed" bales being made for overseas export. Heavy hydraulic machinery compresses ordinary bales to about twice their normal density – in this case, 18 pounds per cubic foot [288 kg/m3] – and reties them with polypropylene strings at 3" [76 mm] oc. In this test, 24" x 24" x 16" [610 x 610 x 406 mm] bluegrass bales were loaded on edge, i.e., on the 16" x 24" face. Unlike the Bou-Ali on-edge tests in which the bales failed suddenly because the strings broke, these bales showed a classic linear behavior up to the proportional limit of 17 psi [120 kPa] with half an inch [13 mm] of deflection, and then sustained additional load as deflection increased. The Elastic Modulus was 992 psi [6839 kPa], several times larger than for ordinary bales. Poisson's ratio was not reported.

A4 Zhang, 2002

Zhang, John, 2000. *Load-Carrying Characteristics of a Single Straw Bale Under Compression*
University of Western Sydney, Australia

Two-string wheat bales were tested flat and on edge, in some cases under low frequency cyclic loading. Plastered bales were also investigated – see section 4.2.2C #C1 for results and discussion.

4.2.2b Tests on Unplastered Bale Walls

B1 Bou-Ali, 1993

Bou-Ali, Ghailene, 1993. *Straw Bales and Straw-Bale Wall Systems,*
University of Arizona, Tucson

Three wall assemblies of flat, three-string wheat bales 12 feet long by 8 feet high [366 cm x 244 cm] were each loaded axially up to 15,800 lbs.

4

STRUCTURE

4

[70.3 kN], or 1317 plf [19.2 kN/m]. The researchers commented that there was deliberately no attempt to pound each bale into place (as is good bale building practice), nor was there any bracing (as is typically provided by crosswalls), so the deflections recorded were conservative. Overlapping re-bar pins of unspecified size and spacing were driven through the cores, as was then the custom. The results were:

	Ultimate load	Deflection
Wall A	1317 plf [19.2 kN/m]	6.9" [17.5 cm]
Wall B	1317 plf [19.2 kN/m]	7.6" [19.3 cm]
Wall C	1317 plf [19.2 kN/m]	7.8" [19.8 cm]

Unlike individual bales which harden under load, the walls had each begun to soften at the maximum load, and wall C had begun to noticeably buckle.

B2 Blum, 2002

Blum, Brandice, and Kris Dick, 2002. *Load Carrying Behavior of On Edge Straw Bale Walls* University of Manitoba, Winnepeg, Manitoba, Canada

Two five-course wall assemblies of two-string wheat bales on edge 7.5 feet long by 6.2 feet high [2.3 M x 1.58 M] were loaded axially. No rebar pins were reported used. The results were:

	Ultimate load	Vertical deflection	Horizontal deflection
			(bulge perp. to plane of wall)
Wall A	350 plf [5.1 kN/m]	2.8" [7.2 cm]	8.1" [20.6 cm]
Wall B	288 plf [4.2 kN/m]	3.0" [7.6 cm]	3.1" [7.9 cm]

Both walls partially buckled under ultimate load, and both, with the load left in place for three days, lost about half of their resistance (stiffness creep). The author also made reference to an earlier test by Ester Arbour at the same university, but this author was unable to obtain a copy. Blum reported that Arbour's test used similar wall assemblies of flat oat bales, with these results:

	Ultimate load	Vertical deflection	Horizontal deflection
			(bulge perp. to plane of wall)
Wall C	754 plf [11 kN/m]	6.5" [16.6 cm]	1.0" [2.5 cm]
Wall D	480 plf [7.0 kN/m]	6.0" [15.3 cm]	2.0" [5.1 cm]

B3 Walker, 2004

Walker, Peter, 2004. *Compression Load Testing Straw Bale Walls*
University of Bath, Bath, United Kingdom

Five six-course high wall stacks of dense, two-string barley bales laid flat measuring 39 inches long by 7.5 feet high by 20 inches thick [990 mm x 2.25 M x 500 mm] were loaded axially. In all but the fourth wall, hazel-wood pins of one to two inch diameter [25 – 50 mm] were driven down the wall center. The third wall's second, fourth, and sixth courses were made up of two half-bales. The fifth wall was plastered with two coats of hydraulic lime plaster – compressive strength at the time of the wall test was 2.9 N/mm2 [421 psi], 29 days after applying the second coat – after precompressing the wall 1% of its height. The total plaster varied from 20 to 60 mm thick, averaging 40 mm [1.6 inches]. The results were:

	type	Ultimate load	Vertical deflection	failure mode
Wall 1	standard	6205 lb. [27.6 kN]	8.7" [22 cm]	global buckling
Wall 2	pre-compressed	4316 lb. [19.2 kN]	4.7" [12 cm]	global buckling
Wall 3	w/ half-bales	2450 lb. [10.9 kN]	5.5" [14 cm]	global buckling
Wall 4	no hazel spikes	2630 lb. [11.7 kN]	6.7" [17 cm]	global buckling
Wall 5	lime-plastered	9240 lb. [41.1 kN]	2.2" [5.5 cm]	type 2/5*

see failure modes illustration 4.2A at start of this section

4.2.2c Tests on Plastered Bales

C1 Zhang, 2002

Zhang, John, 2000. *Load-Carrying Characteristics of a Single Straw Bale Under Compression*
University of Western Sydney, Australia

Two-string wheat bales were tested flat and on edge, plastered and unplastered, in some cases under low frequency cyclic loading. Wishing also to investigate load path within the wall, the author applied load in three ways:

1. directly through the straw core only, top and bottom of wall,

2. directly through the straw core at top, but straw and plaster skins supported at bottom, and

3. through both straw core and plaster skins at both the top and bottom. Both cement and earth plasters were tested, but the author did not describe the mixes or cure times other than that there were two weeks between cement coats; thicknesses averaged 1.6" [4 cm]. Bales averaged about 12% moisture content and a density of 6.2 pounds per cubic foot [100kg/m³]. Probably of more interest than specific results were the author's comments:

a. *Low-frequency cyclic loading has no significant impact on the load-resistance properties of the* [unplastered] *straw bales. (p. 8)*

b. *There is always delayed (viscous) effect on the recovery of the deformation as the* [unplastered] *straw is unloaded. (p. 8)*

c. *There is substantially different adhesion of the plaster to opposite sides of the bale (p. 11)* [ed. note: this is partly why, when stacking a wall, experienced bale builders alternate between exposing the "cut" side and the "folded" (or uncut) side – a result of the baling process.]

d. *There is an initial set phase of the test in which the "fluff" between bales is compressed; the author identified this as 3 to 4% of height. In other words, at least for these particular bales, a stacked wall of bales should ideally be precompressed 3 to 4% of its height before applying plaster. (p. 13)*

e. *…different from the familiar plastic flow as seen in steel after yielding, straw bales can further develop a significant amount of strength after the yielding… although having little significance for service load design…[this behavior] does offer a significant safety buffer and energy dissipation if overloading does occur. (pp. 13-14)*

f. *different loading regimes for the rendered tests do not make a significant difference in the load resistance behavior. (p. 14)*

C2 Mar, 2003

Mar, David, 2003. *Bearing Test of Plastered Straw Bales*
Ecological Building Network, Sausalito, California

Rice straw half-bales were fabricated and stacked flat, two high (so as to fit in the testing apparatus), giving a cross-section perpendicular to load of 23" x 23" [58 cm x 58 cm] plus 1.5" [38 mm] plaster skins each side. Plasters were cured at least one month, and load was applied via a stiffened plywood plate covering the plaster edges; ultimate loads were recorded as follows:

Lime-cement stucco w/ 2" x 2" [5 cm x 5 cm] x14 gauge mesh / avg. of 3:   2810 lbs [12.5 kN]

High straw fiber earthen plaster w/ coconut fiber mesh / avg. of 3:   2340 lbs [10.4 kN]

Low straw fiber earthen plaster w/ coconut fiber mesh / avg. of 2:   1575 lbs [7.0 kN]

C3 Vardy, 2004

Vardy, Stephen and Colin MacDougall, 2004. *Compressive Testing of Plastered Straw Bales and Straw Bale Plasters*, Queen's University, Kingston, Ontario, Canada

In the authors' words: *The main focus of the experiments was to determine the difference in behaviour between bales plastered flat and those plastered on edge. A secondary focus of the experiments was to determine how the plaster thickness and plaster strength affected the overall plastered bale strengths...a number of compressive experiments were conducted on individual plastered straw bales. Bales were tested both flat and on edge, with three different plaster strengths and three different plaster thicknesses. Each combination of bale orientation, plaster strength and plaster thickness was repeated three times in order to determine the variability of the results:*

The plaster used in the experiments was a cement-lime plaster with varying w/[c+l] (water to [cement + lime]) proportions, applied to its full thickness on the bales in a single layer. The types of bale (wheat, rice, oat, etc.) and the types of cement and lime were not reported, but results were presented in graphic form, and the authors commented in conclusion:

Effect of Bale Orientation

...with everything else held equal, the bales plastered on edge had a lower ultimate strength than those plastered flat. The bales plastered on edge with a plaster thickness of 12.7 mm and plaster strength of 1.72 MPa had an average ultimate strength of approximately 25 kN/m while the bales plastered flat had an average ultimate strength of approximately 35 kN/m. The reason for the difference is believed to be the superior bond between plaster and bale observed for the flat bales.

Effect of Plaster Thickness

...bales with thicker plaster had higher ultimate strengths than those with thinner plaster skins. The flat bales with plaster thickness of 38.1 mm had an average ultimate strength of 72 kN/m while the bales with plaster thickness of 25.4 mm had an average ultimate strength of approximately 58 kN/m and those with plaster thickness of 12.7 mm had an average ultimate strength of approximately 32 kN/m. Doubling the plaster thickness from 12.7 mm to 25.4 mm increased the strength 1.8 times, and tripling the plaster thickness from 12.7 mm to 38.1 mm increased the strength 2.25 times. Thus, increasing the plaster thickness increases the plastered

bale compressive strength, but it is less than a 1:1 increase. The reason may be that the thicker layers have a greater portion of plaster that is not directly bonded to the straw.

Effect of Plaster Strength

Increasing the plaster strength increases the compressive strength of a plastered straw bale. For the bales plastered flat with a plaster thickness of 25.4 mm, and plaster strengths of 1.72 MPa, 1.20 MPa, and 0.69 MPa the ultimate strength of the plastered straw bales was found to be approximately 58 kN/m, 45 kN/m and 35 kN/m respectively. Increasing the plaster strength 1.7 times from 0.69 MPa to 1.20 MPa increased the strength 1.29 times, and increasing the plaster strength 2.5 times from 0.69 MPa to 1.72 MPa increased the strength 1.65 times. Thus, as with plaster thickness, increasing the plaster strength increases the plastered bale compressive strength, but it is a less than 1:1 increase.

The results highlight the importance of architects, engineers, and builders involved in the design and construction of straw bale structures providing a combination of bale orientation, plaster strength, and plaster thickness to ensure the walls have adequate compressive strength.

Conclusions

It was determined that the most significant parameter regarding the compressive strength of plastered straw bales is the plaster thickness. The bale orientation was found to be of lesser significance than the other parameters ... The specific conclusions from this work are:

1) *The bales plastered on edge had a lower ultimate strength than those plastered flat.*

2) *Increasing the plaster thickness increases the plastered bale compressive strength, but it is less than a 1:1 increase.*

3) *Increasing the plaster strength increases the plastered bale compressive strength, but it is a less than 1:1 increase.*

4.2.2d Tests on Plastered Bale Walls

D1 Platts, Chapman, 1996

Platts, Bob and Linda Chapman, 1996. *Developing and Proof-Testing the 'Prestressed Nebraska' Method for Improved Production of Baled Fibre Housing* Canada Mortgage and Housing Corporation

A partial wall panel was formed by stacking seven wheat-straw bales 14" x 18" x 32-37" [36 x 46 x 81-94 cm], reinforced and pretensioned on each side using inflatable, removable bladders along the top of the wall (the patented "Fibrehouse System") to stretch the 22 gauge [0.8 mm] hexagonal mesh. A total prestressing force of about 700 lbs/ft [10.2 kN/m] reduced the height of the wall by 3" [7.6 cm], or 3%. A 3/4" [1.9 cm] coat of pre-mixed lime-cement stucco was then applied and cured for 11 days for an expected compressive strength of about 1000 psi [7 kPa].

The results of vertical load application were:

Initial load	Vertical deflection	Highest measured load	Vertical deflection
(at calculated service load for two stories)		*(at limit of testing apparatus)*	
2944 plf [43 kN/m]	0.04" [1 mm]	4500 plf [66 kN/m]	0.12" [3 mm]

D2 Carrick, Glassford, 1998

Carrick, John, and John Glassford, 1998. *Vertical Loading, Creep, Transverse Loading, and Racking Loading on Plastered Straw-Bale Walls* Univ. of New South Wales, Australia

Two-string rice bales were stacked in 18" wide x 9'-2" high (seven courses) x 11'-10" long [45 cm x 2.80 m x 3.6 m] wall specimens, and then compressed between 4 and 8 inches [10 - 20 cm] using the Fibrehouse System (see preceding test report) and 20 gauge [1 mm] hexagonal mesh. Three walls were built and compressed; one was tested under vertical load prior to rendering, then all were rendered with a sand/cement/lime plaster in relative proportions 8:2:1. The authors do not say how long the plaster (applied in three coats) was cured before testing, but since failure mode was typically by crushing of the wooden top plates against the top edge of the plaster, the curing period was likely at least a month. The results were:

	Ultimate failure load	Deflection	Unplastered load	deflection
Wall A	1617 plf [24 kN/m]	.28" [7.5 mm]		
Wall B	1412 plf [21 kN/m]	(not reported)		
Wall C	1466 plf [21 kN/m]	.18" [4.5 mm]	144 plf [4.2 kN/m]	2.6" [66 mm]

Notes: The same three wall specimens were simultaneously subjected to large racking and transverse loads – with attendant deflections – while increasing the vertical load to ultimate. This surely skewed the apparent vertical load capacity downward (note the relatively low failure loads compared against other reports using similar specimens).

D3 Ruppert, Grandsaert, 1999
Ruppert, Jeff, and Matt Grandsaert, 1999 *A Compression Test of Plastered Straw-Bale Walls*, University of Colorado, Boulder, Colorado

Three types of 8' high [2.4 M] stuccoed barley bale wall assemblies were loaded to failure in compression. All were stacked flat and rendered with a sand/cement/lime plaster in relative proportions 4:1:1, in two coats, and cured on average at least forty days to an average tested compressive strength of about 1,000 psi [6900 kPa]. Three 12' long [3.7 M] samples of each type were tested by applying a linear load 1/6 eccentric to the wall centerline (per ASTM standard E-72), with results as follows:

Ultimate failure load (avg. of 3)	Deflection (avg. of 3)	Apparent Em
Wall 1 - 24 inch [610 mm] wide 3-string bale wall with polypropylene fiber reinforcing		
3239 plf [47 kN/M]	.91 inches [23 mm]	4.1 ksi [28.3 Mpa]
Wall 2 - 24 inch [610 mm] wide 3-string wall with 20 gauge hexagonal mesh reinforcing		
3590 plf [52 kN/M]	.46 inches [12 mm]	6.9 ksi [47.6 Mpa]
Wall 3 - 18 inch [457 mm] wide 2-string wall with polypropylene fiber reinforcing		
6156 plf [90 kN/M]	.42 inches [11 mm]	12.9 ksi [88.9 Mpa]

Notes: It has been widely noted that, contrary to expectation, the 18" thick walls (Wall 3) carried substantially more load than the 24" walls, and were stiffer. Though there were some irregularities in load application, and in the quality of plastering, this dramatic difference has yet to be fully explained or understood. Every possible failure mode was seen among the nine specimens (see figure 4.2A), and the authors commented that polypropylene fiber-reinforced stucco (vs. mesh-reinforced stucco) bonded much better to the straw, as evidenced by conditions exposed during demolition. On the other hand, the presence of mesh reinforcing helped substantially in resisting local skin buckling.

D4 Black, Mannik, 1997
Black, Gary, and Henri Mannik, 1997. *Spar and Membrane Structure*
The Last Straw #17: Winter 1997

A proprietary "spar and membrane" system was developed and reported in *The Last Straw,* in which lightly reinforced 2" [5 cm] gunite skins are interconnected with extended "X"-shaped light rebar in the bale head joints. The system was mocked up at one-half scale, tested under out-of-plane load with some nominal vertical load, and modeled and analyzed using SAP90 software. Besides being under patent, this system is somewhat unusual in that it treats the bales purely as formwork, entirely expendable after the gunite cures. The report's authors do not comment on or speculate as to what may happen to the bales in the event of water infiltration behind skins that are effectively moisture and vapor traps, a serious cause for concern with any thick cement-based plaster system (see chapter 5, *Moisture)*. Nor do they comment on the extensive thermal bridging created by the "wrap-around" gunite skin that connects inside to outside at every door and window.

The authors reported very good strength and ductility in the out-of-plane load tests. Based on their tests and computer modeling, they also claim a vertical load carrying capacity on the order of 50,000 pounds per foot, but did not report loading a specimen to that extent.

D5 Dreger 2002
Dreger, Derek, and Kris Dick, 2002. *Compression Resistance of a Stuccoed Straw Bale Wall,*
University of Manitoba, Winnepeg, Manitoba, Canada

Two-string oat straw bales were stacked in two six-course walls 7.5 ft. x 8 ft. [2.3 M x 2.4 M], reinforced with 2" x 2" [5 x 5 cm] 16 gauge mesh tied through the walls with polypropylene baling twine at 16" [41 cm] oc. All were rendered with a sand/cement/lime plaster in relative proportions 4:1:1, in two coats separated by two days, and cured about seven days. (This very short cure time will generally only bring a high lime plaster, at best, to half its ultimate strength, but as events transpired the ultimate reported test loads were limited by the loading mechanisms, not the soft plaster.) The results of vertical load application were:

	Ultimate load	Vertical deflection	Horizontal deflection *(bulge perp. to plane of wall)*
Wall A	1938 plf [28.3 kN/m]	1.1" [2.8 cm]	1.4" [3.5 cm]
Wall B	1973 plf [28.8 kN/m]	0.34" [0.9 cm]	0.2" [0.6 cm]

The author reported that the excessive bulge in wall A was largely due to unwanted flexure in the top plate causing a global bending of the wall, as well as to poor (spalling) stucco. Wall B showed a 15% loss of resistance (stiffness creep) over 24 hours as load was maintained.

D6 Faine, Zhang, 2002

Faine, Michael, and John Zhang, 2002 *A Pilot Study Examining the Strength, Compressibility and Serviceability of Rendered Straw Bale Walls for Two Storey Load Bearing Construction* University of Western Sydney, Australia

Two different walls were constructed from 33" x 18" x 14" [84 x 46 x 36 cm] two-string wheat bales laid flat in a running bond at 12% average moisture content. Continuing on from the preliminary work of Zhang on individual bales (see test #C1), the authors were specifically interested in investigating the load-carrying capacity of walls both loaded and supported only on the straw cores (i.e., with plaster skins free to slide at supports). Both walls were vertically precompressed at about 20" [52 cm] oc with high-tension fencing wire, which was used to cinch them down to 97-98% of their original height before plastering.

Wall 1: An eleven-course wall 13'-1" high by 8'-6" long [4.0 x 2.6 M] was built and plastered both sides with two coats totalling 2.3" [58 mm] of cement-lime-sand plaster in proportions 2:1:8, reinforced with ½" x ½" x 18 gauge [12 mm x 12 mm x 1.2 mm] wire mesh tied through the wall at about 24" [60 cm] each way. Lapped half-inch [12 mm] rebar pins 47" [120 cm] long were also driven through the wall core at about 24" [60 cm] oc.

Wall 2: A seven-course wall 8'-4" high by 8'-11" long [2.56 x 2.6 M] was built and plastered both sides with two coats totalling 1.5" [40 mm] of earth plaster in proportions 3:3:1 of earth, sand, and straw chaff. The plaster's compressive strength was measured at 98 psi [680 kPa], average of 9 cylinders. A ⅛" [3-5 mm] finish coat of the same plaster with lime added was then applied; that plaster's measured compressive strength was 33 psi [230 kPa], average of 9 cylinders. *[Ed. note: the addition of lime to earth (clay) plaster can weaken or strengthen it, depending on many things: quality of lime and clay, proportions of each, quality of mixing, application and cure, and age of applied plaster.]* This wall had no pinning or mesh reinforcing, and failure modes were not reported.

The results of vertical load application were:

Yield load	/	Vertical deflection	/ Ultimate load	/ Vertical deflection
(---- at proportional limit ----)			(---- at failure ----)	
Wall 1 1919 plf [28 kN/m]		0.8" [20 mm]	3221 plf [47 kN/m]	4.4" [112 mm]
(two-story/cement plaster)		(.005H)		(.028H)
Wall 2 1233 plf [18 kN/m]		0.37" [0.9 cm]	2467 plf [36 kN/m]	7.0" [178 mm]
(one-story/earth plaster)		(.004H)		(.070H)

D7 Faine, Zhang, 2005
Faine, Michael, and John Zhang, 2005. *Preliminary Discussion of Bale on Edge Wall Test* University of Western Sydney, Australia

This was a test of an earth–plastered wall constructed of bales on edge, using the same apparatus and protocol as test D6. The authors reported:

The main difference for the test set up was that the bales were laid on edge (five bales high). The wall dimensions were 2700 mm [8'-10"] long by 2210 mm [7'-3"] high (after 3% pre-compression) by 390 mm [15.3 inches] wide.

Earth render was about 40 mm [1.6 inches] thick, applied in two coats to give an overall wall width of 470mm [18.5 inches]. The mix design was 3:2:1 for earth:sand:chaff. Otherwise the testing regime was exactly the same as the three previous tests carried out in the University's test frame.

For the purposes of house construction, the wall would be built to six courses high to give a pre-compressed height of 2620 mm [8'-6"] (from 2700 mm nominal height). This test wall was built to be five courses high due to the physical limitation of the steel test frame.

It appears that the orientation of the straw (acting as "randomly bundled columns") has increased the stiffness of the wall construction. Secondly the earth render has also contributed by being fully loaded by the overlapping top plate design (as in previous tests).

It was anticipated that the render would be more difficult to apply to bales on edge due to the orientation of the straw and it was also thought that the polypro-pylene string binding the bales would break early under the load. Neither of these issues were a problem either during construction or during the test.

Failure occurred when the total applied load exceeded 89.52kN [20,125 pounds, or 2279 plf]. Failure mode was severe horizontal cracking.

From this brief discussion it would appear that straw bale construction with "bales on edge" is a reasonable construction mode for SB houses.

D8 Walker, 2004 (See B3)

Walker, Peter, 2004. *Compression Load Testing Straw Bale Walls*
University of Bath, Bath, United Kingdom

4.2.3 Summary of Ultimate Wall Loads

Test #	Ultimate wall load plf / kN/m	Comments
B1	1317 / 19	unplastered bale wall
B2	350 / 5.1	unplastered bale wall
	288 / 4.2	unplastered bale wall
D1	4500 / 66	failed testing mechanism before wall
D2	1617 / 24	simultaneous high racking and out of plane loading
	1412 / 21	" "
	1466 / 21	" "
D3	3239 / 47	average of three walls
	3590 / 52	" "
	6156 / 90	" "
D5	1938 / 28	failed testing mechanism before wall
	1973 / 29	" "
D6	3231 / 47	two-story cement-plastered wall
	2467 / 36	one-story earth plastered wall
D7	2279 / 33	slightly less than one-story earth plastered wall
B3	2888 / 42	one-story lime plastered wall

4.2.4 Design Methodology

Having reviewed the tests done to date, we have at least a general sense of the range of ultimate failure loads for straw bale bearing walls. The tests, reflecting actual practice, represent a wide array of bales, bale orientation, plasters, and rein-forcing. Even in the few cases in which several samples of the same wall type were tested, irregularities in the bale stacking and plastering – as is common in the field

– made for distinctly different results and failure modes from one specimen to the next. Review figure 1 at the start of this section, and note that the most common failure modes were 2, 3, and 4 – and that mode 4 is easily avoidable just by detailing the system to transfer load through the plaster skins.

A description of internal load-transfer mechanisms within the wall can be found in section 4.3, on out-of-plane loading. To some extent that also informs our understanding of what happens in a wall under vertical load and even under in-plane load where an internal "compression strut" must activate to resist shear loads.

Useful though that model may be, however, it still is only an approximation; the strength, thickness, reinforcing, and planarity (smoothness) of the plaster skins, their connections at the top and bottom of the load path, the quality of the straw-plaster bond, and the qualities of bales themselves all vary, even within one project. In the case of earth plasters, strength will vary enormously with moisture content. Many of those variables can be controlled with great attention to the design and construction of details, and with care in the selection and installation of the various materials. But that level of control and care is rare in construction and certainly rare to date in straw bale structures. With that in mind, we seek now to identify a simplified but conservative methodology for designing straw bale bearing walls.

Using the Allowable Stress Method, the plaster skins can be designed as thin but well-braced bearing walls, albeit ones with many components of varying strength. If you have reasonably good-quality bales, good load-path detailing, and knowledge of the thickness, bond, and compressive strength of the plaster on both sides of the wall, then you can calculate the working capacity of the wall as:

$$P_{allowable} = (FS)f'_c(A_p), \text{ in which:}$$

$P_{allowable}$ is the calculated allowable bearing capacity of the wall.

FS   is the Factor of Safety, reflecting the degree of uncertainty about the strength of the assembly and its components. As we shall see, this number must be chosen by the wall designer with an eye towards how well all of the above-listed variables are known, and to what extent field controls will assure that the wall is built as intended. Engineering tradition holds that, even with very well-understood materials, a minimum factor of safety of 4 for a load–bearing wall is appropriate.

f'_c is the measured ultimate compressive strength of the fully cured plaster.

A_p is the cross-sectional area of the plaster.

Below is a series of calculations for $P_{allowable}$ for different plasters, in which f'_c values have been culled from a variety of sources, and using the lower values. $P_{allowable}$ is calculated per foot [30 cm] of wall, assuming an average plaster thickness of one inch [25 mm] each side, or $A_p = 24$ in² [155 cm²] per foot:

PLASTER	COMPRESSIVE STRENGTH	UNFACTORED LOAD CAPACITY
cement:lime:sand 1:1:6	426-711 psi at 28 days	10224 plf at 426 psi
cement:lime:sand 1:2:9	284-426 psi at 28 days	6816 plf at 284 psi
lime:sand 1:3 (non- or slightly hydraulic lime)	60-190 psi at 28 days	1440 plf at 60 psi
Clay 2:3:3 earth:sand:straw	90-130 psi when completely dry	2160 plf at 90 psi

With some study we can see that these numbers correlate well with the test results: the calculated un-factored values for earth and pure lime plasters are less than the tested values, while the calculated unfac-tored values for cement or lime-cement plasters are more. The range of compressive strengths for all of the plasters is wide, so choos-ing the appropriate safety factor is, again, a matter for engineering and common sense judgment.

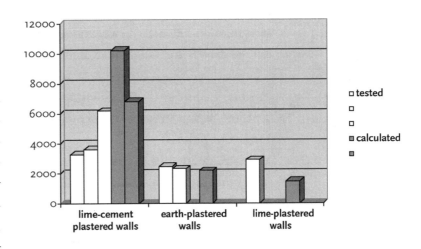

4.2E
COMPARISON OF TESTED VS. CALCULATED UNFACTORED BEARING CAPACITY

(strengths in pounds per linear foot [divide by 67 for kN/m])

These numbers all compare favorably with California's current "straw bale code," Health and Safety Code #18944, which allows an 800 plf [11.7 kN/m] vertical load on a wall with cement or lime-cement plaster. Many have also investigated and commented on the reserve strength provided by the straw bale core alone (e.g., test C1). Comparing that allowable load against the most complete test to date (D2, for which the least average ultimate load was 3239 plf), we have a factor of safety of 3239/800 = 4.0.

*Originally built with
load-bearing bales on
edge plastered with
local gumbo mud, this
structure was eventually
replastered with cement
stucco and remains in
good shape today.*

*photo in 2002 courtesy of David
Eisenberg*

Foot Note

A

Stomp *is a poorly-
defined and colloquial
term whose presence in
an engineering discussion
may cause discomfort to
a few readers. However,
after ten years of search-
ing, this author has yet to
find a better-defined and
more dignified synonym.
Until someone does, you
had best just get up there
and stomp those bales
into place.*

Given the many variables involved, and assuming a high quality
of care in design and construction, a factor of safety of 4 against
ultimate load provides a reasonable working load. If the bales
have short fibers or are soft; if the plaster is not well-worked into
the straw or is not well-cured, or is of uncertain strength; or if
the plaster is not well-reinforced and detailed for load transfer
at the top and bottom (see chapter 10, *Details and Design*), then
the FS should increase accordingly.

4.2.5 Creep, Initial Settlement, and Precompression

Straw bale builders everywhere have observed the tendency of stacked bales to
creep, that is, plastically settle over extended periods of time. This is a well-known
phenomenon in structural engineering that can and does happen with any material or structure, and must often be accounted for in design. A stack of straw bales,
even just under its own self-weight, can and will settle anywhere from several
percent of its height to an almost immeasureable fraction of a percent, depending
on the density and firmness of the bales.

An important distinction should be noted here, as has been regularly observed
by those testing straw bale structures: *Creep* is the long-term settlement of an assembly or material under load (even if only self-weight), whereas *initial settlement*
connotes the short-term height loss in a stack of bales due to the compressing of
the course joints (see, for example, test D6). Bales are big, fuzzy bricks, and good
bale builders know to stomp[A] or pound them into place in order to squeeze, as
much as possible, the fuzzy joints together. This is good practice for any kind of
bale wall, be it load-bearing or not, and should be considered standard practice,
especially where the bales are known to be soft.

Even so, with most bales, all the stomping in the world won't stop them from
creeping over a long period of time (several months or more). As noted in section 4.1.3, recognition of this propensity leads many builders to mechanically
precompress the stack before applying plaster. Your decision on the need for precompression, and the means of achieving it, will vary from project to project, but
knowledge of how much a bale stack can be expected to creep is key to smart
building. Following are the results of one among several creep studies that have
been conducted – the Ecological Building Network tests designed, administered,

4.2F
EBNET STRAW BALE
CREEP TEST SETUP

*illustration by
Dan Smith & Associates*

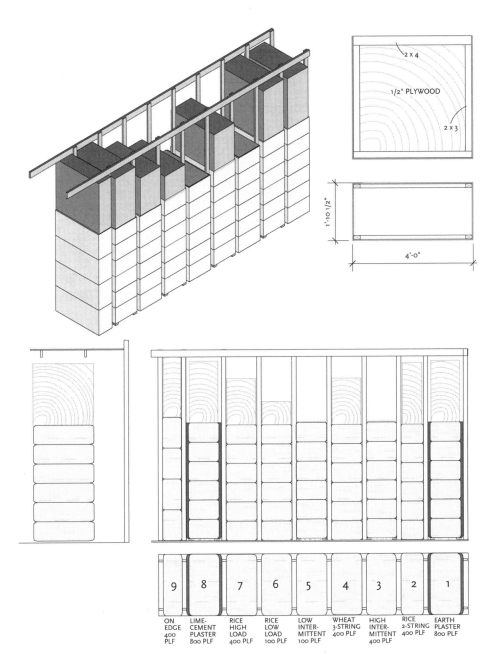

2 x 4

1/2" PLYWOOD

2 x 3

1'-10 1/2"

4'-0"

9	8	7	6	5	4	3	2	1

ON EDGE 400 PLF | LIME-CEMENT PLASTER 800 PLF | RICE HIGH LOAD 400 PLF | RICE LOW LOAD 100 PLF | LOW INTER-MITTENT 100 PLF | WHEAT 3-STRING 400 PLF | HIGH INTER-MITTENT 400 PLF | RICE 2-STRING 400 PLF | EARTH PLASTER 800 PLF

and reported by architect Dan Smith. In the author's words:

The tests were aimed at determining the vertical creep or settlement of various bale walls loaded vertically for 12 months. In the base group are two stacks of six un-plastered rice three-string bales which are tested with uniform low (100 plf) [1.44 kN/M] and high (400 plf) [5.75 kN/M] loads. A comparative group includes wheat three-string, rice two-string, and rice three-string on-edge, all at high loading.

A third group tests the effect of intermittent load, to simulate the effect of a later seismic event, at low and high load. Last, two plastered wall stacks, a lime-cement and an earth plastered, are tested.

Description of Tests (see drawing of test assembly, Fig. 4.2F)

The test format consists of nine stacks of six bales each, with measured weight at the top, with one stack per test. Bales are contained horizontally within an open wood frame to avoid buckling and measure vertical displacement. The weight is added by sand in a plywood bin atop the stack. Settlement is measured initially, and then approximately at days 1, 2, 7, and 14, and at months 1, 2, 6, and 12, though all stacks had largely stabilized after 18 weeks (see graph).

Test stacks

Base Group:	This is the control group, of California three-string rice bales, typically 23"wide, 47" long and 15" high, with various continuous loads.
stack 6	Low load: 400 lbs total, (102 plf, 53 psf, 0.37 psi)
stack 7	High load 1600 lbs, (404 plf, 210 psf, 1.46 psi)
Comparative Group:	Individuals in this group are designed to test specific variables.
stack 2	Tests a change in bale thickness, to 18" wide, 46" long two-string rice bales Two-string rice 1600 lbs, (418 plf, 279 psf, 1.9 psi)
stack 9	Turns the three-string bale on edge, changing the direction of the bale "grain" and effectively switching the width and height, with a 4-bale stack in this case. Three-string rice on edge 1024 lbs, (267 plf, 213 psf, 1.48 psi)
stack 4	Wheat three-string 1600 lbs, (436 plf, 227 psf, 1.58 psi) (with some minor changes in bale dimension, 44"long, 16" high).
Intermittent Load Group:	This group has the same initial conditions as the base group; however, 2" x 2"x 14 gauge welded wire mesh is wrapped up and over the bale stack to hold the compression. The load is applied, the bale stack takes its initial compression, the mesh is stretched tight and stapled to the plates to keep the bales from expanding upwards, and then the load is removed. The load gets reapplied after 44 weeks.
stack 5	Low load intermittent 400 lbs, (102 plf, 53 psf, 0.37 psi)
stack 3	High load intermittent 1600 lbs, (408 plf, 213 psf, 1.48 psi)
Plastered Group:	This group is designed to test the effects of plaster on creep. The walls were plastered on the two 48" faces after the full weight had been applied for ten days, with 2" x 2"x 14 gauge welded wire mesh and with the plaster detailed to bear on the base.
stack 1	Earth plaster, 400 lbs, (100 plf, 52 psf, 0.36 psi)
stack 8	Cement lime plaster, 1600 lbs, (408 plf, 213 psf, 1.48 psi)

4.2.5a Creep Test Summary and Conclusions

Initial Settlement (measured right after loading) This varied in unpredictable ways, and since it was not the central focus, the comparative creep graphs (Fig. 4.2G) start after the initial settlement. The walls were not carefully or uniformly stomped into place or otherwise precompressed, as is often done in actual bale wall construction. Generally we interpret this phase as the period when the bale inconsistencies, especially the bale surfaces, are compressed and the bale shapes conform to one another. Creep is considered the period when the individual straw fibers deform over time. Since both effects happen simultaneously to a certain extent, it is somewhat difficult to separate the two phenomena. Initial compression averaged 1" for the 400 lb. load, or 1.1%, and 2.25" for the 1600 lb. load, or 2.5%. Note that the two-string wall compressed about 4.5%.

Early Creep There seemed to be relatively fast creep over the first one to two weeks, at least on the higher loads.

Slowing Creep After the initial period, most walls settled much less over the subsequent five to eight weeks.

Stabilization After ten weeks, most walls were stable, with no measurable additional creep. Overall, the creep in the rice three-string was about .8" for the low load (0.9%), and 1.1" for the high load (1.2%). The creep-to-compression ratio was 73% (0.8 to 1.1) for the low load, and 49% (1.1 to 2.25) for the high. Unlike the other specimens, the most heavily loaded wall, the two-string rice bales, at 1.9 psi, continued to settle throughout the period. The rice on-edge stack had a much longer creep period (43 weeks) before noticeable stabilization, although the amount of creep was similar at 1.4%.

Intermittently-Loaded Walls This test showed that the walls retained 75-80% of their previous compression after 8 months. In other words, the walls only deformed another 20-25% as compared to the initial compression after the load was reapplied. For example, the initial compression on wall 3 was 2.75", and 50 weeks later when the load was reapplied, it had settled 0.75". This seems to support the value of precompressing bale walls before plastering when the walls might be subjected to severe loading such as seismic or high snow loads.

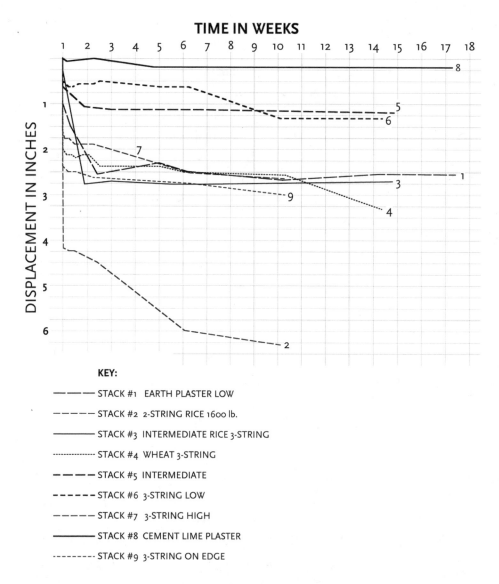

TIME IN WEEKS

DISPLACEMENT IN INCHES

KEY:

— — — STACK #1 EARTH PLASTER LOW

— — — — STACK #2 2-STRING RICE 1600 lb.

———— STACK #3 INTERMEDIATE RICE 3-STRING

·········· STACK #4 WHEAT 3-STRING

– – – – STACK #5 INTERMEDIATE

- - - - - STACK #6 3-STRING LOW

— — — STACK #7 3-STRING HIGH

———— STACK #8 CEMENT LIME PLASTER

··········· STACK #9 3-STRING ON EDGE

4.2G
EBNET STRAW BALE
CREEP TEST RESULTS

Plastered Walls The cement-lime plastered wall, at 400 plf, showed no noticeable settlement at all. This was to be expected, since these are service loads far below ultimate measured loads. The earth-plastered wall, however, at 100 plf did show some settling, 1½" in the initial weeks as the first coat of plaster was still curing. We had provided some precompression, with the load applied for 1.5 weeks before plastering.

These numbers all compare favorably with California's current "straw bale code," Health and Safety Code #18944, which allows an 800 plf [11.7 kN/m] vertical load on a wall with cement or lime-cement plaster. Many have also investigated and commented on the reserve strength provided by the straw bale core alone (eg test C1). Comparing that allowable load against the most complete test to date (D2, for which the least average ultimate load was 3239 plf), we have a factor of safety of 3239/800 = 4.0.

See also section 4.5 for general comments about design recommendations, and also see chapter 10, *Details and Design*.

4.3 Out-of-Plane Load

with Kevin Donahue

4.3.1 Introduction

Forces applied perpendicular to a surface are called *out-of-plane* loads. Below grade, they are the pressure of earth, liquid, or both against basement and retaining walls. Above grade, the most common is simple wind pressure, which can cause many problems for structures as a whole, but very rarely for the walls themselves unless they are particularly tall or poorly supported. Although the pressures caused by wind are in fact anything but simple, varying and reversing both with specific location and with time, engineers designing residential-scale structures typically treat wind loads as uniform pressure applied towards (pressure) or away from (suction) the surface of a wall or roof.

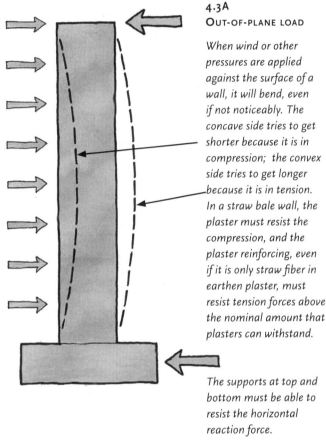

4.3A
OUT-OF-PLANE LOAD

When wind or other pressures are applied against the surface of a wall, it will bend, even if not noticeably. The concave side tries to get shorter because it is in compression; the convex side tries to get longer because it is in tension. In a straw bale wall, the plaster must resist the compression, and the plaster reinforcing, even if it is only straw fiber in earthen plaster, must resist tension forces above the nominal amount that plasters can withstand.

The supports at top and bottom must be able to resist the horizontal reaction force.

In the case of plastered straw bale walls, wind loads are demonstrably non-problematic, as shown in laboratory tests [endnotes 2, 3, 4, and 5] and in field experience – on at least two occasions, unplastered and unbraced straw bale walls withstood hurricane-force winds without distress. The remaining issue in designing for such pressure forces, then, is to model wall behavior as a basis for design of very tall or large wall panels. That discussion will comprise the bulk of this section.

There are other types of out-of-plane forces, however, that are both rare and far more destructive. In the extreme are the effects of bomb blasts or errant vehicles driven into the side of a building, for which there is no economical way to design with *any* building material. If you want a bunker, build a bunker, with three or ten feet of reinforced concrete all around as has been done for decades. If, however,

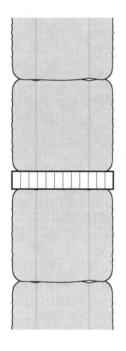

4.3B HORIZONTAL GIRT

A common method of adding horizontal (out-of-plane) support to a tall wall is to set a glulam beam (with a depth equal to the bale thickness) between two courses at mid-height. The girt must have slotted supports at its ends to allow some vertical movement as the bales are stacked, and should be attached to plaster mesh just before plastering.

you only want a reasonably safe structure – one that meets minimum requirements of your local building codes and can withstand the range of foreseeable environmental forces to be expected in its lifetime, then forget about the bombs and runaway trucks. Some events are both infinitesimally unlikely and dramatically costly to protect against. If a big meteor strikes your home, you can only hope that it hits the far end, away from your family, and you can make a lot of money selling your story to Hollywood.

Less extreme but more common are two quite different types of dynamic loading: the effects of objects *carried* by extreme winds, and the shaking effects of earthquakes. The former is recognized as the main problem for buildings in tornado and hurricane zones, for which tests have been developed and carried out on all manner of wall systems (including plastered straw bale walls; see section 4.3.7 on *projectile loads*).

As discussed in section 4.1, buildings in the proximity of known active earthquake faults will get mildly or even rudely shaken up a lot during their lifetime, and might very easily get whacked by The Big One. At the very least, you must allow for that in design and construction – a process somewhat like the wind pressure analysis you would or should do anyway.

To date most engineers have introduced horizontal girts (figure 4.3B) or some other type of additional support when the wall became taller than anything with which they were intuitively comfortable. The need remains, then, to explain how the various materials in the wall assembly work together in order to to lay out a design methodology for larger and taller walls. That is what follows.

4.3.2 Two-Phased Wall Behavior Under Out-of-Plane Load

Some early and relatively crude out-of-plane load tests on plastered straw bale walls, as well as recent and more sophisticated ones, began with a horizontal plaster crack appearing at or near the mid-height bale course on the tension face. This led many to conclude that the walls were more or less exhibiting classic bending behavior for stress-skin panels. Their conclusion was correct – up to that point of first cracking. However, like a concrete beam transitioning from the uncracked to the cracked mode, the behavior of the wall changes substantially with the appearance of that first crack in the tension face. In residential-scale walls, the first crack has always appeared well above design or service loads, but would nonetheless be of concern in two cases:

1) If the wall is underdesigned and experiences this cracking in extreme wind or a moderate earthquake, there would be no structural failure, but the wall could now be vulnerable to water intrusion, leading to longer-term moisture problems in the core (this is another reason for a good roof overhang.)

2) When (not if) the crack appears during major seismic shaking, it will compromise the wall's ability to carry in-plane loads. Emphasis here is on "compromise," not "lose"; the plaster's bond to the straw, along with the reinforcing mesh, will hold the skin together so that even a full-depth crack can transmit some shear via friction – similar to a phenomenon witnessed in seismic tests of adobe construction.

In section 4.1 we found that a plastered straw bale wall is in many ways like a stress-skin panel and can be modeled as a *sliced transformed section*. That model is conservative in that it assumes no frictional shear between bales and treats the course joints as slots in the web of the transformed section. The friction factor between bales laid flat, μ, has been measured[1] to be about 0.63, but the normal force between bales can vary widely from project to project, with time, and even within a single wall; the conservatism seems well-warranted. The sliced transformed section model also intimates that shear behavior will govern over bending, and out-of-plane tests to date have consistently shown evidence of exactly that: shear distortion of the bales dominates wall behavior.

Kevin Donahue conducted and studied several tests with the hope of identifying behavior and establishing a design methodology. All of those tests were conducted on wall specimens about eight feet [2.4M] high, a typical residential scale, and none showed anything like failure until they were loaded far beyond service loads.

In the first test[2], a 7.5 foot high [2.3 M] wall was built and plastered both sides with a two-inch [50 mm] sprayed soil-cement known as *Pisé* [A] (a "semi-soft skin" plaster in the parlance of chapter 3, like a low-strength concrete), reinforced with 2" [5.1 cm] x 2" x 16 gauge welded wire mesh. The wall was then slowly rotated

FOOTNOTE

A
"Pisé" is both the historic french word for rammed earth, and an acronym coined by David Easton for Pneumatically-Applied Stabilized Earth.

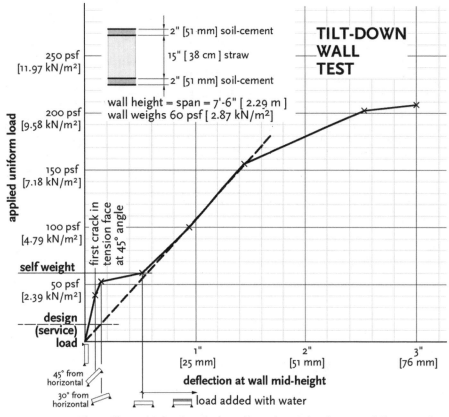

The wall was built, plastered, and cured upright, then carefully rotated on hinged supports to the horizontal, measuring deflections at 45 and 30 degrees from horizontal. After it was flat, load was added with water in a plastic-lined box framed over the flat wall.

4.3C

TWO-PHASED WALL BEHAVIOR UNDER OUT-OF-PLANE LOAD

on hinged supports to a horizontal position, at which point it had an out-of-plane load of 1g (100% of self-weight), and had deflected 0.56 inches [14 mm]. Substantial additional load was then added by building a plastic-lined frame on top and adding water in measured increments. A detailed illustration of that test, showing the two-phased behavior just described, is given in figure 4.3C.

4.3.3 Pre-Cracking Wall Behavior Under Out-of-Plane Load

A complete analysis of most beams of most materials requires checking both bending and shear stresses, and deflections. As a practical matter, except for very short, heavily-loaded beams, shear is often a minor consideration, and most beams (and walls under out-of-plane load) are checked only for bending loads. As it turns out, with plastered straw bale walls the situation is different, as evidenced by every test to date. The straw bales, being relatively very soft, distort under load from rectangles to parallelograms within the wall, while the bonded sections of plaster try to remain rectangular; shear is by far the dominant force in both stress distribution and deflection.

In the Tilt-Down test, the first crack appeared in the tension face when the wall had been rotated down to 45 degrees from horizontal – a 42 psf [2 kN/m²] load perpendicular to the surface – and the wall had deflected 0.09" [2 mm]. Up to that point, the plaster skins tried to act as shallow beams in bending to resist the load, as follows:

4.3D

The tilt-down wall in horizontal position with water-filled box on top for adding load.

For a 12-inch-wide vertical strip of wall:
- the moment on the wall is $M = wl^2/8 = 42(7.5^2)/8 = 295$ ft-lbs, or 3544 in-lbs
- the section modulus of the two-inch-thick plaster skins is $S = bh^2/6 = 12(2^2)/6 = 8$ in³ (two skins = 16 in³)
- the bending stress at the point of cracking is $M/S = 3544/16 = 222$ psi
- check against predicted $MOR = 1.6\sqrt{f'_c} = 1.6\sqrt{1200}$ (allowable stress design) = 55 psi

Given the level of precision (or imprecision) of the structural model, plaster thickness, and material strength, this is a very satisfying correlation; the plaster skins tried to resist the load as beams, and cracked when the tension reached the plaster's predicted capacity of four to five times the allowable stress. Further evidence of

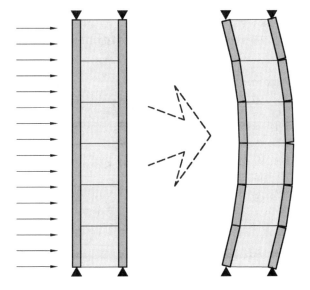

4.3E

When loaded out of plane, the soft straw bales distort from rectangles to parallelograms, forcing cracks to appear along course joints.

This behavior is consistent with every test done to date, but had been incorrectly interpreted to be due to sliding of the bales relative to one another.

Until the first crack appears, then, the load is resisted largely by the two plaster skins acting like wide, shallow beams – not very strong, but nonetheless stiffer than the global structural assembly. The first cracks occur when the tension face exceeds its tensile capacity – the Modulus of Rupture (MOR).

this behavior is the shape of the cracks; were there pure stress-skin-panel-type behavior, the cracks would evenly split the tension-side plaster skin and would be uniform in thickness. Such was not the case, as can be seen clearly in figure 4.3F

The crack is wide at the bottom (the face of extreme tension), occurs at a bale coursing joint, and narrows to nothing within the thickness of the plaster, indicating that the plaster skin was trying to act as a very shallow beam and quickly reached failure (though at a load far above design load). This indicates that the wall has created a "hinge" point that shifts its behavior from bending-dominated to a complex combination of shear in the bales, and tension/compression/bending in the skins, as will be modeled below. The 2" x 2" 16 gauge mesh in the plaster is now fully engaged, similar (but not the same) to the way steel reinforcing is more fully engaged when a concrete beam cracks.

**4.3F
BENDING CRACK
IN TENSION FACE
PLASTER**

4.3.4 Post-Cracking Wall Behavior Under Out-of-Plane Load

Donahue modeled the cracked section, as shown in figures 4.3C and 4.3G, and developed a seven-step design methodology by which any wall, of any size and material makeup, can be analyzed. Following is a depiction of the method, using as an example a one foot wide [30 cm] strip of an eight foot high [2.4 M] wall subject to a 100 psf load, which "becomes" an 800 pound point load at mid-height. The reactions at points 1, 2, 5 and 6 are each 800/4 = 200 pounds. Use also the material properties used in the tilt-down wall test depicted above:

2 inch thick soil-cement plaster ("Pisé")

f'_c = 1200 psi +/- (based on cube tests)
Modulus of Elasticity E_s = 57,000$\sqrt{f'c}$ $\cong$ 1,975,000 psi [13,617,000 kN/M^2]
(Allowable Stress Method (ASD))

2" x 2" x 16 gauge welded wire mesh

A_s = 6 x (.031^2 x π) = 0.018 in^2 / ft. [11.6 mm^2] per linear foot [30 cm] of mesh
F_y = 60,000 psi   [413,685 kN/M^2]

16 gauge galvanized staples with 1³/₄" legs, 4 inches oc

National Evaluation Report NER 272 gives an allowable pullout force of 32 lbs. [142 N] each (which incorporates a safety factor of 5, i.e., average failure load was 5 x 32 = 160 lbs [712 N]). The allowable load per foot is, then, 3 x 32 = 96 pounds per foot [1401 N/m].

rice straw bales

E_c (core, i.e., straw) = 130 psi + [871 kPa]+

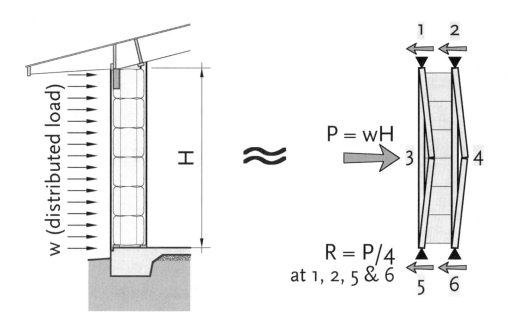

$$P = wH$$

$$R = \frac{P}{4}$$
at 1, 2, 5 & 6

4.3G
DESIGN MODEL FOR POST-CRACKING WALL BEHAVIOR

Notes:

1) Any engineer will look at this and note the factual error of basic static analysis: P does *not* equal wH. To get an equivalent bending moment on the wall, P would be wH/2. However, in the shear-dominated behavior of the post-cracking mode – the subject at hand – a P of wH gives the same reaction loads at points 1, 2, 5 and 6, and thus is the more representative approximation for analysis. This approximation, though apparently crude, fits very well with the data from all the tests.

2) In this model no vertical load is applied, i.e., the wall is assumed to be non-bearing. If the reader is analyzing a load-bearing wall, the vertical loads can be added to the model above, applied at points 1 and 2, reacted at points 5 and 6, and the static analysis as depicted in the following pages carried through. However, since tests have shown that residential scale walls eight or nine feet high [2.4-2.6 M] of just about any construction can easily resist conventional demand loads, the underlying assumption here is that a design is necessary because the wall is substantially higher than nine feet – a condition that for several reasons invariably calls for a post and beam structure with no vertical load (by definition) on the bale walls.

3) If the wall is part of a post-and-beam system, as is assumed in note 2, then there will be support on all four sides of the wall panel; that is, the vertical posts in the wall will also resist lateral load and brace the straw bale wall panel on its sides. Discounting that effect, substantial as it may be, renders this analysis conservative.

4.3.4a Example Seven-Step Calculation (steps listed as A through G)

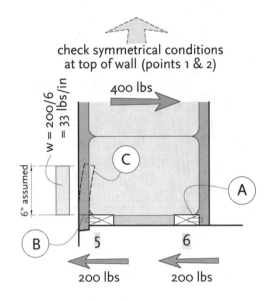

check symmetrical conditions at top of wall (points 1 & 2)

400 lbs

$w = 200/6 = 33$ lbs/in

6" assumed

C

A

B

5

6

200 lbs   200 lbs

4.3H

A) Check staple tension at points 2 and 6

R (demand) = 200 lbs, and the listed capacity is 96 lbs (but no staple failure was observed in tests at this load level; $\Longrightarrow$ the staple tension factor of safety is less than that which generated the NER report allowable value but is still serviceable. Bearing at points 1 and 5 may be carrying more than half the load.

B) Check plaster shear at points 1 and 5

R (demand) = 200 lbs, and the shear stress on the 2" x 12" cross section just above the sill plate is:

200 x 1.5 / (2x12) = 12.5 psi

Plaster (soil-cement) is like a weak concrete;

$\Longrightarrow V_{allow} = 1.1\sqrt{f'c} = 1.1 \sqrt{1200} = 38$ psi (ASD)   *OK*

C) Check plaster in bending at points 1, 2, 5, and 6

R (demand) = 200 lbs; treat as a uniform load of 33 pounds per inch on a section of plaster six inches high above a "fixed base" at the top of the sill plate. (The six-inch height is a judgment call, a somewhat arbitrary number agreed upon by the three engineers involved with developing these criteria: Kevin Donahue, David Mar and Bruce King. Six inches is slightly less than half the height of most bales and probably the most that a section of plaster can "span" in cantilever.)

section modulus of plaster (neglecting reinforcing) is $S = bh^2/6 = 12$ x $2^2/6$ = 8 in^3

Moment on section $M = w|^2/2 = 33$ x $6^2/2 = 594$ in-lb.

bending stress $f_b = M/S = 594/8 = 74$ psi (conservatively neglects effect of mesh reinforcing)

Modulus of Rupture MOR $\approx 1.6 \sqrt{f'c} = 1.6 \sqrt{1200} = 55$psi

$\Longrightarrow F_b \approx 55 < 74$ *OK w/implicit safety factor of 5 used in ASD values*

D) Check tension in bales

Shown as a freebody diagram, each bale in the wall will look like figure 4.3J, and will distort into a parallelogram as shown. Mar[3] postulated a "compression strut" acting within a wall assembly that must be activated to carry shear loads; likewise, a tension and compression strut will activate within the bale cross-section to resist – or try to resist – the distortion shown. Bale dimensions vary, but for the purposes of this exercise assume a 15 inch high by 12 inch wide section; the tension (and compression) stress is then: $(400\sqrt{2}) / (12\text{x}15\sqrt{2})$ 2.2 psi [15.2 kPa] – the demand load. This translates to 317 psf [15.2 kN/m²], and though we have no measurement (and can't imagine how to make one) of internal tensile strength, this is more than we would expect the bale to be capable of.

The tensile strength of straw is known to be higher than most softwoods, but that has little relevance here. The internal tensile strength in a bale is a function of fiber lengths, and the degree to which they "grab" each other (be it by friction, mechanical interlock, or something else) determines how strong the bale is. That being the case, the orthogonal compression stress would be sqeezing the fibers together in a way that would increase frictional bond and therefore tensile capacity.

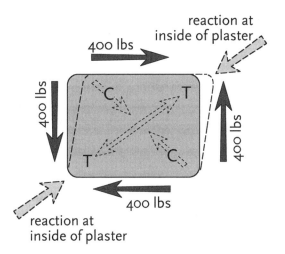

FIGURE 4.3J

In the preceding load-deflection diagram, the wall had deflected almost an inch [24 mm] under a (very high) 100 psf [4.8 kN/m²] load, so we know the bales were distorted, and that by extrapolation 2 psi +/- is higher than the bale's tensile yield point. And *that* means that the distortion of the bale must be resisted by the diagonal reactions shown at the plaster in combination with whatever tensile capacity the bales in fact have.

The skins are both acting as the facings of a stress-skin panel and holding the wall assembly together, and shear is flowing from bales to plaster to bales and so on. These point loads at the bale corners – the bale course joints – explain the horizontal cracks that have appeared in every out-of-plane test to date. It may well be that there is no slippage at all between bales, as had been thought before; the diagonal point reactions shown in the freebody diagram would be enough to crack most plasters. The "slotted transformed section" model (in section 4.1) probably still applies, but appears to be conservative.

This discussion also suggests the purpose, and perhaps need, for wire or string ties that connect the mesh through the wall at bale courses. A tie would in theory carry the tension force, relieving both the bale and the plaster skin from having to do so. (We say "in theory" because the test results to date do not necessarily confirm this; as is ever the case, more research is needed to clarify this behavior.) Wall ties will certainly strengthen and stiffen a wall against out-of-plane loading, and should be considered essential in conditions of very high seismic risk and/or in very tall walls.

The diagram also shows that there is shear (bond) stress at the straw-plaster interface. For a fifteen-inch-high bale, that stress is $f_v = 400/(12 \times 15) = 2.2$ psi [15 kN/m^2] (as per basic mechanics, the same as the previously-computed tension stress). As with the tensile bond to be discussed in the section that follows, we have no measurement of what the failure stress may be, but have seen no overt slippage in tests to date. Furthermore, innumerable reports from the field portray plaster and straw as being *very* difficult to separate when circumstances require it. The implication is that this shear bond is not a limiting link in the complex mechanism that is a plastered straw bale wall.

E) Check tensile bond between plaster and straw at points 1 and 5

We checked in steps B and C that the plaster skin bearing against the sill plate can resist the 200 pound reaction, but we must also look at the tendency of the bales to pull away from the plaster at those same locations. Using the same model as for step C, the tensile bond stress would be distributed over a six inch x twelve inch area: $f_t \approx 200/(6 \times 12) = 2.8$ psi [19 kN/m^2]. Once again, we have no measured values against which to compare this demand load, but wall tests to date show no evidence of this being a problem.

The shear and tensile bond between straw and plaster both depend primarily on three things:

1) the average length of straw fibers (the longer the better),

2) the number of fibers per unit area that engage the plaster enough to have "development length," and

3) the amount those same embedded fibers engage, or "grab," the mass of straw in the bale.

All of this, though hugely difficult to quantify, emphatically points to the value of using bales with the longest possible fibers (see chapter 1, *Straw and Bales*), and the need to work the first coat of plaster well into the straw (see chapter 3, *Plaster and Reinforcing*).

F) Check mesh tension at point 4

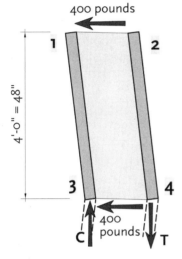

400 pounds

4'-0" = 48"

1

2

3

4

400 pounds

C T

$D = d_1 + t(1/2 + 3/4)$
$= 15" + 2"(1/2 + 3/4) = 17 1/2"$ say 17"

3

4

$t_c = t/2 = 1"$

4.3K

A freebody diagram of the top half of the wall, showing the shear, tension, and compression forces at the mid-height hinge.

4.3L

Detail of the hinge joints at wall mid-height (points 3 and 4)

The tension and compression forces T and C are easily calculated to be 400 x 48" / 17" = 1129 pounds [5 kN]. The mesh area was calculated to be 0.018 in²/foot, so the mesh tensile stress f_t = 1129/0.018 = 63 ksi [434,370 kN/m²]. This is roughly equal to the ultimate strength of most galvanized wires, more than enough to cause some yielding.

G) Check compression on plaster at point 3

Assuming that half the plaster thickness remains engaged, as shown, then the plaster stress is f_c = 1129/(1"x12") = 94 psi [648 kN/m²]. Compared to the allowable compressive stress of 0.33 f'_c, or 400 psi, this is well within allowable limits.

4.3.5 Comments

In the foregoing example we analyzed a wall almost exactly like the "tilt-down" test wall depicted in the preceding load-deflection diagram, the difference being that we used a slightly taller wall (8 feet high, not 7.5 feet). More importantly, the applied load of 100 psf [4.8 kN/m²] is far higher than any but the most rare and extreme wind or earthquake demands on a residential-scale structure anywhere in the world. Walls of that size (roughly 8 feet/2.4 M high), plastered with just about anything, seem to be abundantly stiff and robust; even unplastered walls of that scale have passed without problem through hurricane-level winds.

We have tentatively presented a design methodology that treats the wall as a simple span from foundation to roof or floor above (and conservatively ignores the bracing effect of vertical posts within the wall, where they occur). In doing so we have necessarily speculated, since the whole wall assembly, as should by now be obvious, is an ungainly combination of bales (about whose properties we know comparatively little), plaster (about which we may know a lot, or little, circum-

4.3M

ECOLOGICAL BUILDING NETWORK OUT-OF-PLANE TESTS, DECEMBER, 2003

All walls are eight foot high stacks of 16" x 23" x 48" bales (23" perpendicular to load) with plaster, mesh, and attachments as shown (the same on both sides of the wall). Load was applied in a semi-cyclical way, in that the bladder that applied the load (see figure 4.3N) could be inflated up to the point of applying a desired pressure but would not sustain it; there was load relaxation between each reading.

(The full report can be downloaded at www. ecobuildnetwork.org)

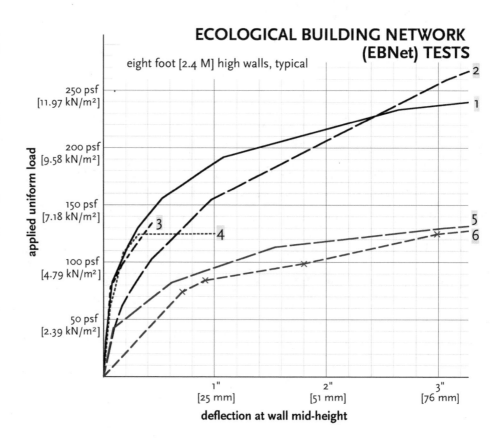

stances depending), staples, and mesh (about which we generally know more). Still, this is educated speculation, well-matched to test results,[2,3,4,5] and articulates a much more detailed and logical model of wall behavior than has previously been described.

(See also section 4.5 for general comments about design recommendations.)

4.3.6 Summary of Recent Tests

Wall 1:

Plaster: one-inch stucco applied in two coats

Plaster reinforcement: 2 x 2 x 14 gauge welded wire fabric stucco mesh

Top and bottom connection: 16 gauge, 7/16"crown x 1.75" leg staples @ 2"

Wall 2:

Plaster: one-inch stucco applied in two coats

Plaster reinforcement: 17 ga x 1.5" hexagonal woven wire lath

Top and bottom connection: 16 ga 1/2"crown x 1.25" leg staples @ 6"

Wall 3:

Plaster: one-inch stucco applied in two coats

Plaster reinforcement: 1% 1.5" Xorex steel fibers by volume (13 lbs per side)

Xorex specs: deformed 0.045" x 1.5" 120 ksi fibers

Wall 4:

Plaster: one-inch stucco applied in two coats

Plaster reinforcement: 0.8% 2" Xorex steel fibers by volume (10.5 lbs per side)

Xorex specs: deformed 0.045" x 2.0" 120 ksi fibers

Wall 5:

Plaster: two-inch earth plaster applied in one coat

Plaster reinforcement: 2 x 2 x 0.047" Cintoflex C plastic mesh

Through-ties: two loops (of 2) baling twine spaced @ 24" each course (seven courses) tied to 5/8" x 4' horizontal bamboo dowels outside mesh both sides

Wall 6:

Plaster: two-inch earth plaster applied in one coat

Plaster reinforcement: 2 x 2 x 0.047" Cintoflex C plastic mesh

Thru ties: two loops (of 2) baling twine spaced at 24" above the second and fourth courses

(third points) tied to 5/8" x 8' vertical bamboo dowels outside mesh both sides

4.3N

OUT-OF-PLANE TEST APPARATUS, WALL IN FAILURE-LEVEL DEFLECTION, AND FIRST CRACK

illustration by David Mar
photos courtesy of Kevin Donahue

4.3.7 Projectile Loads – What Happens in Hurricanes and Tornadoes?

Straw bale walls of normal dimensions and construction can easily withstand the enormous horizontal wind pressure created in hurricanes, tornadoes, and the "Santa Ana" or "Chinook" winds that periodically occur at the base of some mountain canyons. It is well known, however, that the damage caused by such extreme wind storms – at least for one- and two- story structures – is rarely from the wind pressure itself as much as from the debris picked up by the wind and tossed forcefully about. Lots of things get picked up in a big wind and then fly along at 60 or 80 or more miles per hour [30-40 m/sec] in a zone as much as several dozen feet [10m +/-] above the ground surface. Each of those objects is then effectively a small missile, and those missiles can cause substantial damage. Recognizing this, the U.S. Federal Emergency Management Authority (FEMA) recommends that people living in the path of such winds build extra-strong core areas in their homes in which they can take safe refuge for a few hours. The question then becomes, What wall assemblies qualify as "core walls"?

Engineers have devised tests to simulate the projectile loads described, one of which involves shooting a 15 pound [6.8 kg] 2x4 [38x89 mm] wood stud perpendicular to the wall to be tested. Researchers conducted such a test[6] on both unplastered and plastered straw bale walls. The value of their results is somewhat compromised by incomplete reporting – the type of straw (wheat, rice, etc.) and, more importantly, the gauge of mesh reinforcing and the length and manner of plaster curing were not reported. They constructed four course high (56"/1.4M]) x 24" [61 cm] thick walls with 7 pcf [112 kg/M^3] bales and #4 (1/2"/13mm diameter) rebar at 24" [61 cm] on center impaled through the wall centerline. One set of tests was on an unplastered wall, the second set was on a wall with either "older chicken wire" or "light gauge expanded metal" on unspecified areas of a single specimen, each tied through the wall at 12 inches [30 cm] on center each way. The plaster mix was given as "18 parts brick sand, 2 parts portland cement, 1 part type S masonry cement, and one cup of 1 inch plastic fiber," which would give a substantially weaker plaster than the 1 cement : 1 lime : 6 sand mix used on typical straw bale projects using lime-cement plaster. The plaster was applied in three coats for total thickness ranging between 1.5 and 3 inches [3.8 to 7.4 cm].

Shooting the 15 pound [6.8 kg] 2x4 [38x89 mm] wood stud straight at the wall, they reported results as follows:

1) Unplastered	2x4 velocity[A]	effect at far (non–impact) side of wall
A	104 / 152	hit seam between bales and penetrated 3 feet beyond far side
B	101 / 148	hit center of bale and penetrated 2 feet beyond far side
C	101 / 148	hit end of bale (bale parallel to force) and stopped in straw
D	52 / 76	hit center of bale and pushed some straw out far side
E	35 / 51	hit end of bale (bale parallel to force) and stopped 7" into straw
2) Plastered		
F	101 / 148	spalled large pieces of stucco from far side
G	91 / 134	hit seam between bales and penetrated 2 feet beyond
H	84 / 123	penetrated 15" and spalled pieces of stucco from far side
J	71 / 103	penetrated 21" and spalled pieces of stucco from far side
K	63 / 92	penetrated 13" and caused some radial cracking in far side stucco

[A] *velocities in miles per hour (mph) / feet per second (fps) [1 mph = 1.6 km/hr, 1 fps = 0.3 M/s]*

By way of giving context to these results, the authors state that a 15 pound 2x4 "missile" traveling at 100 mph, which is considered to require a 250 mph sustained wind, comprises the threshold tornado standard for occupant protection. (They do not state the source standard.) They further state that in 99% of the tornadoes in the United States, wind speeds do not exceed 250 mph, and in 90% maximum wind speeds are 150 mph. They further point out the conservatism of their test in the sense that a projectile is highly unlikely to strike perpendicular to a wall, as was the case in all the tests.

ENDNOTES

1   Ramirez, Juan Carlos, and David Riley, 1998. *Strength Testing of Stucco and Plaster Veneered Straw-Bale Walls*, University of Washington, Seattle, Washington

2   Donahue, Kevin, and David Arkin, 2001. *Preliminary Report on Out-of-Plane Testing of an 8 foot by 8 foot Straw Bale/Pisé Wall Panel* and Donahue, Kevin, 2002, unpublished calculations on application of classic beam theory to out-of-plane loading on straw bale walls, Berkeley, CA

3   Mar, David, 1998. *Full Scale Straw-Bale Vault Test*, Berkeley, California

4   Carrick, John, 1998. *Vertical Loading, Creep, Transverse Loading, and Racking Loading on Plastered Straw-Bale Walls* Building Research Centre, University of New South Wales, Australia

5   Platts, Robert, 1996. *Developing and Proof-Testing the 'Prestressed Nebraska' Method for Improved Production of Baled Fibre Housing*, Fibrehouse, Ltd. with Scanada Consultants Ltd., Ottawa, Ontario

6   Bilello, Joseph, and Russell Carter, 1999. *Missile Perforation Threshold Speeds for Straw Bale Wall Construction with a Stucco Finish* The Wind Engineering Research Center, Texas Tech University, Lubbock, Texas

4.4 In-Plane Load

4.4.1 Introduction to In-Plane Loads

When force is applied to a wall parallel to its largest surfaces, most typically at the top of the wall, then the wall is loaded *in-plane,* and is acting as what is generally known as a *shearwall.* Most buildings, especially houses, rely on shearwalls to remain upright and safe when affected by wind or earthquake forces.

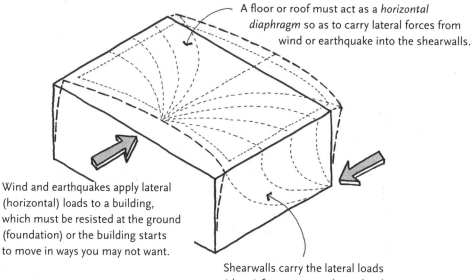

A floor or roof must act as a *horizontal diaphragm* so as to carry lateral forces from wind or earthquake into the shearwalls.

Wind and earthquakes apply lateral (horizontal) loads to a building, which must be resisted at the ground (foundation) or the building starts to move in ways you may not want.

Shearwalls carry the lateral loads (shear) from upper to lower levels.

The extremely simplified version – virtually all buildings are more complex than this. In typical engineering practice, the walls perpendicular to the direction of loading are considered to resist out-of-plane load only (see section 4.3), while the walls parallel to load carry the force on the building as a whole. This is for the simple reason that the walls parallel to load are much stiffer, and will tend to "grab" all the load to the building. (Here's a simple, illustrative experiment showing the difference between in-plane and out-of-plane stiffness: take a large, thin hardcover book, such as an atlas, and balance it on a table on its edge, with the binding facing up. Now push at the top against the broad face – it falls right over. Now try it again, only push against and parallel to the edge; it may slide, yes, but it's pretty hard to get it to tip over. For almost any wall of any material, out-of-plane stiffness is relatively low, in-plane stiffness is relatively high.) Engineering convention is to analyze a structure in each of two perpendicular directions, sometimes more for very oddly-shaped floor plans.

The design of shearwalls starts with understanding the entire building – knowing the forces that may affect the wall, the way these forces "travel" through the structure to each wall and from the wall to the foundation, and the strength of the wall assembly under in-plane load. It also requires understanding the *boundary conditions* – the connections that tie the top, bottom, and sides of the wall to the surrounding building, and how the entire structure hangs together when blown by the wind or given a shake. As the saying goes, the chain is only as strong as its weakest link, and very often building designers (whether owner-builders or professional engineers) fail to pay adequate attention to the boundary conditions – frequently the weak link – that commonly govern the strength of the overall assembly.

A shear force at the top causes point 2 to move away from point 3, opening a tension crack between them ...

...and will cause point 1 to move away from point 4 when the load reverses direction ...

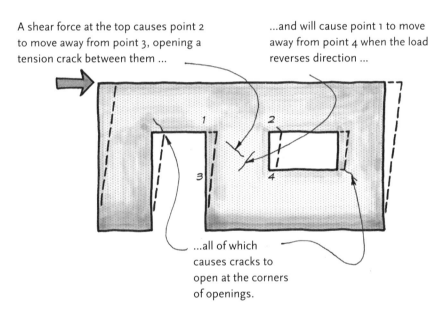

...all of which causes cracks to open at the corners of openings.

4.4B
A SHEARWALL AND ITS INTERNAL CRACKING

The way walls crack tells us where the tension forces are – perpendicular to the cracks. We reinforce concrete, and plaster for straw bale walls, to resist tension forces because no plaster by itself is very good at that.

A similar inattention to boundary conditions will skew the results of laboratory tests. In the view of some engineers, many of the in-plane load tests on straw bale walls done over the past fifteen years, though they revealed a lot, have been compromised by inadequate consideration of the test setup, yielding unduly conservative or unconservative results. This is not said as a criticism but rather to point out that, as with building itself, tests of building assemblies require a great degree of art, knowledge, and experience. Both building and test designs are invariably better if subjected to review by two or more knowledgeable people. In any case, the bulk of the reference, discussion, analysis and conclusions drawn in this section derive from the EBNet cyclic in-plane tests conducted by the authors[1] (the results are reproduced in some detail at the end of this chapter).

Furthermore, it bears pointing out that the construction industry is still refining its understanding of wall assemblies far more common and well-tested, such as plywood-sheathed stud walls and steel-reinforced concrete walls. We cannot presume to have definitive answers to the many questions an engineer may ask, but at the same time can now speak about straw bale shearwalls with a far better understanding than ever before.

In this section we describe the in-plane load resistance and behavior of bale walls and their boundary conditions, based on tests to date, in resisting wind and seismic forces. With that we propose design recommendations and code provisions (chapter 11) for the use of plastered straw bale shearwalls in buildings.

4.4.2 General Considerations for In-Plane Wall Design

The art and science of seismic engineering could be said to consist of both knowing and controlling the way forces, especially dynamic forces, act within the building. It is an imperfect science, if only because we can predict only roughly the intensity and direction of the three-dimensional shaking, continuing and changing over the seconds of a temblor, that will affect any particular building. We *can,* however, know more precisely about the materials with which we assemble and connect the building. The goal, again, is always to have *ductile yielding,* which is to say, guide the forces into connections and elements that can stretch, bend, crinkle, rock back and forth, or otherwise deform so as to absorb the energy of the shaking without collapse. Yielding – *controlled* yielding – is the way of the Tao, and the way of surviving major earthquakes.

Intense ground shaking caused by earthquakes is only rarely extreme, occurring every one, two or three hundred years, whereas small and moderate temblors are far more frequent; this fact affects the way we think of and design all seismic load-resisting systems. Under the relatively modest loading of wind and medium-to-small earthquakes, a structure should be strong enough to resist the load without damage. When The Big One hits, however, it's a new ball game – again, the structure and its components must be able to deform so as to absorb the energy of the shaking. The lateral strength of plastered straw bale walls is primarily attributable to the reinforced plaster skins – the "eggshells" of the analogy in section 4.1. The stiff plaster, braced by the straw core, is intended to absorb the shaking energy of a large earthquake by cracking and locally crushing, resist damage to the structure in the more frequent small-to-medium earthquakes, and provide resistance to wind loads without damage.

Many seismic design engineers, trained in conventional structural materials, are surprised and positively impressed with the behavior of straw bale walls in the laboratory. The latest experiments[1] showed that well-detailed lime-cement plastered walls with steel mesh reinforcement could resist the same range of lateral loads as common, well-built plywood-sheathed stud walls. Even earth-plastered walls with plastic mesh reinforcing proved roughly comparable to a wood stud wall with very light plywood sheathing. The straw bale walls also appeared tougher, meaning they could still carry vertical loads even when highly distorted by lateral loads; equipment constraints limited displacement to $\pm$ seven inches at the top of the wall with no sign that the walls were approaching collapse at these very high distortions. The toughness is due to the flexibility (elastic compressibility) of the bales, the bonding and bracing between straw and plaster, and the width of the bales. The geometry alone makes for a sturdy wall that is resistant to buckling because of its small aspect ratio (wall height / wall width).

The evidence suggests that well-plastered one-story straw bale walls have little risk of collapse under intense seismic shaking. While reassuring, there is more that can and should be considered to reduce or eliminate earthquake-induced damage to the walls and the building in general:

1) the configuration and extent of the walls with respect to the building plan,
2) the provision of a complete load path from the roof to the foundation (i.e., boundary conditions for mechanically connecting or tying the various components of the structure together), and
3) the design and detailing of the walls.

4.4.3 Wall Layout

General rules about ideal wall lengths and layout are fairly intuitive, but also vary greatly depending on the degree of seismic risk at the building site and the softness of site soils. (Soft soils generally intensify seismic shaking and the resulting damage.)

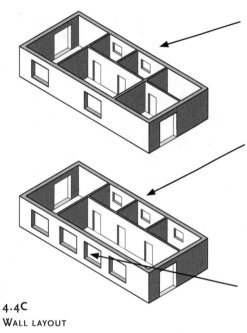

4.4C
WALL LAYOUT

Rule 1a Walls, be they exterior straw bale walls or interior partition walls, should be distributed throughout the building plan as uniformly as possible. That way, the loads of wind or earthquake are spread around fairly evenly. Boring architecture, maybe, but safe structure.

Rule 1b If, however, there are large open areas, or large glazed walls such as for passive solar design, then the rest of the building has to make up for the "soft spot" – the other walls must work that much harder to hold things together when the wind blows or the ground shakes.

Rule 2 Wall openings should be limited with respect to wall lengths and thickness. Again, the more doors and windows you have in the walls, the more light you will have, but the harder the remaining walls will have to work when needed.

Rule 3 Heavier buildings are shaken harder by earthquakes than lighter ones.

Rule 4 Taller buildings are harder to hold down.

Rule 5 As buildings begin to get damaged, the weaker parts bend or break first.

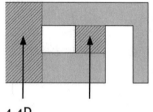

4.4D
WALL PIERS

Doors and windows break up a wall into "miniwalls" that must sometimes be checked independently of the overall wall system.

The gravity load due to the self-weight of the wall and any weight of the roof tributary to the wall (where the wall is load-bearing) confers some lateral strength and stability, but the use of well-attached, reinforced plasters is the primary means of reliably strengthening and stabilizing walls. Wall segments, or piers, can be defined by the penetrations used for windows and doors; a typical pier is the rectangular section of wall between a door and a window, or between a door and a wall corner. Piers, when part of a shearwall, must often be analyzed separately as "miniwalls" within the surrounding wall.

4.4.4 Load Path and Design Philosophy

Straw bale wall systems are composite systems requiring the cooperation of many components to develop a complete load path for carrying lateral loads from the roof to the foundation. In current practice in California, straw bale shearwalls use and engage wood plates at the wall's top and bottom (along with their attachments to the surrounding structure), wire nails or staples fastening reinforcing mesh to the plates, plaster (see chapter 3 for material properties of meshes, fasteners, and plasters), and the stacked assembly of straw bales at the literal and metaphorical core of the wall. Ductile behavior will be obtained when these assembled components can sustain relatively large deformations with little loss of carrying capacity. Testing to date suggests that reinforced concrete design methods can be applied to the plaster skins so as to design the elements and assembly for under, over, or balanced reinforcement.

The best prospects for obtaining ductile seismic response are associated with several alternative (but not exclusive) possibilities:

1) rocking of the wall (over-reinforcing), involving the opening of gaps at the base of the wall, with gravity loads providing a restoring moment;
2) flexural yielding of the wall (under-reinforcing), involving yielding of the mesh, and/or
3) development of compression struts in the bales (following skin degradation);
4) crushing of plaster edges at wall ends.

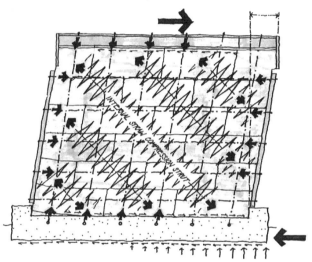

4.4E
A STRAW BALE
SHEARWALL AND
ITS INTERNAL
COMPRESSION STRUTS

illustration by David Mar

Any plaster is much stiffer than the straw bale core, with the straw acting to brace the relatively slender plaster facing materials. If "compression struts" in the bales are to be fully mobilized, the facings would first have to degrade significantly under previous load reversals. Prior to this degradation, stress will develop throughout the field of each face, and these stresses will redistribute as the facings crack or fail locally due to the tension and compression stresses of the applied lateral and gravity loads.

Yielding of the mesh in flexure is akin to the behavior of an under-reinforced concrete member, and is achievable with cement plaster facings. The compressive strength of earth plasters is so low that even with relatively light plastic mesh (such as polypropylene), crushing of the plaster at the base may occur like an over-rein-

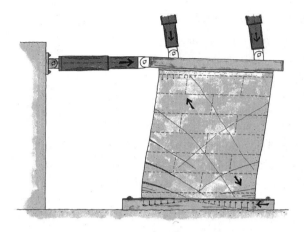

4.4F

In tests as well as buildings, a straw bale shearwall must absorb the energy of earthquake forces by deforming, locally crushing and stretching, rocking back and forth, or some combination of these in order to absorb the energy of the shaking without collapse. Tall, narrow walls are dominated by bending; short, squat walls by shear; and most walls – of any material – resist load by a combination of the two.

illustration by David Mar

forced concrete member. However, loss of the flexural resistance associated with failure of the mesh or facing is not tantamount to failure of the wall. Test walls exhibited substantial toughness, not losing their integrity or their capacity to carry gravity loads through drifts of 7.5% (the limit of the test setup). Hence it seems unlikely that earthquake displacement demands would be sufficient to cause collapse in light single-story residential construction having a relatively dense network of interconnected straw bale (and other) walls. (See the hysteretic curves from the EBNet tests at the end of this section.) Nevertheless, for purposes of code design, sufficient lateral strength must be demonstrated by analysis and provided through adequately detailed walls. Three levels of detailing were developed for each set of three walls, aiming for a flexural yielding mechanism in the case of the plaster walls and a flexural crushing or rocking mechanism in the case of the earth plaster walls.

4.4.5 Selecting Wall Details and Materials

4.4.5a Bales (see also chapter 1)

There is often no choice here; you use what is available in the area. If there is a choice, as in coastal California, there is a preference for rice straw bales, which tend to be more dense and more resistant to moisture problems. In many places, available bales are too soft for use in structural walls, and therefore must be compressed and retied. Likewise, the stacked bale wall will function better in every way if it is precompressed (see section 4.1), but this is not always necessary.

4.4.5b Plaster (see also chapter 3)

Plaster serves many functions in determining the wall's moisture, thermal, fire-resistive, and aesthetic properties, and is an integral part of the structure as well. Where the wall must serve as primary structure, either as a load-bearing or shear wall, that will often determine the appropriate plaster and curing regimen to use. If the building is not in a high wind or seismic risk area, you are much freer to choose the plaster based on other considerations.

4.4.5c Reinforcing (see also chapter 3)

Earth plasters are relatively soft and are generally reinforced with a comparably flexible mesh such as polypropylene, natural fiber meshes such as coir or hemp, or just natural fibers such as chopped straw from the bales. Natural fibers have been used in earth structures and plasters for centuries to provide structural reinforcing, but must be protected from moisture and decay. Many polypropylene fencing materials are strong enough for use in structural walls, and of course are far less vulnerable to moisture degradation. Metal meshes may or may not be compatible with earth plasters, but to our knowledge they have not been tested or tried in the field.

Gypsum and pure lime plasters are somewhat stronger than earth plasters, but in general, if reinforced at all, they use the same types of mesh or fiber reinforcing materials.

Lime-cement and soil-cement plasters are far more strong, brittle, and stiff, and should be reinforced with a galvanized steel mesh. Relatively light-gauge mesh must be used so it can be stapled at its edges, and to promote yielding of the mesh rather than failure of the cement plaster in compression. So far, experience in the lab[2] (see section 3.6) indicates that 14-gauge galvanized steel 2" x 2" [5 cm] fencing works well, whereas premature failures develop at the welds of 16-gauge fencing (the transverse wires separate from the longitudinal wires). Thus, in highly-loaded walls, we currently have a strong preference for 14-gauge galvanized mesh, although future tests might identify an adequate 16-gauge fencing product.

In concrete, steel reinforcement is normally protected from corrosion because the alkaline cementitious environment causes a passivating oxide layer to form on the surface of the reinforcement, providing a barrier that prevents oxygen and water from reaching it, and thereby preventing the chemical reactions that cause rusting. However, the concrete's alkalinity is gradually diminished over time as atmospheric CO_2 causes carbonation of the concrete's outermost (typically one to two inches [2.5 − 5 cm]) layer. In the case of plaster over bales, the thickness of the plaster cover over mesh reinforcement is much less than that required for reinforced concrete, and thus it is likely that the plaster's alkalinity in the vicinity of the mesh will be reduced. For this reason it is always preferable to use galvanized steel lath and meshes with cement-based plasters. The zinc coating provides the barrier to prevent oxygen and water from chemically reacting with the steel even if carbonation occurs; it also provides galvanic protection because the zinc is anodic to steel. Further protection for the mesh is afforded by topically applying sealants such as siloxane, by spray-painting the bottom horizontal (most exposed) band of mesh and staples with zinc-rich primer paint prior to plastering, and by generally protecting walls from rain (see chapter 5, *Moisture*).

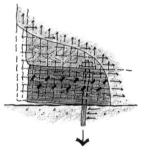

4.4G WALL CORNERS

This part of the wall is the most important to structural performance. Sill plates must be sized to carry the bending loads imposed by earthquakes, the plaster must bear against the foundation, and the mesh must be adequately stapled to the plates so as to carry both shear and tension loads (or shear only if a post with hold-down device is introduced).

illustration by David Mar

4.4.5d Fasteners and Anchorage (see also chapter 3)

Mesh details must be carefully attended to in providing a complete load path. This involves designing attachments at both the top and bottom of the wall, and to a lesser extent at door and window openings.

In the large-scale tests, the mesh extended vertically from mud sill to bond beam with overlaps at the vertical joints of 6 inches [15 cm] for the steel mesh and 12 inches for the polypropylene mesh. An additional horizontal band of mesh was placed at the top of the wall to strengthen the attachment of the mesh to the bond beam, and a similar horizontal mesh band was placed at the bottom to strengthen its attachment to the mud sill. These bands, which extended up to or beyond the mid-height of the first course of bales, and were stapled to the sill or bond beam as well as the full-height mesh proved to be beneficial and are recommended for future construction.

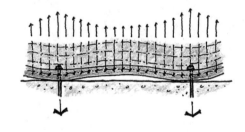 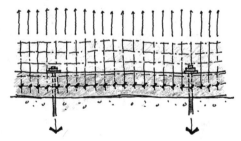

4.4H

In a high seismic risk design, the sill plates must be thick enough both to resist bending and cross-grain tension, and to receive a multitude of staples. Wherever possible, staples should stagger with the mesh joints as shown in figure 4.4G.

illustration by David Mar

It is well known that in wood stud shear-walls, thin base plates simply don't work under high seismic loading because they either split between anchor bolt holes or split in cross-grain tension under uplift loads. The same was seen in the large-scale straw bale wall tests, so heavier plates (such as 4x4 [10cm x 10cm]) are needed to receive the staples. Problems related to pressure treatment corroding the light metal staples can be averted by using untreated 4x4 plates bolted to the foundation over a capillary break such as plastic or asphaltic membrane. In such cases, a layer of asphaltic building paper or similar moisture barrier must be attached to the untreated sill and all untreated framing in contact with the plaster (see figures 4.4K and 10A).

Anchorage tests[2] also showed that manually-driven staples (electro-galvanized 15 gauge x $^7/_8$ inch rounded shoulder staples, slash point, with $^3/_{16}$ inch inner spread) are adequate to anchor the polypropylene mesh. If pneumatically driven staples are used, electro-galvanized 16 gauge x 1.25 inch medium crown staples are adequate for the polypropylene mesh, while electro-galvanized 16 gauge x 1.75 inch medium crown staples are adequate for the 14 gauge mesh. The staples should be driven diagonally over the mesh intersections, aiming for a snug contact that does not crimp the mesh. Staples generally did not fail when they were installed diagonally over the wire intersections, whereas they routinely pulled out when installed parallel to the mesh wires.

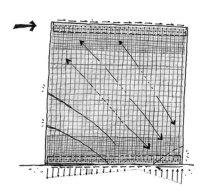

4.4J

In a high seismic risk design, the mesh should completely cover both the inside and outside of the wall, and be well-fastened to the top and bottom (sill) plates. Mesh sheets should lap at least 6 inches [15 cm]; an additional horizontal band of mesh along both top and bottom courses, also fastened to the plates, ensures a relatively smooth load path from plate to field of plaster and back to plate – akin to the transition in your body from bone to tendon to muscle to tendon to bone, a gradation of stiffness rather than abrupt changes.

illustration by David Mar

4.4K

Wall base details specific to seismic load-resisting shearwalls. If the rain exposure of the wall is severe, additional durability should be added by treating the exterior plaster with siloxane (with an extra coat along the bottom course), and by spray-painting the mesh and staples with zinc-rich paint in the bottom two feet [60 cm] +/-.

Bottom of the wall / seismic details

*As with most wall assemblies, this is where connections matter most.
If the wall is not intended to function as a shearwall,
then many of the comments below do not apply.
In any case, detail 10D applies here as well.*

Sill plates should be:
1) Non-ammonia-based pressure-treated, or
2) Any pressure-treated lumber with stainless steel staples, or
3) Untreated lumber bolted over a moisture barrier from the foundation, and with a capillary break such as Grade D paper separating it from the plaster.

Plaster
should be designed, mixed, applied, protected, and especially cured with much greater care than is customary in most places, because it is here a structural material.

Mesh
should be chosen for compatibility with the plaster, and based on structural demands.

A second layer of mesh
should be added in a horizontal band along the bottom (shown) and top courses of the wall. (see also figure 4.4J)

Anchor bolts
should be sized and spaced as needed for loads, for reducing bending in the sill plate, and have oversized washers under the nuts as is now done in wood stud construction (see figure 4.4H)

Plaster
must bear firmly on the foundation or floor -- provide framing members or blocking under all plaster skins.

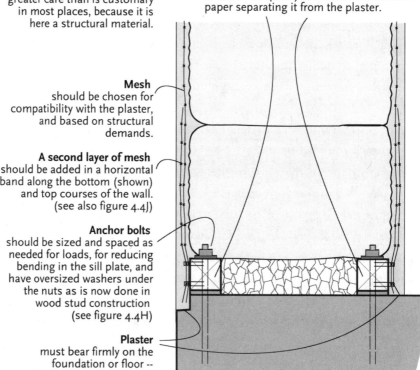

4.4.6 Summary Review of Cyclic In-Plane Load Tests

Full scale (8 foot x 8 foot) wall envelope curves

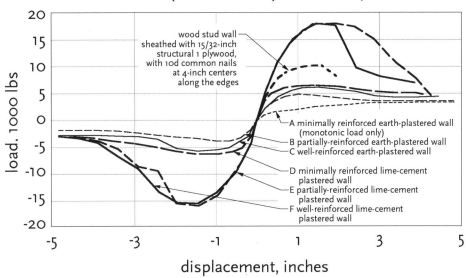

wood stud wall sheathed with 15/32-inch structural 1 plywood, with 10d common nails at 4-inch centers along the edges

A minimally reinforced earth-plastered wall (monotonic load only)
B partially-reinforced earth-plastered wall
C well-reinforced earth-plastered wall
D minimally reinforced lime-cement plastered wall
E partially-reinforced lime-cement plastered wall
F well-reinforced lime-cement plastered wall

y-axis: load, 1000 lbs
x-axis: displacement, inches

4.4L

COMPARISON OF WALL BEHAVIORS UNDER SAME LOADING PROTOCOL

from the EBNet test program, 2001

See the following pages for complete hysteretic curves for each wall, each wall's construction, and comments on failure modes for each.

4.4.7 Hysteretic Curves From Cyclic Wall Tests[1,3]

Typical Specimen Description – Walls A – F

Six plastered straw bale assemblies were constructed and tested. Internally, each wall was similar, with six bale courses stacked flat in a running bond. Each course was the length of two bales, a nominal eight foot [2.4 M] length per course. The nominal height of each wall, from bottom of bale to top of bale, was also eight feet. Two different skin materials, earth plaster (walls A, B, and C) and lime-cement plaster (walls D, E, and F) were used. Reinforcement details were used with each plaster type representing light, medium, and heavy reinforcement. All walls had a total nominal thickness of 1.5" [3.8 cm] for all plasters applied. (Download test descriptions at www.ecobuildnetwork.org for a more complete description of the walls and results.)

WALL A WAS SUBJECTED TO A MONOTONIC TEST PROTOCOL:

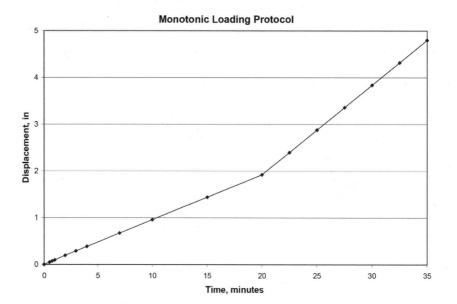

4.4M

WALL LOADING
PROTOCOLS

WALLS B – G WERE SUBJECTED TO A CYCLIC TEST PROTOCOL:

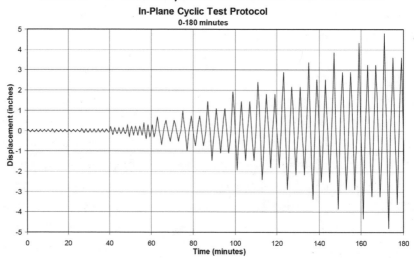

4.4.7A WALL A EARTH-PLASTERED WALL / LIGHT DETAILING (monotonic load)

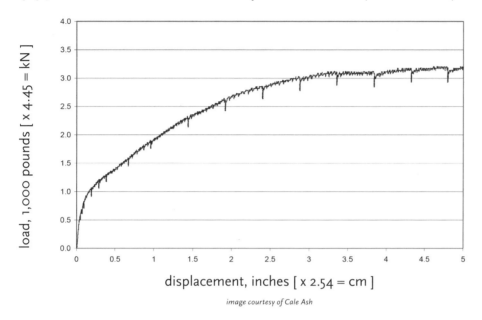

image courtesy of Cale Ash

Wall A was coated with earth plaster consisting of earth, sand, water, and straw fibers. Compression tests yielded inconsistent results, with average compressive strengths ranging between 290 psi and 160 psi. Five loops of 350 lb. polypropylene baling twine, running continuously over the header beam and under the 2x4 mudsill, comprised the only reinforcement.

Comments: Prior to loading, as it dried the earth plaster pulled away from the box beam leaving visible gaps of one to two inches [2.5 to 5 cm] between the plaster and box beam around approximately half of the box beam's perimeter, probably due to the lack of mesh reinforcement for the plaster to adhere to. The peak capacity of Wall A was 3.2 kips, which was reached at 4% drift (3.84 inches) and was maintained for higher displacements. During loading, the header beam was observed to slip relative to the top course of bales as evidenced by cracking in the plaster returns at the top of the wall. At lower displacements (less than 2.4 inches), the failure mode appeared to be dominated by the box beam slipping relative to the top course of bales, corresponding to lateral loads less than 2.85 kips. Above this 2.5% drift level, crushing of the earth plaster in the compression zone commenced as lateral load capacity increased to the maximum value of 3.2 kips. There was no evidence to suggest the poly-twine failed at any point during the tests, as it was found to be taut when inspected at the gaps that opened at the base of the wall during testing.

4.4N

Box beam slipping away from the top of wall A

image courtesy of Cale Ash

4.4.7B WALL B EARTH-PLASTERED WALL / MEDIUM DETAILING

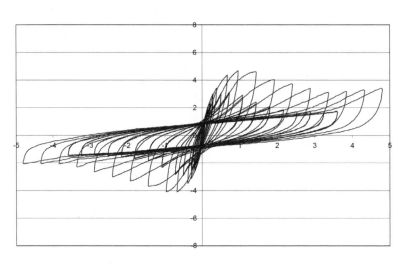

load, 1,000 pounds [x 4.45 = kN]

displacement, inches [x 2.54 = cm]

image courtesy of Cale Ash

4.40

*Flexural crack openings
at base of wall B*

image courtesy of Cale Ash

Wall B was coated with earth plaster (see Wall A description). The reinforcing was two layers of Cintoflex™ polypropylene mesh consisting of 0.05 inch nominal diameter legs 1.9 inches on center as reinforcement, which came on an 96 inch wide roll (see mesh and fastener tension tests in chapter 3, *Plaster and Reinforcing*), An additional horizontal band of mesh was laid over the top and bottom courses. All mesh layers were attached at once to 4x4 plates top and bottom with 16 gauge staples (1.25 inches deep with 7/16 inch crowns) at each mesh intersection (i.e., 2 inches +/- oc), and mesh was tied through the wall at each course (23 inches on center vertically) and at 24 inches [61 cm] on center horizontally.

Comments: The plastic mesh provided additional skin reinforcement relative to that in Wall A. A side benefit to using some form of mesh is that the plaster has something to bond to, reducing or avoiding the peeling problems of Wall A, which had no mesh reinforcement. During testing, the predominant failure modes observed were compression zone crushing and base sliding, with the base sliding becoming more pronounced at later stages of the test. The peak capacity of 4.7 kips was reached on the eighth load step, at a drift level of 1% (0.96 inches). Looking at the load-displacement plot, the change in the hysteresis loops with increasing displacements suggests that sliding of the wall becomes more significant at higher displacements. The higher amplitude cycles were observed to wear down the earth plaster at the base, which gradually reduced it to sand, clay, and straw components. The height of the wall was correspondingly reduced due to this wearing and crushing. The resulting soil debris served as a wedge to push the plaster out of plane, away from the bales, when the plaster was loaded in compression. As this occurred, the plaster would crush down over the test frame, thereby creating a form of interlock and shear resistance that might not be available in field settings. However, this behavior began only after drifts of 2.5%.

4.4.7c WALL C EARTH-PLASTERED WALL / HEAVY DETAILING

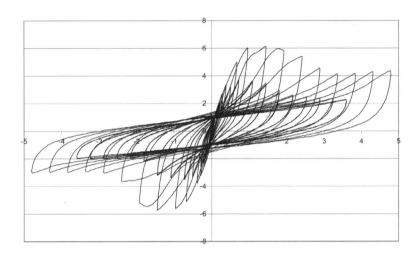

load, 1,000 pounds [x 4.45 = kN]

displacement, inches [x 2.54 = cm]

image courtesy of Cale Ash

Wall C was the same as Wall B except as follows: Welded wire mesh was used, and 5/8 inch diameter bolts at 24 inches on center were installed on each side from the base up to plywood "shear cleats" set between the first and second bale courses. Mesh was tied through the wall at 24 inches on center horizontally and at every bale course vertically with poly twine.

Comments: Wall C used a heavy 2" x 2" 14 gauge wire mesh with the first course of bales anchored to the base via plywood plates and threaded rods. As shown above, these modifications caused an increase in the lateral strength of this wall relative to that of Wall B, with a peak load of 6.1 kips occurring at 1.5% drift (1.44 inches). At 1% drift, the 6.0 kip resistance was an increase of nearly 30% over the corresponding resistance of Wall B at this drift level. The overall structural response of this wall was similar to that of Wall B, with predominant failure modes consisting of crushing of the earth plaster and sliding of the wall at its base. The heavier mesh was observed to reduce the slip at the base of Wall C from a peak-to-peak amplitude of ¾" in Wall B to ½" amplitude in this specimen at a drift of 4%. No flexural tension cracks were observed during the testing of Wall C, indicating the mismatch of plaster compressive strength to wire mesh tensile strength. Like Wall B, this wall experienced the plaster interlocking with the base of the test frame at drifts above 3%.

4.4P

Fracture of wire mesh at 5% drift at base of wall C

image courtesy of Cale Ash

4.4.7D WALL D LIME-CEMENT-PLASTERED WALL / LIGHT DETAILING

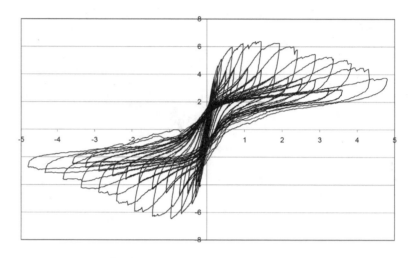

displacement, inches [x 2.54 = cm]

image courtesy of Cale Ash

4.4Q

Cross-grain tension failure of 2x4 plate at base of wall D at 5% drift

image courtesy of Cale Ash

Walls D, E, and F were plastered with lime-cement plaster: 30 gallons of sand, 8 gallons of cement, 2 gallons of slaked lime, and 6-1/2 gallons of water. The lime was prehydrated by mixing 6 gallons of water (as measured in water containers) with a 50 pound bag of slaked finish lime. The lime was then allowed to sit and hydrate for five days until it ceased absorbing water. Compressive test results using two inch cubes were 2210 psi at 36 days. Wall D was reinforced with a 17 gauge hexagonal wire mesh (standard plaster netting), 16 gauge staples (1.25 inches deep x 7/16 inch crown), and 2x4 base plates to receive the mesh.

Comments This combination of a strong skin and a relatively weak reinforcement led to a failure mode different from that of Wall C. The walls with cement plaster skins were stiffer than those with earth plaster skins. The figure above shows the load-displacement plot for this test, and the pinching nature of the hysteresis loops suggests the rocking behavior that was observed at higher displacements. The peak load of 6.4 kips was only marginally higher than that observed for Wall C, but the post-peak behavior was dominated by rocking rather than sliding. As higher displacements were reached, the base of the wall exhibited two distinct failure modes. In some locations the weak mesh was elongated and had fractured, while at other locations the 2x4 sill plate receiving the mesh staples failed in cross-grain bending. By the end of the test, the combination of mesh fractures and sill failure had progressed along the full length of the wall, allowing the observed rocking behavior to continue unimpeded. None of the staples anchoring the mesh were observed to fail or pull out.

4.4.6E WALL E LIME-CEMENT-PLASTERED WALL / MEDIUM DETAILING

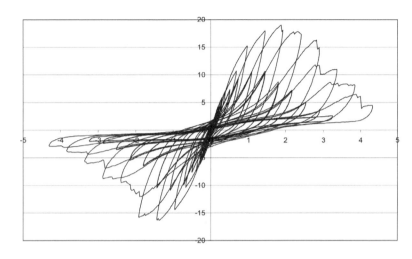

displacement, inches [x 2.54 = cm]

image courtesy of Cale Ash

Wall E plaster was the same as for Wall D. Reinforcing was a welded wire mesh consisting of 14 gauge wires intersecting at right angles every 2 inches on center and a roll width of 48 inches, 16 gauge staples (1 inch deep x 7/16 inch crown), and 4x4 base plates to receive the mesh.

Comments: For this medium-detailed cement plaster wall, 14-gauge 2" x 2" mesh was used to reinforce the plaster, and additional staples were used to attach the plaster to both the sill plate and the header beam. To reduce the likelihood of skin buckling under compressive loading, through-ties running through the thickness of the wall and anchored by dowels in the body of the plaster were installed at every other course. Instead of the 2x4 sill plate, which failed in Wall D, a 4x4 sill plate was used, and the 4x4 plate was anchored more frequently. The combination of cement plaster skins and heavier wire mesh resulted in an increased lateral strength, having a peak value of 19 kips at 2% drift, as shown above. This increase of nearly 200% over Wall D was associated with the development of several flexural cracks within the bottom third of the wall height. Wall E ultimately failed because the reinforcing mesh lost its tensile capacity from both mesh fracture and staple pullout. The mesh fracture was attributed to a combination of tensile elongation and low-cycle fatigue associated with the load reversals, which appeared to work the vertical wires of the mesh. The failures primarily occurred at the staple locations, with some failures also occurring at the intersections of the horizontal and vertical wires where the wires are spot-welded together during manufacture.

4.4R

Flexural crack at base of wall E at 2.5% drift

image courtesy of Cale Ash

STRUCTURE

4.4.6F WALL F LIME-CEMENT-PLASTERED WALL / HEAVY DETAILING

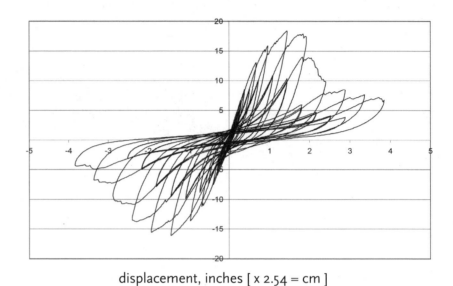

displacement, inches [x 2.54 = cm]

image courtesy of Cale Ash

4.4S

Failure of the mesh and staples at base of wall F at 7.5% drift

Wall F plaster, mesh, and stapling was the same as for Wall E. The heavily-detailed Wall F added spikes from the header beam, additional cross ties, and confinement of the first bale course in addition to the details of Wall E.

Comments: The figure above shows the load-displacement response of this wall, which had a peak lateral strength of 18.2 kips at 1.5% drift, and, at 2% drift, 17.9 kips. A comparison of plots for walls E and F shows the limited benefit gained from Wall F's additional detailing. The confinement of the first bale course was intended to shift the failure above this level while distributing the yielding of the reinforcing mesh over more of the wall height, aiming to achieve a more ductile behavior. The ultimate failure was indeed observed at this level, although there was not an appreciable difference in the ductility or strength of this wall compared to Wall E.

4.4.7G Wall G Lime-cement-plastered wall with medium detailing and 2:1 aspect ratio [3]

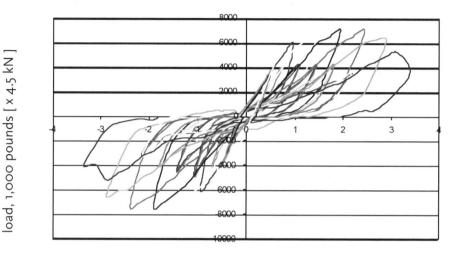

load, 1,000 pounds [x 4.5 kN]

displacement, inches [x 2.54 = cm]

Wall G This wall specimen consisted of six 15.5 x 23 x 48 inch (height, depth, width) three-string rice straw bales. The bales were stacked vertically to create a wall with a nominal height of 7.5 feet [2.3 M] from the bottom to the top of the bales, a length of 4 feet [1.2 M] and a nominal width of 2 feet [0.6 M]. Reinforcement was lapped wire mesh as for Wall E. The wire mesh was manufactured in 14 gauge 2" x 2" right angle squares and was overlapped 12 inches [30 cm] at the top, bottom, and around the corners of the bales. The skin of the wall was a lime-cement-plaster similar to that of Wall E applied in three coats.

Comments: As expected, the 4 x 8 foot high wall's behavior was governed primarily by flexure due to the 2:1 aspect ratio. Before testing, the centerline of the wall was marked, did not move during testing, and few shear cracks occurred. The first signs of permanent damage occurred in the form of cracks at a displacement of .67 in. [1.7 cm]. Cracks continued to form, eventually causing spalling on the rear left side at a displacement of 1.68 in. [4.3 cm] and a corresponding load of 6500 lbs. [2948 kg.]. The largest opening of a crack was measured to be 1 inch on the right side of the specimen, and occurred above the one-foot area where the bottom U-shaped second-layer wire mesh overlapped with the panel wire mesh. Uplift of up to one inch [2.5 cm] at the corners of the wall was observed. As displacements were increased and the wall continued rocking, uplift increased and hence bearing failure occurred in the cement plaster. As this failure occurred, the neutral axis was observed to migrate towards the ends of the wall, slowly decreasing and thereby engaging the wire mesh more. Once the main crack spanned across the length of the specimen, the neutral axis began returning toward the center of the wall as the rocking action occurred primarily at the crack location instead of the base of the wall.

4.4T

Plaster cracking in Wall G just above the area of doubled mesh.

images courtesy of Sarah Faurot, Krista Kelly, and Hyung Kim

4.4.8 Commentary

A) Walls with 1:1 aspect ratios: Based on the full-scale in-plane tests of plastered straw bale wall assemblies supporting imposed nominal dead loads of 200 plf [2.9 kN/M], we concluded about the first six wall tests (with 1:1 aspect ratio):

1) The details used in Walls B, C, E, and F provided good control over the mechanisms of inelastic deformation.

2) The low compressive strength of earth plaster governed the behavior of Walls B and C, resulting in a crushing failure that has parallels to an over-reinforced concrete member.

3) The welded wire mesh used in Walls E and F yielded as intended so as to develop a ductile flexural mode of response in these walls.

4) All walls maintained their integrity and continued to carry gravity loads through drifts of 7.5% of their height, with no sign of impending failure. Larger drifts could not be imposed because of limitations in the test setup.

5) For resisting seismic loads, the details used in Walls B, C, and E can be recommended for walls having about a 1:1 aspect ratio. Further testing and analysis will lead to guidelines for walls having a broader range of aspect ratios.

6) All walls are recommended for resisting wind loads with appropriate safety factors or load reduction factors. (Wall A is not recommended for seismic loading because it is simply not robust enough for even modest seismic shaking; Wall D because hexagonal mesh can and does deform under load, though use of a thicker sill plate might improve its peformance; Wall F because it required a lot more work but gave essentially no better performance than its easier-to-build counterpart, Wall E.)

B) Wall with 2:1 (tall and narrow) aspect ratios: Based on the full-scale in-plane test of Wall G, which was similar except as noted to Wall E; unlike Wall E, 16 gauge (not 14 gauge) staples were used, and a 200 plf [2.9 kN/M] simulated dead load was applied before stapling the mesh, but it was not made clear in the report if that load was left on during lateral loading. Even if it were removed, however, the stapled mesh would retain at least some precompression. From this test we concluded:

1) We expected a maximum capacity of Wall G with the 2:1 aspect ratio to be 25% of that of Wall E with an aspect ratio of 1:1. The actual maximum load was 37% of that of Wall E: 7 kips [31 kN/M] for Wall G versus 19 kips [84 kN/M] for Wall E.

2) The discrepancy in the expected maximum load values was most likely due to Wall G's increased ratio of area of overlapped steel mesh to area of single-layer steel.

3) The cracks formed on both Walls E and G just above the cutoff of the overlapping layers of wire mesh. Cracking in these locations is preferable to base cracking as it increases the wall's overall load capacity and ductility.

4.4.9 Design Recommendations

1) A preliminary comparison with the measured response of plywood walls indicates that a ductility R factor of 5.5 (per the 1997 Uniform Building Code seismic design formula) would be conservative for the design of walls having geometry and details corresponding to Wall E (that is, walls with detailing as used in Wall E, and an aspect ratio of 1:1 or wider).

2) An allowable shear of 610 plf [8.9 kN/M] for straw bale walls having cement stucco skins and 14 gauge mesh, as well as details comparable to those used in Wall E, is suggested for squat walls having nominal aspect ratios not exceeding 1:1. Measured peak strengths were approximately 3.7 times this value. For more slender walls, ultimate flexural strengths should be estimated; allowable values may be determined by dividing the ultimate strength by 3.7.

3) Lacking more extensive cyclic testing of narrow walls (aspect ratio higher than 1:1), and of walls in general, a lower (more conservative) R factor of 3 is recommended for narrow walls, over-reinforced earth plaster walls, and over-reinforced lime-cement plastered walls.

4) For wind design in non- or low-seismic risk areas, see the draft building code, section 11.3, for recommended allowable shear values. See section 4.5 for general comments about design recommendations.

4.4.10 Conclusions

A) Based on the full-scale in-plane tests of plastered straw bale wall assemblies supporting imposed nominal dead loads of 200 plf, we concluded about the first six wall tests (with 1:1 aspect ratio):

1) The details used in Walls B, C, E, and F provided good control over the mechanism of inelastic deformation that occurred in those walls.

2) The low compressive strength of the earth plaster was critical for Walls B and C, and resulted in a crushing failure that has parallels to an over-reinforced concrete member.

3) The welded wire mesh used in Walls E and F yielded successfully in developing a ductile flexural mode of response in these walls.

4) All walls maintained their integrity and continued to carry gravity loads through drifts of 7.5% of their height, with no sign of impending failure. Larger drifts could not be imposed because of limitations in the test setup.

5) The details used in Walls B, C, and E can be recommended for future use for the construction of walls having a nominal 1:1 aspect ratio. Further analysis and review of test data is required to make recommendations for walls having a broader range of aspect ratio.

B) Based on the full-scale in-plane test of Wall G (with 2:1 aspect ratio), we concluded:

1) Based on the difference in length of the specimens, the maximum expected capacity of the wall with the 2:1 aspect ratio was expected to be 25% of that of Wall E with an aspect ratio of 1:1. The actual maximum load of the wall at a 2:1 aspect ratio was better; Wall E reached a maximum load of 19 kips [8618 kg.] whereas Wall G reached a maximum load of 7 kips [3175 kg.], or 37% of that of Wall E.

2) The discrepancy in the expected maximum load values was most likely due to the increased ratio, in Wall G, of area of overlapped steel to area of single-layer steel.

3) The cracks formed on both Walls E and G just above the cutoff of the overlapping layers of wire mesh. Cracking in these locations is preferable to cracks forming near the base of the wall which would decrease the wall's load capacity.

4.5 Design Recommendations – Final Thoughts

It bears repeating here a few things that were discussed earlier: a reinforced, plastered straw bale wall, with its attachments to structure above, below, and at its ends, is only somewhat similar to structural materials and assemblies already known to the engineering community. It really is a new kind of structure and, though simple enough in concept – stack up some bales and plaster them, just like those settlers in Nebraska did one hundred years ago – the structural model is quite complex. The strength and behavior of a wall, under every kind and direction of load, depends on:

- the stiffness and strength of top and bottom sill plates or assemblies,
- the fasteners used to attach plaster reinforcing to those assemblies,
- the stiffness of the stacked straw bale assembly,
- the strength and stiffness of both the reinforcing and the plaster,
- the firmness of support provided at the top and bottom of the plaster skins,
- and especially, (as always in construction), on the skill and care that goes into design and installation, and to proper curing of the plaster.

In chapters 3 and 4 we have presented findings on the strength of materials commonly used in straw bale construction, such as mesh, staples, and plasters, and on the results of large-scale tests of a range of assemblies. But we have been by no means comprehensive. People build with what is available to them, and what is common in coastal California may not be practical or even available in Denmark, Peru, India, or even the interior of California. You will have to make do with what you have, drawing whatever reasonable inferences you can from the information provided herein. As is always the case in engineering design, you must allow for uncertainty (e.g., How strong is this mesh, and this plaster? How much field quality control will be exercised to assure the wall is built as intended?). You must also keep in mind that uncertainties compound; if you're 50% certain of the plaster strength, and 50% certain of the mesh strength, then you are, arguably,

ENDNOTES

1
Ash, C, Mark Aschheim, David Mar, and Bruce King 2004.
Reversed Cyclic In-Plane Tests of Load-Bearing Plastered Straw Bale Walls
13th World Conference on Earthquake Engineering, Vancouver, B.C., Canada

2
Ash, C, Mark Aschheim, David Mar, and Bruce King, 2005.
Recommended Mesh Anchorage Details for Straw Bale Walls
Ecological Building Network, Sausalito, CA

3
Faurot, S., Krista Kelly, and Hyung Kim, 2005.
In-Plane Cyclic Straw Bale Shear Wall Testing
California Polytechnic University, San Luis Obispo

only 25% certain of the strength of the combination. In performing a structural analysis by the Allowable Stress Method or Ultimate Strength Method, you must consider all of the above factors, and perhaps others as well, in deciding on an appropriate factor of safety or strength-reduction factor.

It would surely make many readers happy if we were to provide clear, certain "cookbook" details and formulas for structural (and moisture) design in these pages, but we just can't, at least no more than already presented. Notwithstanding the general public's impression that engineers know very exactly what they're doing because we use impressive mathematics and numbers to the 3rd decimal place, in reality a great deal of judgment is required in any engineering analysis. The design of straw bale buildings is not different; you as a building designer must balance physics, material science, and the realities of your local construction industry to arrive at reasonable conclusions for design. This is the art of engineering.

That said, we join with many other engineering and construction books, and building codes, in providing prescriptive – and still tentative – allowable loads in the tables of section 11.3. That document is a draft still working its way through the many reviews and edits necessary to becoming part of the California Building Code; it is not an official code document, but certainly aspires to eventually be one. The values given there must also be used with a great deal of judgment.

Having now presented all of these qualifiers, hedges, and warnings, we must finish by pointing out that we now know far more than even a few years ago about how to design straw bale buildings, and can do so with some confidence anywhere in the world. There is certainly more that we would like to learn and test, especially as straw bale construction itself evolves as a building technology. But we are no longer just shooting in the dark; the big questions have been largely answered, leaving only the thousand smaller ones to now be addressed.

Perhaps the most important testament of all, not yet mentioned, is the one provided by Nature. There are now load-bearing straw bale structures all over the world, from one to one hundred years old, using innumerable combinations of bales, plasters, and other materials, and this author has yet to hear of a structural failure or even a significant structural problem. This observation is offered to give you some perspective on the choice, for your particular project, of safety factor. There is a toughness and reserve strength in plastered straw bale walls that laboratory tests to date have only hinted at, but to which the century-old homes on the Nebraska prairie attest. Be cautious, yes – this wall is what holds the roof over your head – but make your judgment call with one eye each on reports from the lab, and on the readily-available wealth of field experience.

The Seventh Inning Stretch

*I'm fixing a hole where the rain gets in
And stops my mind from wandering
Where it will go...
Where it will go...*

— John Lennon and Paul McCartney
Fixing a Hole

MOISTURE

5.1 Moisture, Materials, and Straw Bales

by John Straube

5.1.1 About Water

Water is the majestic and mysterious chemical foundation of life on earth, without which we wouldn't even be here to admire, wonder, or worry about it. But if you're in the construction business, you had better worry about it, as water is your nemesis, and moisture is involved in most building problems. The most serious tend to be structural damage due to wood decay, unhealthy fungal growth, corrosion, freeze-thaw, and damage to moisture-sensitive interior finishes. Avoiding these problems requires an understanding of materials, moisture, and the way moisture moves through a straw bale wall and the building enclosure in general. This chapter deals with the fundamentals of moisture in buildings, and more specifically with moisture that moves through enclosure walls. The principles are the same for all buildings, but moisture control is particularly significant for straw bale buildings because of the moisture sensitivity of the materials.

The first part of this chapter (5.1) deals with materials, moisture physics, and the theoretical framework of moisture control. The second part (5.2) deals with practical applications and discusses the specifics of straw bale construction in more depth. The final section (5.3) examines the conditions that initiate and foster straw decomposition.

The moisture tolerance of houses can be dramatically improved through intelligent design of building location, orientation, geometry, HVAC systems, and materials. These are the least expensive and most effective approaches – and ones rarely used because they must be considered very early in the design stage. All too often, a building has been fully "designed" or conceptualized before anyone with a knowledge of building science gets involved – if in fact any such person is ever involved – at which point the easy solutions have been designed out.

> *The best moisture control strategies always involve designing problems OUT – not solving them after they have been needlessly designed into the enclosure.*

5.1.3A
MOISTURE STATES AND PHASE CHANGE PROCESSES

Moisture, in all its states, is a molecule with two positively charged hydrogen atoms and one negatively charged oxygen atom (H_2O). The molecule is only about 0.3 nanometers in diameter: one billion laid end to end would be about one foot long.

5.1.2 Materials

It is common to classify materials in different ways. For example, organic materials are based on carbon and hydrogen molecules, whereas mineral-based materials are based on molecules with silicates and calcites. Another useful distinction is that between porous and non-porous materials; many materials are porous, and if the pores are microscopic (e.g., on the order of thousandths of an inch) they will have very large internal surface areas. For example, the interior surface area is about 0.2 m²/gram [50 ft²/ounce] for gypsum board, 20 m²/gram [5000 ft²/ounce] for cement paste, and even more for wood or cellulose. Materials such as glass, steel, and most plastics have essentially no porosity. Consequently they have no internal surface area and hence allow neither water absorption nor moisture transmission.

5.1.3 The Water Molecule and its States

Water, like most materials, exists in liquid, solid, vapor, and adsorbed states or phases. Unlike most materials, we experience water in all of its states during our daily lives. Iron and gasoline also exist in all of the states shown in Figure 5.1.3A, but only at temperatures outside our normal range of experience. Of these states, the adsorbed state is the least understood, and will be described in more detail later.

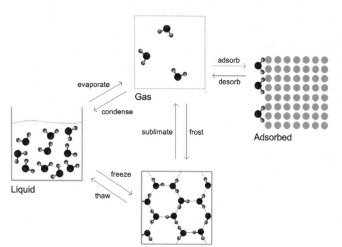

5.1.4 Water's Interaction with Materials

The polar water molecule "magnet" is attracted to many materials in both the vapor and liquid state. For example, water drops will cling to your skin and to the mirror after a shower. Liquid water is actually sucked into the very small tubes (termed *capillaries*) present in porous materials: the smaller the tube the greater this *capillary suction*. The suction (or wicking) of interconnected capillaries explains how water is drawn up into celery, into brick, and to the top of tall trees. A few materials, like silicone, oils, and some plastics, repel water, and this repulsion causes water to bead up (e.g., rain on oil-soaked concrete or water on waxed paper).

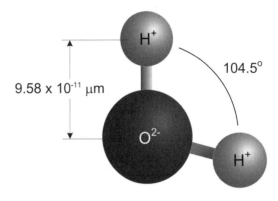

9.58×10^{-11} μm · 104.5°

5.1.3B THE WATER (H$_2$O) MOLECULE

Notice that the centroid of the two positive charges is not coincident with the centroid of the two negative charges. This spatially-unbalanced distribution of charges means that H$_2$O is a polar molecule that behaves like a tiny magnet, i.e., the hydrogen end is permanently positive and the oxygen end is permanently negative.

The manner in which water molecules interact with other water molecules is also due to their polar nature. The hydrogen of one molecule attracts the oxygen of another and causes the water molecules to group together. Hence, liquid water tends to exist in large clusters. As the temperature increases, the clusters gain more energy and break up into smaller clusters. When liquid water is evaporated, the molecules gain so much energy that they act individually as lone vapor molecules. The difference in size between the liquid water molecule clumps and the lone vapor molecule explains how materials such as Gore-Tex™ and Tyvek™ can simultaneously be watertight and highly vapor permeable.

5.1.5 Moisture Storage and Material Response

Many surfaces in contact with water vapor molecules have the tendency to capture and hold those molecules because of the molecules' polar nature; this process is called *adsorption*. These materials are called *hydrophilic*, whereas materials that repel water are called *hydrophobic*. Most building materials are hydrophilic. As water vapor molecules in the air adsorb to the internal surfaces of these materials, the materials' water content increases significantly. Such materials are described as *hygroscopic*. Materials such as glass, plastic, and steel do not have internal pores and therefore are not hygroscopic – they do not pick up moisture from water vapor in the air. (*Desiccants* are a special type of hygroscopic material. They can absorb a very large amount of moisture, typically several times their dry weight at high relative humidities).

When a material has **ad**sorbed all the moisture it can, further moisture will be stored in the pores and cracks within the material by capillary suction, or by **ab**sorption. For example, wood will adsorb vapor from the air up to approximately 25 or 30% moisture content at 98% relative humidity, but fully capillary-saturated wood wetted by liquid water may hold two to four times this amount of moisture. Once a material is *capillary-saturated* it will generally not be able to store any more moisture. When this moisture content is exceeded, a material is called *oversaturated;* no more water can be wicked into the material and drainage mechanisms, if available, will begin to remove the excess moisture.

In summary, *liquid* water is *ab*sorbed into capillary pores, where significant amounts of water *vapor* can be *ad*sorbed to the surface of pore walls.

5.1.5a Moisture Storage Regimes

Figure 5.1.5A shows the three different regimes of moisture storage: the sorption or hygroscopic regime (Regions A–C), the capillary regime (D) and the oversaturated regime (E). It is very important to recognize that the moisture content varies primarily with relative humidity (RH), not with absolute humidity.

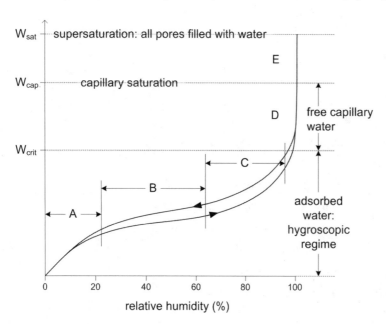

A: Single-layer of adsorbed molecules
B: Multiple layers of adsorbed molecules
C: Interconnected layers (internal capillary condensation
D: Free water in Pores, capillary suction
E: Supersaturated Regime

In the hygroscopic regime, water vapor adsorbs to the pore walls. As RH increases, more layers adhere, although the first few layers are more strongly attached (Regions A and B). In Region C, the layers grow to such a size that they begin to interact and interconnect, and the surface tension of water causes meniscuses to form within the smallest pores. At the highest relative humidities, all but the largest pores are filled with water. The capillary regime (Region D) is somewhat arbitrarily designated as that part of the moisture storage function above the critical moisture content. Physically, it is presumed that a continuous liquid phase forms. Finally, in the supersaturated state, the RH is always 100%, and no more water will wick into a material – external forces must force it in.

5.1.5b Practical Implications

Materials such as wood, mortar, gypsum, and concrete begin life with all of their pores filled with water. As the material dries, the water content in the pores drops, and adsorbed water will try to leave the surface of the pores. However, the strength of the bond between water molecules that make up the adsorbed layers results in tension forces as drying progresses. It is these internal tension forces that cause drying shrinkage stresses and the consequent cracking in wood, clay, concrete, and plaster.

Conversely, brick begins life in a high temperature oven: completely dry. When water vapor subsequently enters the pores, compressive stresses are developed as water molecules force themselves close to the brick material and other adsorbed water molecules. This internal compressive force causes the initial expansion of brick and the wetting expansion of other porous materials like clay and wood.

Hence, wetting and drying due to adsorption will cause expansion and contraction in many materials. This explains why wooden doors tend to be tight in a humid summer and loose-fitting in a dry winter, and vice versa.

5.1.5B
SORPTION ISOTHERMS FOR MANY BUILDING MATERIALS

Time, temperature, and relative humidity are the most important environmental variables affecting durability. (The moisture content can be related to the relative humidity by the sorption isotherm; see figure 5.1.5B). In the upper portion of the hygroscopic regime (typically once the relative humidity exceeds about 80%), the adsorbed water vapor is attached so loosely that it may be available for fungal growth and corrosion. However, for dangerous levels of corrosion and mold growth, much higher humidities and even liquid water may be needed. Fungal growth can begin on most surfaces when the stored moisture results in a local relative humid-

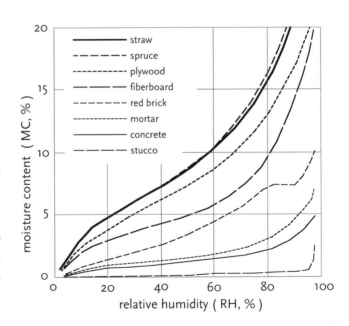

ity of over about 80% after many months. Corrosion and decay, to proceed at dangerous rates, require higher levels of humidity (well over 90%) and temperatures over 60° F (15° C) for months. It is for these reasons that the RH around a material should be controlled, *not* (necessarily) the moisture content. Freeze-thaw damage and dissolution (of, for example, gypsum) require the material to be at or near capillary saturation (100% RH).

To dry out a material previously wetted, one must reduce the relative humidity within the material as quickly as possible. Drainage is not sufficient for this purpose since it will leave a large amount of saturated (100% RH) material. Capillary and adsorbed moisture can only be dried by evaporation followed by diffusion.

5.1.6 Moisture Problems

Moisture in buildings causes a wide range of problems. The most serious tend to be structural damage due to wood decay, steel corrosion or freeze-thaw, unhealthy fungal growth on interior surfaces, and damage to moisture-sensitive interior finishes.

For a moisture-related problem to occur, at least four conditions must be satisfied:
1. a moisture source must be available,
2. there must be a route or means for this moisture to travel,
3. there must be some driving force to cause moisture movement, and
4. the materials and/or assembly must be susceptible to moisture damage.

Elimination of even one condition can prevent a moisture-related problem. This is, however, often practically or economically difficult. In practice it is impossible to remove all moisture sources, to build walls without imperfection, to remove all forces causing moisture movement, or to only use materials that are never susceptible to moisture damage. Hence, designers take the approach of reducing the probability of having a problem by addressing two or more of these prerequisites. The best way to design moisture-tolerant buildings is to control or manage moisture while reducing the risk of failure by judicious design, assembly, and material choices.

5.1.7 The Moisture Balance

If a balance between the amount of wetting and drying is maintained, moisture will not accumulate over time and moisture-related problems are unlikely. Therefore, when assessing the risk of moisture damage you should always consider rate and duration of wetting and drying together with the ability of a material or assembly to safely store moisture.

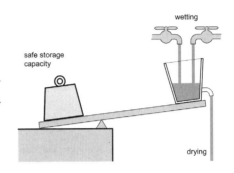

**5.1.7A
THE MOISTURE
BALANCE**

Moisture sources and wetting mechanisms, moisture sinks and drying mechanisms, and moisture storage and material response will each be considered in turn below.

Most moisture control strategies of the recent past attempted to reduce the amount of wetting, for instance by increasing an enclosure's air tightness and vapor resistance or by reducing the volume of rain water penetration. However, it has become generally accepted that most building construction will not be perfect, and thus wetting will occur – windows tend to leak into walls, cladding stops only some of the rain, some amount of air leakage is inevitable, etc. Old homes often allowed a significant amount of wetting but matched this with a large amount of drying and a significant amount of safe storage. The drawback to this historic approach was often excessive space conditioning energy consumption and material use. (For example, a drafty and uninsulated house would require far more wood for heating in the fireplace and stove than its sealed, insulated counterpart.) Therefore, modern approaches to enclosure wall and roof design emphasize balancing a reduced wetting potential with the provision of greater drying potential and safe storage. Straw bale walls perform more like historic enclosures in that they have a significant amount of storage and high drying capacity.

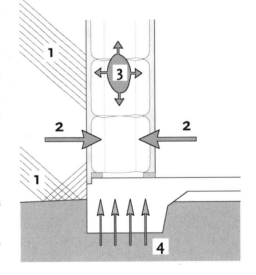

5.1.8 Moisture Sources and Wetting

The four major sources of moisture and the wetting mechanisms involved for a building's enclosure are:

1. precipitation, especially driving rain, whether wicked, leaking through the cladding, or splashed upward from grade,

2. water vapor in the air transported by diffusion and/or air movement through the wall (from either the interior or the exterior),

3. built-in and stored moisture, and

4. ground water, in liquid and/or vapor form, wicked up through the foundation or through cladding that touches the ground.

**5.1.8A
MOISTURE
SOURCES AND WETTING
MECHANISMS FOR
STRAW BALE ENCLOSURES**

Driving rain, generally the largest source of moisture entering into a building, must be controlled. Various strategies exist for managing driving rain, but accepting and managing (by storage and drying) some leakage is often the most successful and practical.

Water vapor – whether generated by occupant activities (bathing, cooking, laundry, drying out of materials) or from the outdoor air in warm, humid conditions – often causes problems in conditioned homes. Control of the interior moisture levels by ventilation in cold weather and dehumidification in warm, humid weather can be used to reduce the amount of interior moisture. *Vapor transport by air movement is by far the most powerful mechanism, and all homes with conditioned space require an air barrier system.* Vapor transport by diffusion is usually much less important, and low-permeance vapor diffusion barriers are often not necessary (but are often confused with *air* barriers, which are).

Moisture is also often built into buildings: lumber may contain well over 25% moisture by weight, straw is often installed at over 12%, and concrete contains large quantities of water (over one gallon per cubic foot is common) when poured. This source of moisture may be controlled by limiting the use of wet materials or by allowing drying before closing in the building.

Ground water is present in vapor form almost everywhere, even in deserts, whereas liquid is present only in areas with high water tables and during rainfalls and snow melts. Low vapor permeance ground covers are required between the soil and the enclosure (walls, slabs, crawlspaces) in almost all climates to prevent the diffusion of moisture into the enclosure. Similarly, a capillary break (hydrophobic or water-resistant material) prevents liquid water from wicking into the enclosure from the soil.

Another important source of moisture can be plumbing leaks and surface water floods. These can be managed by using disaster pans below appliances, locating drains to remove plumbing leaks, and siting the building above flood levels. Wetting events from these sources usually will cause damage, and must be avoided if at all possible.

5.1.9 Moisture Sinks and Drying

Moisture is usually removed from an enclosure by:

1. evaporation of water transported by capillarity to the inside or outside surfaces;

2. vapor transport by diffusion, air leakage, or both, either outward or inward;

3. drainage, driven by gravity; and

4. ventilation (ventilation drying), which is not usually effective for straw bale enclosures.

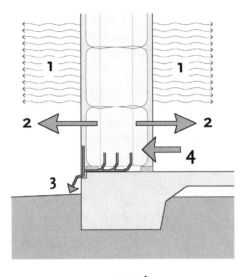

**5.1.9A
DRYING
MECHANISMS
FOR STRAW BALE
ENCLOSURES**

Wet materials such as historic solid masonry or thatch will dry directly to their environment, but this mechanism is less important for modern multi-layer enclosure assemblies. Straw bale walls are similar to solid masonry buildings – they must be allowed to wick and dry by diffusion to the interior and the exterior.

Water vapor, whether generated internally or resulting from evaporation from wet materials, can be removed by diffusion and air movement. Some materials (low vapor permeance materials like steel and plastic) resist diffusion drying. In hot weather, drying can occur to the interior and the exterior, and in cold weather it tends to occur toward the outside. In most climates, buildings should be designed to allow drying in both directions; the actual direction will vary with weather conditions.

Drainage is the fastest and most powerful means of removing water that may penetrate cladding or leak into a basement. Drainage layers outside of basements and drainage gaps behind cladding and below windows have all been shown to be very effective. When drainage stops, materials are still saturated and surfaces wet, so other drying mechanisms must be employed. Drainage, however, is not useful as a general means of moisture control in a straw bale building as the amount of water needed to initiate drainage is so high, it will likely not dry fast enough to avoid damage to the bales. Experience has shown that a bale or bale wall can hold a lot of moisture – more than enough to cause decay – without releasing it by drainage. However, drainage is nevertheless essential to provide in bale walls in the event of an unforeseen accident, such as a plumbing or other major leak.

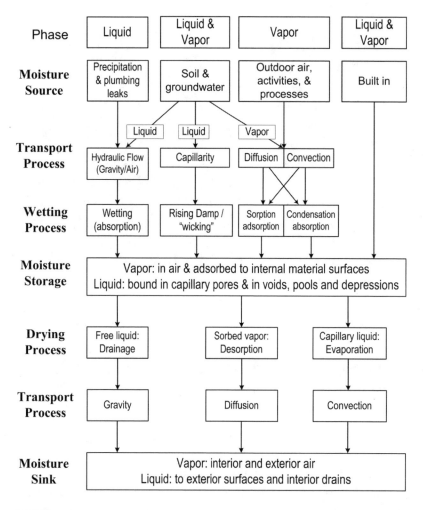

5.1.10A
SUMMARY
OF MOISTURE
SOURCES, SINKS,
AND TRANSPORT
MECHANISMS

Ventilation behind cladding and roofing can be an effective mechanism of drying in many climates and situations. On the other hand, if dry, cool spaces such as crawlspaces are ventilated during warm, humid weather, wetting will occur via condensation on cold surfaces, so ventilation is not recommended for crawlspaces. Moreover, ventilation of the straw bales themselves behind plaster skins is not useful because the resistance of compressed straw to airflow is quite high (and because for many other reasons the plaster should be applied directly to the straw). Ventilation could, however, be used to aid the drying behind a rainscreen overcladding mounted over the outer plaster skin of a bale wall (see chapter 10, *Details and Design*).

5.1.10 Moisture Storage

A building material's or assembly's ability to store moisture is important as it represents the amount of time that can separate wetting and drying events before problems begin.

Moisture can be stored in a variety of ways in enclosure assemblies — as vapor, water, or solid (frost, ice). The volume of water that is stored in an enclosure can be large, on the order of a few to tens of kilograms per square meter. This moisture can be stored as vapor, liquid, or solid in a variety of ways:

1. trapped in small depressions or in poorly drained portions of assemblies,

2. adhered by surface tension as droplets (or frost, or even ice) to materials and surfaces,

3. adsorbed within hygroscopic building materials (especially brick, wood, fibrous insulation, and paper),

4. retained by capillarity (absorbed) in porous materials, and

5. stored in the air as vapor.

The sources, transport mechanisms, and sinks of moisture are shown generically in Figure 5.1.10A. This is a general diagram which applies to all buildings, straw bale or not.

5.2 Moisture Control Practices

by John Straube

As presented in section 5.1, managing moisture requires a balance of wetting, drying, and safe storage. The primary durability concern for straw bale buildings is wetting by rain, particularly driving rain. However, plumbing leaks, air leakage, ground water, and roof leaks can be problems as well, and must be addressed.

What we said before bears repeating: The moisture tolerance of houses can be dramatically improved through intelligent design of building location, orientation, geometry, HVAC systems, and materials. The most effective approaches — rarely used because they must be considered very early in the design stage — are the least expensive because they anticipate and avoid problems rather than inadvertently creating them. **The best moisture control strategies always involve designing problems OUT — not solving them after they have been needlessly designed into the enclosure.**

5.2.1 Rain Control

Keeping out the rain is one of the oldest and most important functions of building enclosures. In part this is because the amount of water deposited by rain on the above-grade building enclosure, especially wind-driven rain on walls, is generally larger than that from any other moisture source. Despite thousands of years of experience, avoiding rain-related building damage is still one of the most difficult tasks that designers and builders face. Hence, the choice of rainwater control strategy and the design and quality of construction details are critical.

Traditionally, rainwater control meant preventing rain from reaching the interior of the building and wetting interior finishes and furnishings. Avoiding rainwater penetration through the enclosure, therefore, was critical. It is still a critical criterion, but contemporary and straw bale enclosures typically must perform at a higher level and control damage within the enclosure. Rain-related problems can affect appearance through discoloration, staining, and efflorescence; can induce damage (freeze-thaw damage, corrosion, and decay), and can cause human health problems related to mold growth.

Regardless of the approach taken to wall design, building shape and site design choices can reduce the amount of rain deposited on walls. Depending on materials, details, workmanship, and exposure, a wall can be designed to drain any water that penetrates, store and subsequently dry it, or exclude all rain perfectly. Straw bale walls tend to use the storage approach, although rainscreen designs are possible and desirable in high exposure applications. Finally, despite our best efforts, some rain is often absorbed into materials or penetrates through imperfections, so drying must be provided to remove this incidental moisture.

The Canadian holistic approach to rain control can be described by the three D's[1]:

1. **D**eflection,
2. **D**rainage/Storage/Exclusion, and
3. **D**rying.

The next three sections will investigate each component of this strategy in turn.

5.2.1a Deflection
Climate
Both climate and site (i.e., microclimate) play a large role in determining a building's rain exposure. The climate zone is important for assessing the wetting potential (driving rain potential) and drying potential, since hot and dry or cold weather accelerates drying. Many parts of the world experience a significant amount of wind-driven rain, and high-rise buildings in suburban settings are usually seriously exposed. Choosing appropriate siting and massing can significantly reduce the amount of rain deposited on walls.

Site
The role of siting is critical to rain control, and any type of protection, such as berms, plantings, and other buildings, will reduce the driving rain load. Exposure to the prevailing driving rains can be reduced in low-rise buildings (one to two stories) by planting, landscaping, and placement near other buildings. Buildings or topography of equal height located within two building heights will provide a significant amount of protection. (This is more than just a moisture consideration; building codes have for many years allowed an appreciable reduction in structural wind design loads in sites surrounded by a lot of trees, irregular topography, and/or buildings.)

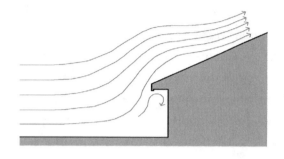

5.2.1A
INFLUENCE OF
OVERHANGS AND
PITCHED ROOFS ON
WIND AND RAIN FLOW

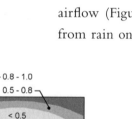

0.8 - 1.0
0.5 - 0.8
< 0.5
RDF

Low-rise Building H/W << 1

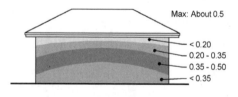

Max: About 0.5

< 0.20
0.20 - 0.35
0.35 - 0.50
< 0.35

5.2.1B
RAIN DEPOSITION
FACTOR DISTRIBUTION
ON RECTANGULAR
BUILDINGS

*Note: an RDF of 1 is
the amount of driving
rain deposited on the
upper corner of a
cuboidal building
on an unprotected
site; "H/W" is the
height-to-width ratio.*

Building Shape and Mass

The shape and massing of a building influences the amount of wind-driven rain that can strike a wall.

The shapes of the roof and overhang also have an important impact, especially for low-rise buildings. Field measurements[2] and computer modelling[3] have shown that overhangs and peaked roofs reduce rain deposition by approximately 50%. A damage survey of wood frame buildings in British Columbia[4] found that the size of a building's roof overhang correlated directly (that is, inversely) with the probability of rain-related damage. Peaked roofs and overhangs protect a wall from rain by both shadowing and redirecting airflow (Figure 5.2.1A). Hipped roofs provide an opportunity to shelter walls from rain on all four sides of the building. Laboratory studies[5] suggest that the same strategies can also be used on high-rise buildings by reducing both peak deposition rates and the area over which these peaks occur.

Field measurements,[6,7,8,9] computer modelling,[10,11] and wind tunnel testing[12] have provided an indication of the quantity of driving rain deposition that can be expected on vertical walls. For low-rise situations, the amount of rain deposited is on the order of 10 to 20% of the product of wind speed and rainfall intensity. The amount of rain deposited on the walls of low-rise buildings erected on exposed sites could be in the order of gallons per square foot (hundreds of litres per square meter) per year. Sheltered locations and single-story houses with wide overhangs will be exposed to much less rain deposition (e.g., less than a tenth as much).

Exposed cubical buildings tend to have very high rain deposition in the upper corners, top, and side edges (Figure 5.2.1B). The higher deposition is due to the higher wind speeds and unrestricted flow patterns around such buildings. The amount of rain deposition on the upper corners of a tall building will often be two to four times that on a similarly shaped low-rise building.

Rainwater on Walls

The rainfall intensity and duration, the absorbency and storage capacity of the wall material, the smoothness and wettability of the wall surface, the wall's shape, the effect of the wind and gravity, and the previous wetting and drying history of the cladding all affect the migration of rainwater once it has been deposited on the wall's surface.

Any surfaces above and/or beside the wall of interest also play a role, since water draining or blown from these surfaces will add to the water on the wall. If water is deposited on a wall at a high rate, a surface film will form, ensuring that any extra water will be drained away on the surface. If a porous building material like brick or plaster becomes saturated, it will begin to behave like an impervious material; that is, any deposited moisture will simply be drained away. For example, most rainwater driven onto a dry earth plaster will be absorbed. If, however, the plaster's surface becomes saturated, or if the intensity of rainfall is higher than the plaster's ability to absorb the rainwater, the water will begin to be both shed and transmitted through the plaster (and into the straw bale wall core). A sheet of metal or glass will respond quite differently. Shedding will begin very shortly after rain is deposited on the wall, and large surface flows of water can be expected during most rainfalls.

Surface drainage must be considered and controlled as much as is practical. Water spilling over roof drainage systems or collected by glazing and other impervious cladding materials can increase the amount of water on a wall below by an order of magnitude. For example, a band of windows or a metal-topped parapet above a plastered straw bale wall will dramatically increase the wall's "exposure" unless the driving rain collected is distributed and removed from the wall surface by projecting sills with a drip (Figure 5.2.1C).

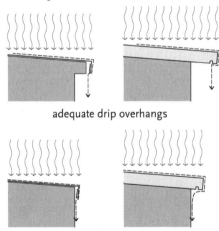

adequate drip overhangs

inadequate drip overhangs

5.2.1C
THE ROLE OF DRIPS AND PROJECTIONS IN SHEDDING RAIN DEPOSITION

Water flowing on a wall surface will tend to concentrate in streams where it encounters projections from the flat wall surface. Surface tension will act to adhere smaller water streams to the leeward side of corners and projections such as flutes and window mullions. The concentration of flow can increase the volume of water on small areas of a wall to levels many times that predicted by the rain deposition equation. Highly-varied concentrations of surface flow can cause unsightly staining, streaking, and dirt washing, (such as, typically, under the ends of windowsills), and the possibility of potentially damaging differential moisture expansion.

5.2.2 Drainage/Storage/Exclusion

Siting, building shape, and surface rainwater control rarely provide complete rain control (although deep wraparound porches may eliminate the need for rain control under them). Hence, some strategy to deal with the rainwater that strikes the surface of the wall must be employed.

Rainwater

There are three fundamental rain control strategies available to the designer[12]. In order of historical priority, they are:

1. Storage (storage or mass walls),
2. Exclusion (perfect barrier walls), and
3. Drainage (drained and screened walls).

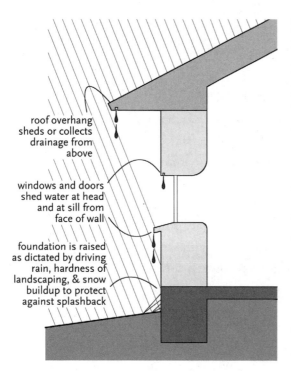

roof overhang sheds or collects drainage from above

windows and doors shed water at head and at sill from face of wall

foundation is raised as dictated by driving rain, hardness of landscaping, & snow buildup to protect against splashback

5.2.1D
SUMMARY OF
PRINCIPLES OF RAIN
DEFLECTION

These categories have been developed from basic observations and physical facts. Rain deposited on a wall can either be face-drained (shed), absorbed (by capillarity), or transmitted (penetrating further into the wall). Each layer of a multi-layer wall responds to rain in these ways. If water penetrates through the entire wall assembly, the wall is generally considered to have failed. However, transmission of rain water into any sensitive layer of a wall assembly may also cause damage, degrade performance, and affect durability. In fact, hidden water penetration into moisture-sensitive materials within walls causes the most problems for modern wall systems just as it does for straw bale walls.

The primary classification in this context is whether a wall is a *perfect barrier* or an *imperfect barrier,* and there are two classes of imperfect barriers: *storage* and *drained.*

Storage or mass walls are the oldest strategy. This approach requires an assembly with enough safe storage mass to absorb all rainwater that is not drained or otherwise removed from the outer surface. In a functional massive storage wall this moisture is eventually removed by evaporative drying before it reaches the wall's inner surface. Although enclosures employing this strategy might be best termed "moisture storage" systems, the term "mass" is often used because a large quantity of material is required to provide sufficient storage. The maximum quantity of rain that can be controlled is limited by the storage capacity available relative to drying conditions. Some examples of mass walls include adobe, solid

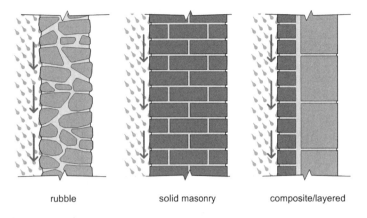

rubble   solid masonry   composite/layered

5.2.2A
EXAMPLES OF
MASS OR STORAGE
WALL SYSTEMS

multi-wythe brick masonry, and single-wythe block masonry (Figure 5.2.2A). *Perfect barrier systems* stop all water penetration at a single plane. Such perfect control requires modern materials. Perfect barrier systems that use the outermost layer as the rain control plane are termed *face-sealed*. Because it is very difficult (if not impossible) to build and maintain a perfect barrier wall, most walls are designed as, or perform as, imperfect barrier wall systems of either the mass type or the screened type. The rain control plane in face-sealed walls is exposed to the full range of environmental conditions and also has strong aesthetic requirements. These demands often result in compromises in the choice of materials, and the result is, all too often, premature deterioration.

The joints between perfect barrier elements may also be designed as – or rather hoped to be – perfect barriers as well (e.g., a single line of caulking). Such joints, however, have a poor record of performance and should not be relied upon to control rain entry. Some representative systems that are designed as perfect barrier wall elements are metal panels, some window frames, and face-sealed Exterior Insulated Finish Systems (EIFS) (Figure 5.2.2B). In practice, each of these systems exhibits failures not in the field of the wall, but at the face-sealed joints.

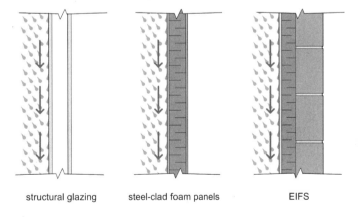

structural glazing   steel-clad foam panels   EIFS

5.2.2B
EXAMPLES OF
PERFECT BARRIER
WALL SYSTEMS

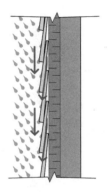

lap siding

panel cladding system

masonry veneer

5.2.2C
EXAMPLES OF
SCREENED-DRAINED
WALL SYSTEMS

Screened-drained walls assume some rain water will penetrate the outer surface (hence the cladding "screens" rain) *and* remove this water by designing an assembly that provides drainage within the wall. Since it has often been shown that lap siding (vinyl, fiber cement, or wood) and masonry veneers leak significant amounts of water, this design approach is the most realistic and practical for walls with such cladding.

Supplementary mechanisms, such as a capillary break and a water barrier (collectively termed a *drainage plane*), are usually employed to resist further inward movement of water that penetrates the inevitably imperfect cladding. Some examples of drained wall systems include cavity walls, masonry and natural stone veneers, vinyl siding, two-stage joints, and drained EIFS (Figure 5.2.2C). It should be noted that the screen is much more than a rainscreen; it must also resist wind, snow, solar radiation, impact, flame spread, etc.

Field testing and some field experience has shown that small gaps may be sufficient to provide drainage. For example, the space formed between two sheets of building paper (especially if those sheets have a texture or are wrinkled) can allow sufficient drainage. The small space behind lap siding also often allows drainage.

An air space can be provided to improve the drainage capacity and to act as a very effective capillary break between the cladding and the remainder of the wall. An effective drainage cavity space becomes more important as the rain loading and the screen water permeance increases, since it is expected that more water will drain within this space more often. A true drainage cavity should be at least 3 to 6 mm wide, since this is approximately the gap size that can be spanned by water. Since dimensional tolerances must be accounted for, a dimension of 10 mm (about 1/3 inch) is usually quoted. If ventilation drying is desired, a larger airspace must be provided.

Experience from coast to coast in Canada[13] and in the rainy regions of the United States[14] has shown that drained and screened cladding systems are the most reliable for providing rain control. Drainage within the wall complements the drainage on the exterior surface (Figure 5.2.2C). Pressure moderation can help reduce the amount of rain that penetrates systems that are prone to air-pressure-driven rain penetration (primarily joints in non-absorbent materials and metal joints).

Rainscreen approaches are ideal for straw bale walls with high exposure to driving rain, keeping in mind that plaster must still be applied to the straw because it provides fire resistance, airflow resistance, rodent and insect resistance, and structural functions. Cladding is then applied over a drainage gap, and the exterior plaster becomes the secondary drainage plane. Flashing, weep holes, and vent holes are also needed to complete the system. Wood, fiber-cement siding, and even stucco can all be used over the drainage and ventilation gap as the primary drainage plane. (See also chapter 10, *Details and Design*.)

5.2.2D
ROOF, SITE, WINDOW, AND WALL DRAINAGE AND FLASHING CONCEPTS

Ground and Surface Water

Every building should be protected from flowing surface water. This requires that the building be raised above the grade and the site be graded to direct surface drainage. This may require swales and berms to direct both surface and ground water around the home (Figure 5.2.2E).

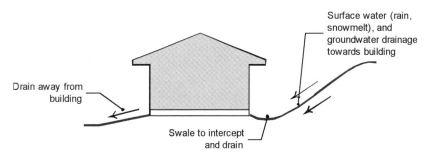

Splashback – the phenomenon of water dripping off a roof or ledge or splashing off of grade back onto the wall – can be controlled by a combination of grade separation and covering of the grade with porous surfaces. It is generally recommended that the grade separation be a minimum of 6" (150 mm), although 8" (200 mm) is recommended for straw bale walls. Smooth, hard grade surfaces such as concrete and asphalt encourage splashing, whereas one inch or more of stone, grass, or mulch tend to reduce it.

5.2.2E
SITE GRADING TO DIRECT SURFACE AND GROUNDWATER AROUND A BUILDING

In climates with significant snowfall, accumulated snow around walls can often be unavoidable. When sun heats the wall, melting can occur at the wall-to-grade interface. Experience with straw bale buildings has shown that the resulting wetting can be a problem. Other than avoiding snow accumulation, the best means of controlling wetting due to melting snow is grade separation or cladding over the drainage space.

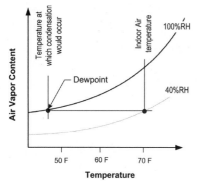

5.2.3 Water Vapor Control

Controlling water vapor, whether to avoid condensation wetting or to encourage drying, is a major part of managing the moisture balance. If you don't quite understand that, conduct a simple experiment that thousands of backpackers have inadvertently tried. Camp outside anywhere — even on a warm, dry evening — with your sleeping bag wrapped in plastic, and you'll wake up in the morning soaking wet. Why? Because the water vapor trying to leave your body got caught against the impermeable plastic and condensed, i.e., became water. This happens to buildings all the time because the builder didn't understand and control water vapor.

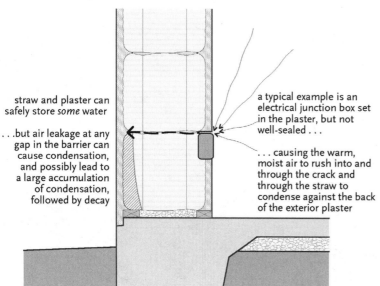

straw and plaster can safely store *some* water

...but air leakage at any gap in the barrier can cause condensation, and possibly lead to a large accumulation of condensation, followed by decay

a typical example is an electrical junction box set in the plaster, but not well-sealed . . .

. . . causing the warm, moist air to rush into and through the crack and through the straw to condense against the back of the exterior plaster

5.2.3A
AIR LEAKAGE
CONDENSATION
IN COLD WEATHER

Air Barriers

An air barrier system is required in all building components that separate two different environments. An air barrier system is an assembly of components that resists airflow. In a straw bale wall, an air barrier system can be made from the plaster skins and the sealed joints between the floor slab, the window frames, and especially the top of the wall-to-ceiling joint.

Airflow control is needed to reduce energy loss, control condensation within the wall, isolate the air in the straw bale from the air in the building interior, reduce fire and smoke spread, and reduce sound and odor transmission.

Condensation occurs because the capacity of air to store water vapor drops dramatically as the temperature drops. If the water vapor content in a volume of air remains the same (none is added or removed) but the volume is cooled, the relative humidity (RH) will rise. If the volume is cooled enough, the RH will climb to 100%, and the *dewpoint,* or point at which condensation can occur, is reached. If air is heated the relative humidity will drop and condensation cannot occur.

Condensation within walls (termed *interstitial condensation*) can occur if warm, humid air leaks out during cold weather (Figure 5.2.3A) or, more rarely, if hot, humid outdoor air leaks inward while the interior is kept cool. Condensation will preferentially occur on solid surfaces, and so, in straw bale walls, condensation will usually occur on the inside of the plaster rather than in the straw itself. To control this condensation an air barrier system should be installed that is strong, durable, air-impermeable, stiff enough not to deform and damage itself, and most importantly, continuous. Even a small hole or a long thin crack can allow too much air to leak through. The plaster skins on a straw bale wall provide an excellent part of the air barrier system, but the joints, especially at the base (behind the baseboard) and the top (at the intersection with the ceiling finish) need to be sealed to provide continuity. Air barrier systems can also be made from sealed assemblies of drywall, wood paneling, concrete, plaster, caulking, plastic, or other materials. Straw, even densely-packed straw, will not be sufficiently air-impermeable to stop air flow. Dense straw-reinforced earth (i.e., a good earth plaster) is, however, air-impermeable.

Despite a builder's best attempts, some leakage of air will still occur. The amount of this leakage can be measured using a blower door apparatus. To avoid problems due to small amounts of leakage, the interior relative humidity should be controlled. This is accomplished by ensuring ventilation (using exhaust fans or passive vents). The direction and quantity of airflow can also be controlled by managing the pressure difference that drives airflow.

Since straw and plaster are hygroscopic, their RH depends on their moisture content (see section 5.1.5). If the exterior of the straw bale cools (at night or during cold weather), the RH of the air around the straw will rise, possibly enough to allow condensation. However, the storage capacity and vapor permeability of both the straw and most plaster skins are quite high. Hence, as the RH of the air in the

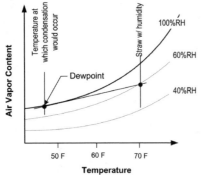

Air Vapor Content

Temperature at which condensation would occur

Straw w/ humidity

100%RH

60%RH

40%RH

Dewpoint

50 F   60 F   70 F

Temperature

5.2.3B
**CONDENSATION ON
COLD SURFACE DUE TO
REDISTRIBUTION**

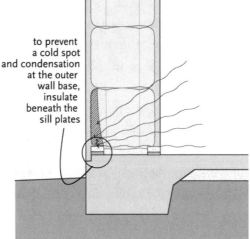

to prevent
a cold spot
and condensation
at the outer
wall base,
insulate
beneath the
sill plates

straw rises during cooling, the hygroscopic materials adsorb the vapor and store it safely. This is a form of redistribution of vapor from the warm side of the wall to the cold side. If non-hygroscopic or vapor-impermeable materials are inserted into or onto the straw in this scenario, condensation could occur on their non-absorbent surface (Figure 5.2.3B). Once liquid water forms, the adjoining straw will wick up the water, and its moisture content may quickly rise to dangerous levels. This scenario can and does occur, and can cause damage, at all non-absorbent *thermal bridges* (locations with low thermal resistance and hence cold temperatures). The most common situation in practice occurs at the base-of-wall-to-foundation detail. Because the top of the concrete is cold (uninsulated) and not very absorbent or hygroscopic, it should be treated with a vapor barrier and capillary break to prevent wicking from the wet soil.

There are several solutions to this problem. The first is to insulate the concrete slab vertically on the exterior. This will solve the problem in cold weather by keeping the concrete slab temperature higher than the adjoining straw bale temperatures. In hot weather, however, the slab may remain quite cool, creating the possibility of condensation, the frequency and severity of which will depend on the climate, the solar exposure, and the interior temperatures. Exterior slab insulation is hard to execute both functionally and aesthetically, but does provide significant benefits. A second solution is to separate the bales from the slab by a vapor-permeable insulating layer. This is usually done with crushed stone and wood plates. The stone resists wicking but provides no insulation. A layer of semi-rigid fibrous insulation would be more effective, as would a layer of stone with a band of insulation along the inside of the outside sill plate.

Drying of wetted bales is driven almost exclusively by vapor diffusion. Air moves slowly through straw bales, but does not move easily enough to allow useful drying. Drainage stops while the straw is still very wet, and straw does not exhibit strong capillary wicking. Hence, only diffusion is available. Wet materials have an RH of 100% or slightly less. As shown in Figure 5.2.3C, a wetted layer of straw on a cool night will dry by vapor diffusion (which always moves from more vapor content to less) to the interior and the exterior at the same time. If the weather is often cold, most drying will occur to the exterior. If the weather is often warm and/or the wall is often heated by solar exposure, then drying will occur mostly to the interior. Therefore, to encourage fast drying, use plaster skins with high vapor permeance.

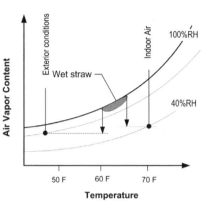

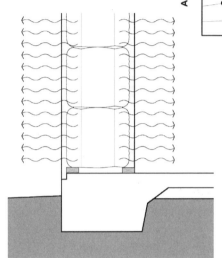

5.2.3C
DRYING TO THE INSIDE AND OUTSIDE OF A WET STRAW BALE WALL

Diffusion Control and Vapor Barriers

Although most condensation problems occur because of air leakage (convection), vapor diffusion can occasionally cause a small amount of wetting. Assemblies should be designed to ensure minimal diffusion wetting, while at the same time allowing as much drying of incidental moisture as possible. In most cases a highly vapor-permeable system is desirable to ensure fast diffusion drying of any accidental wetting that might occur.

Straw does not provide much resistance to vapor diffusion flow, but a thick layer, such as a 24 inch [600 mm] thick straw bale, will have a moderate level of permeance of 2 to 4 US perms. The plaster skins may have a much wider range of vapor permeance. For example, a typical 1.5 inch thick pure cement-sand stucco mix might have a permeance of only 1 US perm (60 metric perms) whereas a 2 inch thick earth plaster could have ten times this permeance. This range of variability has significant implications for the ability of plastered straw bale walls to dry quickly. Table 5.2.3(1) provides some average values, although variations of +/- 50% may occur, depending on the exact mix and application.

Some building codes have required vapor barriers for framed walls. These requirements, based on a limited amount of research conducted over 50 years ago, have recently come under question. The International Residential Code is being changed to remove this requirement for all but the coldest climate zones of North America. Straw bale walls are quite different than framed walls, as the skins and the bales both have significant amounts of vapor diffusion resistance and massive moisture storage capacities. Vapor can only diffuse into the wall at a reasonably slow and measured rate, and the quantities are low enough that the wall can absorb and subsequently release the moisture. This behavior is similar to that of traditional solid masonry or adobe walls, which never required a separate low permeance plastic vapor barrier.

TABLE 5.2.3(1) TYPICAL AVERAGE VAPOR PERMEANCE VALUES FOR PLASTER SKINS

	US PERMS	METRIC PERMS
TYPICAL VAPOR BARRIER (BY DEFINITION)	< 1	< 60
1:3 cement stucco (1.5")	1	50
5:1:15 cement:lime:sand (1.5")	4	200
1:1:6 cement:lime:sand (1.5")	7	400
1:2:9 cement:lime:sand (1.5")	9	500
1:3 lime:sand plaster (2")	9	500
earth plaster (2")	11	600

Based on experience and calculations, a low perm vapor barrier (defined as a layer with a permeance of less than 1 US perm) is neither required or in fact desirable for almost any plastered straw bale wall. **The permeance of the exterior skin should be kept as high as practical without sacrificing structural or other performance requirements.** For a typical residence the vapor permeance of the interior plaster skin should be kept as high as possible to encourage inward drying, but low enough to avoid a significant amount of cold weather diffusion wetting. Striking the correct balance is not always easy. However, for climates with at least one month of cold weather (an average daily temperature of less than 5°C / 40°F), the inner skin should not be less permeable than the outer skin. In climates with significant amounts of cold weather (four months or more), the interior skin permeance (including paint layers) should have a permeance of less than 5 or 6 perms (300 - 350 ng/Pa s m^2). Controlling the interior humidity during cold weather by good ventilation can allow the interior skin permeance to climb to ten perms in this type of climate. If the climate has no cold months, the interior skin permeance can be as high as desired.

5.2.4 Moisture-control layers

Numerous sheet goods or trowel-applied coatings are used as moisture control membranes in building assemblies. The most common type of membranes, so-called "breather membranes," are used to provide a vapor-permeable but water-repellent (capillary-breaking) layer in an assembly. Waterproof and vapor-**im**permeable membranes are used to provide a vapor barrier, capillary break, and long-term water resistance. Each class will be discussed below.

Building Papers and Housewraps

Building papers (Grade D papers and #15 or #30 felt are the most common) and polymeric housewraps (such as Tyvek™) are both widely used to act as vapor-permeable and water-repellent layers. These membranes are not waterproof but will resist water wicking. Cellulosic materials may fail if kept wet for too long, and they may rot. The performance of polymeric wraps is more long-lasting, and rot will not occur, but many of the commonly-available products have, after installation, macroperforations (in the order of 0.01 inch or larger in diameter, most commonly from the staples by which they are attached) that can cause leakage under sustained wetting behind cladding.

Stucco has long been applied over building papers. As the stucco is applied, moisture is absorbed and the paper expands. When the stucco hardens and dries, the paper relaxes but the stucco does not. The result is a small gap that debonds the paper from the stucco and helps to provide a small amount of drainage. Stucco tends to stick to polymeric wraps, even wrinkled ones, and does not exhibit this drainage, or worse, allows water to penetrate at locations of bonding. Testing has shown that two layers of light paper or a layer of paper over a polymeric housewrap will provide good drainage and prevent stucco from bonding to the inner layer.

Breather-type sheathing membranes are all vapor-permeable to allow for outward drying. Although this type of product should have a wet cup vapor permeance of more than about 10 US perms [500 ng/Pa/s/m^2], the resistance to liquid water should often be a higher priority than vapor permeance. Note that almost all building papers and felts exhibit variable vapor permeance properties; when they are wet or exposed to high humidity (i.e., when they need to allow drying), their permeance is well over 1000 metric perms and may be several times higher. All plastic housewraps have an almost constant vapor permeance.

Building papers and wraps can also be used to break the bond between materials. For example, sheets of material have long been used behind stucco over wood to prevent cracks from forming when wood expands and contracts. In straw bale construction, building paper or wrap between the plaster and the straw would assist with moisture control but would result in total debonding and hence would completely compromise the structural performance. Hence, **building papers should never be used over large areas of any straw bale walls, even non-load-bearing ones.**

Papers or wraps *should* be used over wood posts, embedded window frames, and similar components to both debond the stucco locally (to reduce cracking) and to reduce wicking inward. Where mesh is used in the plaster, it should always continue over such debonded areas to provide structural continuity and control cracking.

Waterproof and Vapor Barrier Membranes

Waterproof membranes are sometimes used in areas of high exposure to water such as windows, roofs, and near grade. Typical products include peel-and-stick membranes, trowel- and spray-applied compounds (many asphalt-based, although epoxy and polyurethane membranes exist). Almost all waterproof membranes are very vapor impermeable. A typical self-adhering membrane or flashing has a vapor permeance of less than 0.1 US perms [5 ng/Pa/s/m^2], one hundred times less than most housewraps.

These membranes should be used sparingly in straw bale walls, and only where high concentrations of water are likely such as under windowsills. By using small areas of these materials, water vapor can diffuse around them and thereby allow drying.

5.2.5 Plumbing

Plumbing problems and failures cause a remarkable number of serious wetting events. Plumbing should never be run in straw bale walls, as leaks will be impossible to detect and condensation on cold water piping is almost certain to cause local decay of the straw. Plumbing that must penetrate walls should be placed inside oversized watertight (or jointless) plastic pipe sleeves that are sloped to the exterior to capture and control leaks or condensation.

5.2.6 Wetting During Construction

Because serious wetting is most likely to occur during construction and bale storage, bales should be installed, whenever possible, only after the roof has been installed. This is the main reason why post-and-beam bale structures are far more common than load-bearing structures; it's so much easier to keep the bales protected at all times. In very dry climates it may be possible to build the walls with sufficient speed to avoid wetting, but even in the desert one afternoon thundershower at the wrong time can make for a world of problems. In any case, the bottom of the bales should be installed raised above the slab or floor to avoid wetting from any water that pools on that surface. This is normally accomplished by using slab "toe-ups" or pressure-treated sill plates.

If bales might be exposed to the weather during storage, they should be covered carefully with tarps spaced away from them at least 2 inches [50 mm] to allow air to circulate. Take care to avoid collecting and draining water into a straw bale wall or storage pile in the folds and seams of tarps. **Bales must be protected from water from the day they are harvested until the day they are safely under a roof.**

Glossary

• **Air Leakage or Convection** is the movement of air through the enclosure driven by an air pressure difference. Air can flow easily through small cracks and openings and more slowly but easily through highly porous materials like batt insulation and loose straw. Significant quantities of air cannot flow through typical cement, lime, or thick earth plasters.

• **Air Barrier Systems** are assemblies of materials intended to provide the primary resistance to airflow across enclosures. An air barrier must be strong, durable, continuous, air-impermeable, and stiff enough not to deform and damage itself. Air barriers can be made from sealed assemblies of drywall, wood sheathing, concrete, plaster, caulking, and other materials. Straw bale walls use plastered skins and sealant (at joints) to provide an air barrier.

• **Hygroscopic Materials** are those that change their moisture content in response to the RH surrounding them. Straw, wood, lime, earth, and many natural materials are hygroscopic. A wet material will always have an RH of 100% regardless of its temperature. If a hygroscopic material is placed in air at a given RH it will eventually (from many hours to many days) reach a moisture content in equilibrium with this RH. A plot of RH versus MC is called the sorption isotherm.

- **Moisture Content (MC)** is a measure of the amount of water in a material. It is usually measured as the weight of water relative to the weight of *dry* material, i.e., the dry moisture content (the wet moisture content is the weight of the water relative to the wet material). Hence, 20% (dry) MC in a material with the density of straw (say 10 pounds per cubic foot dry) is equal to 2 pounds of water per cubic foot of straw. Since wood weighs much more, about 45 pcf, 20% MC in wood means 9 pounds of water per cubic foot of wood, and 5% MC in concrete, which weighs about 150 pcf dry, means 7.5 pounds per cubic foot of concrete. Occasionally, especially in Europe, moisture content is measured as the *volume* of water divided by the *volume* of dry material. Moisture content can be related to the equilibrium relative humidity via the sorption isotherm. Hence, 15% MC in straw is **not** equal to 15% RH but closer to 80% RH. A MC of about 16% or lower is usually safe for straw, but if the moisture content exceeds 20-25% for extended periods of time during warm conditions, fungal growth can begin. Serious decay tends to set in at MC of over 25 to 30%.

- **Relative Humidity (RH)** is the amount of moisture or water vapor that air contains compared to the maximum amount it can hold at that temperature.

- **Water Vapor Diffusion** is the process by which water vapor moves through a material as water vapor molecules. The rate at which it migrates or diffuses depends on two factors: the difference between the water vapor pressure in the air inside the building and that in the outside air, and the resistance that the material assembly of the wall (or roof or floor) presents to the migration of water vapor.

- **Vapor Diffusion Barriers or Retarders** are materials that offer a higher resistance to vapor diffusion.

- **Vapor Permeability** is a measure of a material's ability to allow vapor diffusion. Materials with a large proportion of interconnected pores will allow vapor to diffuse through them. For example, straw and batt insulation are quite porous and hence vapor can diffuse easily. Steel, many plastics, and glass are very dense and crystalline, and hence practically stop diffusion. Materials such as rigid foam plastic, earth, and lime slow but do not stop diffusion.

- **Vapor Permeance** is a measure of a material layer or assembly's ability to allow vapor diffusion. The permeance of a homogenous material is the permeability divided by thickness. Hence, thin layers of high-permeability materials allow diffusion almost unhindered. Thick layers of low-permeability materials (e.g., concrete, solid timber, cement stucco) create layers of low permeance. By arbitrary and scientifically questionable convention, a layer with a permeance of less than 1 US perm is defined as a **vapor barrier.** Layers with 5 or even 10 US perms are often called vapor retarders. Normal latex paints on plaster are vapor retarders, whereas vapor barrier paints are vapor barriers. Thin layers of PVC, polyethylene, metal, and aluminum foil are all vapor barriers with a permeance much less than 1 US perm. Thick (1.5 inch or more) cement plaster with latex paint can be a vapor barrier and even 2 inches of lime–cement plaster can be rendered a vapor barrier by the addition of a coat of oil paint.

ENDNOTES

1   *Wood-frame envelopes in the coastal climate of British Columbia: Best Practice Guide,* Canada Mortgage and Housing Corporation, Ottawa

2   Straube, J.F., (1998) *Moisture Control and Enclosure Wall Systems.* Ph.D. Thesis, Civil Engineering Department, University of Waterloo

3   Blocken, B., Carmeliet, J., *Driving Rain on Building Envelopes – I. Numerical Estimation and Full-Scale Experimental Verification,* Journal of Thermal Insulation and Building Envelopes, Vol 24, No 4, 2000, pp. 61-110.

4   *Survey of Building Envelope Failures in the Coastal Climate of BC.* Report by Morrison-Hershfield for CMHC, Ottawa, 1996.

5   Inculet, D.R., Surry, D., (1994) *Simulation of Wind-Driven Rain and Wetting Patterns on Buildings Report* BLWT-SS30-1994, U. of West. Ontario

6   Lacy, R.E., (1965) *Driving-Rain Maps and the Onslaught of Rain on Buildings.* Building Research Station Current Paper 54, HMSO Garston, U.K.

7   Straube, J.F., and Burnett, E.F.P.,"Driving Rain and Masonry Veneer", *Water Leakage Through Building Facades, ASTM STP 1314,* R. Kudder and J.L. Erdly, Eds., American Society for Testing and Materials, Philadelphia, 1997, pp. 73-87.

8   Künzel, H.M., (1994) *Regendaten für Berechnung des Feuchtetransports,* Fraunhofer Institut für Bauphysik, Mitteilung 265

9   Frank, W. *Entwicklung von Regen und Wind auf Gebaeudefassaden,* Verlag Ernst & Sohn, Bertichte aus der Bauforschung, 1973, Vol 86, pp. 17-40.

10   Choi, E.C.C., "Determination of the wind-driven-rain intensity on building faces", *Journal of Wind Engineering and Aerodynamics,* Vol 51, 1994, pp. 55-69.

11   Karagiozis, A., and Hadjisophocieous, G., "Wind-Driven Rain on High-Rise Buildings", *Proceedings of BETEC/ASHRAE/DOE Thermal Performance of Building Envelopes VI,* Dec., 1995, pp. 399-406.

12   Straube, J.F. and Burnett, E.F.P., "Rain Control and Design Strategies". *Journal of Thermal Insulation and Building Envelopes,* July 1999, pp. 41-56

13   *Rain Penetration Control Guide,* Morrison Hershfield for CMHC, Ottawa, 2000.

14   Lstiburek, J., (1999) *Builders Guide for Mixed Climates,* Building Science Corporation, Westford, MA.

5.3 Moisture and Decomposition in Straw: Implications for Straw Bale Construction

by Matthew Summers

5.3.1 Introduction

Straw is a natural fiber that can last many thousands of years under the right conditions. Intact straw has been found in dry Egyptian tombs and buried in layers under glacial ice. However, under typical conditions straw will slowly degrade, as do all natural-fiber materials like wood, paper, cotton fabric, etc. The rate at which this happens is highly dependent on the conditions under which the straw is stored, primarily moisture content and temperature. With proper attention to moisture control, a straw bale structure should be able to last as long as any conventional wood-framed home.

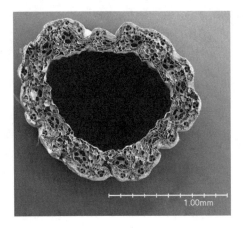

5.3A
RICE STRAW IN CROSS-SECTION

photo courtesy of Delilah F. Wood USDA-ARS-WRRC Albany, CA

Straw is the structural material that makes a plant stand up. Its fiber structure consists of cellulose strands bound in a matrix of hemicellulose and lignin. Some straws, like rice, have a significant amount (up to 20%) of inorganic compounds such as silica that are adsorbed by the plant during growth. After the plant dies, the fiber structure remains intact unless it degrades by biological or chemical mechanisms – exactly what all straw bale builders want to avoid.

Straw is a potential food source for microorganisms such as fungi and bacteria. Under the right conditions, these microorganisms degrade the straw in a process similar to composting. Although straw is not necessarily their preferred meal, it contains adequate amounts of energy and nutrients to provide for their growth and sustenance. Spores of these microorganisms, when baled with the straw as it is harvested from the field, will be ready to reproduce and multiply given the right conditions.

The four main conditions that affect the rate of growth of these microorganisms and, thus, the rate of straw decomposition are:

1. nutrients contained in the straw,
2. availability of oxygen in the straw,
3. temperature of the straw, and
4. free moisture on the straw.

In terms of nutrients, straw is generally lower in nitrogen than is optimum for compost mixes, making it slower to grow and sustain large populations of decomposing microbes. In compost, the optimum ratio of nitrogen to carbon is between 1:20 and 1:40, whereas straw's ratio ranges from 1:70 to 1:120. Hay and grass are higher in nitrogen than grain straws, making them better food sources. Generally, the greener the straw, the more nitrogen will be present in it; thus, allowing a longer period for field drying can reduce the amount of nitrogen in the baled material and reduce potential microbial growth. Other nutrients in straw are typically adequate for biological growth and are not limiting in the rate of microorganism growth.

The availability of oxygen is another key factor for active microbial growth. As animals do, the types of fungi and bacteria that rapidly decompose straw require oxygen to respire while utilizing the carbon food and energy source the straw provides. While a bale of straw is almost 90% air, the oxygen within the bale will quickly be used up and replaced with carbon dioxide during active microorganism respiration. Inhibiting the diffusion of new oxygen into the bale, as wall plasters will do, will limit the rate of decomposition. Although not yet quantified, very likely the rate of decomposition in a plastered straw bale wall, because of limits on the amount of available oxygen, will be lower than a bale with the same moisture content that is open to the environment.

Temperature is an important parameter for microorganism growth. Below zero degrees Celsius (32°F), these tiny life forms do not actively grow or persist because water is frozen. Many fungi and bacteria cannot survive at temperatures below 10°C [50°F], so growth is not very active at low temperatures even above freezing. In the range of 20°C to 70°C [68° to 158°F], fungi and bacteria thrive, each species having its own range and optimum temperature for growth. Above 70°C, most species cannot survive and biological growth ceases.

Moisture is the key ingredient that initiates decomposition in straw, and most people are familiar with the relationship between moisture and mold growth. A major question for straw bale builders is: *How much moisture is too much?*. Much of current understanding is based on rules-of-thumb from the haymaking industry or from straw bale builders' experience. Some recent studies that have looked more carefully at decomposition and moisture in straw are discussed below.

It has been observed that free moisture on the straw is necessary to initiate micro-organism growth and decomposition. Theoretically, straw could be at 99% humidity with equilibrium moisture content as high as 39% on a dry basis (28% on a wet basis)[A] and not support growth. However, on a practical level moisture can migrate and condense, and bulk moisture content is never uniform throughout a bale. **Bulk moisture levels of greater than 25% dry basis (20% wet basis) should be avoided to give a margin of safety.**

5.3.2 Moisture Experiments

The amount of nutrients and the availability of oxygen will not change, or will change only very slowly, for a given bale of straw and installation as long as microbial growth does not occur. However, moisture content and temperature will fluctuate based on outdoor climate, indoor conditions, or the accidental entry of liquid water. Of key interest to straw bale builders is what effect different moisture and temperature regimes will have on the degradation of straw contained within a wall. A study conducted at the University of California, Davis investigated this phenomenon in rice straw (Summers et al., 2002), with more thorough tests performed on rice and wheat straw (Summers, 2005).

In order to quantify rate of decomposition with a high degree of accuracy, the rate of carbon dioxide evolution from the straw can be monitored using sealed containers. As microorganisms break down the carbon in the straw, oxygen is converted to carbon dioxide in a process called *respiration*. By monitoring the quantity of carbon dioxide produced from the sample, one can estimate of the rate of carbon loss from the sample. In practical terms, this rate of carbon loss announces the rate that organic matter is being degraded in the straw. Rapid rates of organic matter loss indicate significant degradation of straw – the condition you want to avoid.

In the first experiment, green rice straw was taken directly from the field in Yolo County, California and dried to various moisture contents for immediate testing. Additional straw was dried to less than 12% dry basis (10% wet basis) and stored for several months. It was remoistened to various different moisture contents between 12 and 150% dry basis (10-60% wet basis) and placed in sealed containers. Containers were placed in environments of 10°C, 20°C, and 35°C, and carbon dioxide evolution was monitored daily for two weeks. Figure 5.3B shows the

FOOTNOTE

A

Dry basis moisture content is the weight of water contained per weight of dry material. *Wet basis* moisture content is the weight of water contained per weight of wet material equal to dry material + water. The building industry typically uses dry basis moisture content but the food and agriculture industry often uses wet basis, and many moisture meters are wet basis. To convert: Wet Basis Moisture = (Dry Basis Moisture)/ (1+Dry Basis Moisture) or Dry Basis Moisture = (Wet Basis Moisture)/ (1-Wet Basis Moisture) where the values are given in decimal form, not percent. Multiply by 100 to obtain the final value in percent.

container setup and locations where the carbon dioxide meter was installed.

The second set of experiments was conducted to give a more detailed description of the activity in the moistened straw. Rice straw was obtained from a composite sample of M-202 variety rice straw collected in Butte County, California in the fall of 2001. Wheat straw was obtained from a single bale of Durham variety wheat grown in New Mexico in the summer of 2001. Straw was dried to 10% moisture in the field or in the laboratory and was maintained in dry storage before the experiments. Containers were filled with 20 dry grams of straw that had been cut into approximately 25 mm pieces and remoistened to selected moisture contents. Filled reactors were supplied 30 mL/min of humidified laboratory air and were placed in incubators at 25°C and 35°C. Outlet air from the fourteen filled reactors and two empty reactors (baseline for each incubator) was dried and directed to the gas sensor system. A carbon dioxide sensor and an oxygen sensor measured concentration of the dried outlet gas on a 15-minute valve cycle so that each reactor was monitored once every four hours. This setup allowed for monitoring the rate of decomposition.

An alternative way to measure microbial activity is to instead measure heat production, using a highly-insulated container like a *Dewar vessel* to monitor the temperature of the moistened straw. Other authors have used Dewar vessels to examine self-heating in straw (Carlyle and Norman, 1941) and compost (Koenig and Bari, 2000). Dewar vessels are used in methods to determine the level of stability of compost (Brinton, 1995). The method is simple, not requiring any sophisticated gas sampling instruments or temperature control. The only required equipment is a Dewar vessel, temperature sensors, and a data collector. The Dewar's insulation allows simulation of real bales that heat up from microbial activity.

5.3B
TESTING SETUP FOR FIRST SET OF EXPERIMENTS.

Carbon dioxide concentration was monitored in the CO2 analyzer.

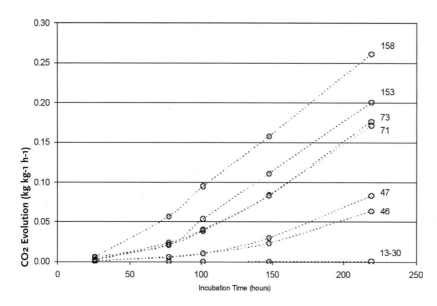

5.3C
CO2 EVOLUTION FROM RICE STRAW OVER 10 DAYS OF INCUBATION AT 25°C.

Dry basis moisture content (%) indicated to the right.

5.3.3 Results

In the first experiments, the total evolution of carbon dioxide, CO_2, is measured as a function of time for each moisture sample. Figure 5.3C shows results for CO_2 evolution per unit mass of straw for containers of rice straw incubated at 25°C. Samples below 30% moisture show little measurable CO_2 evolution over the two weeks of measurement, indicating that little microbial activity exists in straw at these moisture levels. Above this level, the rate of evolution increases with moisture and appears to vary with time depending on the moisture level.

Evolution consistently increases with moisture content above 30% for all temperatures. The data for five-day CO_2 evolution as a function of moisture content are shown in Figure 5.3D for both the green and the remoistened straw. That green samples below 30% moisture (dry basis) continued to decrease in CO_2 evolution with moisture may be due to residual plant respiration or to non-uniform drying. The rehydrated straw shows little respiration below 30% moisture. This indicates that microbial activity in the rehydrated straw initiates somewhere between 30 and 40% moisture content and increases steadily from 30% to 150% moisture.

The second set of experiments gives more detailed information on the growth of microbes with respect to time. Figure 5.3E shows the measured results of oxygen consumption rate for wheat straw at 25°C for the first 250 hours of decomposition. For 100% and 60% moisture, there are two distinct peaks in oxygen consumption rate. This may indicate two types of microbes or two different food sources in the moist straw, although the second peak may also be an artifact of the sampling and analysis system at these higher moistures. The instrument behavior with high resulting humidities is still being investigated. The samples at 40%, 35%, and 30% show a single peak, and 25% and 10% show no distinct peak above the noise in the sensor. Closer analysis of the area under this peak (the first peak for 100% and 60%) shows that the area is reasonably consistent, indicating that the moisture content affects the rate of growth but not the size of the food source available to the microorganisms.

The five-day CO_2 evolution for rice straw at 25°C and 35°C are shown in Figure 5.3F. These data correspond well with the results of the closed isothermal experiments (Figure 5.3D(b)).

Because of excessive moisture in the sampling lines for the 35°C experiments, the data were unreliable after a few days so the kinetics could not be fully evaluated. The first few days of reliable data indicated that the difference between 35°C and 25°C was not dramatic. This is consistent with what was found in the closed isothermal bioreactors.

The relationship between respiration and heating can be demonstrated with the Dewar vessel bioreactors. Figure 5.3G shows the resulting temperature profiles from the self-heating of rice and wheat straw at 100% moisture in a laboratory atmosphere at 25°C. From these data, respiration rate can be estimated. This can be compared with the respiration rate measured at 25°C. There appears to be good correspondence between the respiration rate in isothermal experiments and the total heat generated in insulated vessels.

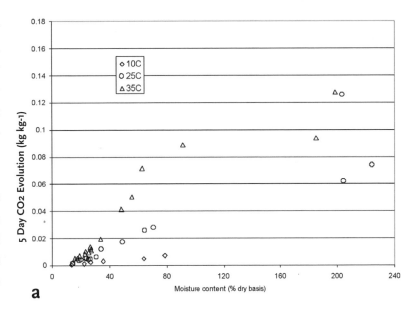

a

5.3D FIVE-DAY CO2 EVOLUTION FROM CLOSED ISOTHERMAL BIOREACTORS FOR

(a) green, and
(b) remoistened rice straw.

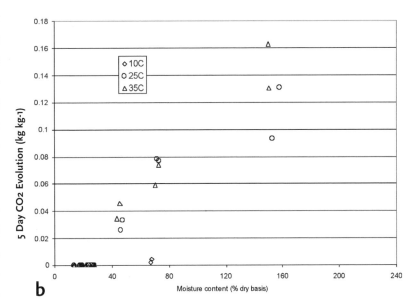

b

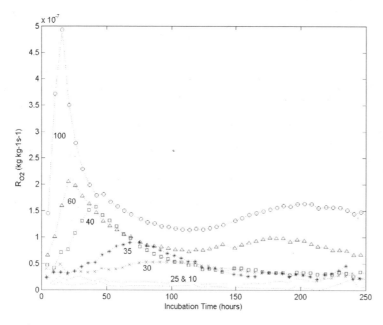

5.3E *Respiration rate from wheat straw samples measured in isothermal bioreactors at 25C. Approximate moisture content is indicated (% dry basis).*

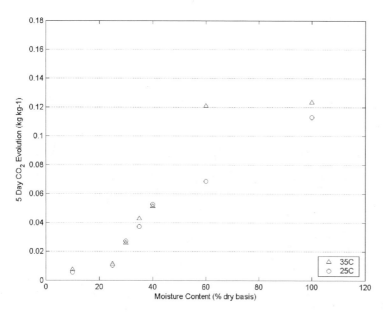

5.3F *Five-day CO2 evolution from flow-through bioreactors for rehydrated rice straw.*

5.3.4 Discussion

Two distinct respiratory behaviors were apparent in both rice and wheat straw. The first initiated at 30–40% moisture content, and growth rate increased linearly to 100% moisture content. The second was not apparent until 60% moisture content and increased at 100% moisture content and above. The wheat straw showed somewhat higher growth rates and biodegradable substrate levels than the rice straw, but the impact of moisture was similar for both.

The effect of moisture content on decomposition in straw can be compared with other substances that decompose from microorganism activity. In these experiments, we did not see the initiation of measurable microbial respiration below 30% moisture in straw. This corresponds to an equilibrium relative humidity of 0.89 in straw. We observed a steadily increasing rate from 40% to above 100% moisture for the first respiration peak, corresponding to a narrow range of relative humidity from 0.93 to 0.98 in straw. We did not see the second respiration peak until moisture content of greater than 60%, corresponding to a relative humidity of 0.95. In foods, fungal activity typically initiates above equilibrium humidity of 0.80 and bacteria above 0.93 (CSIRO, 2005), consistent with these observations.

In soils it has been found that fungi generally require for growth a relative humidity higher than 0.90 and bacteria require relative humidity of greater than 0.95 (Swift et al., 1979). Interestingly, in straw these correspond to estimated moisture contents of 40% and 60% respectively, near the points at which the first and second respiration peaks become apparent. It is possible that the two respiration phenomena observed in straw are related to fungal colonies in the first case and bacterial colonies in the second. Both fungi and bacteria have been found in decomposed straw (Dobie and Haq, 1980, Atkey and Wood, 1983).

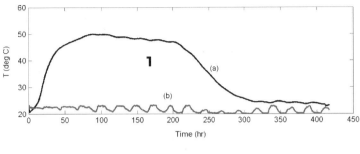

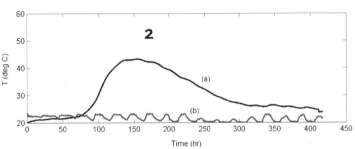

5.3G MEASURED TEMPERATURE PROFILES AND TEMPERATURE RATE IN DEWAR (INSULATED) VESSEL BIOREACTORS FOR:

(1) *wheat straw at 100% moisture, and*
(2) *rice straw at 100% moisture.*
Curves represent:
(a) *average internal temperature, and*
(b) *ambient laboratory temperature.*

In reality, the moisture on the straw samples may not have been uniform in spite of efforts to equally distribute moisture in their preparation. This could cause some of the moisture effect observed in the experiments – wet, decomposing regions interspersed with dry straw – to be discrete, with marked decomposition in moist areas and no decomposition in dry areas. This kind of non–uniform wetting and decay would be even more likely to occur in actual straw bales in a building.

5.3.5 Moisture Management in Straw Bale Buildings

Two central and persistent questions for straw bale builders and building owners are: "What moisture levels should be of concern?" and
          "What should be done when moisture is detected?"

In the experiments, we found microbial growth initiated between 30 and 40% moisture content with a second, more sustained growth activity possibly initiated at 60% moisture content. For the samples compared here, wheat straw showed greater reactivity than rice straw, but both initiated some activity at moisture content as low as 30% and demonstrated the presence of two apparent types of activity. The studies (and experience) indicate that liquid water penetration into straw bales is the most likely cause of decomposition after baling.

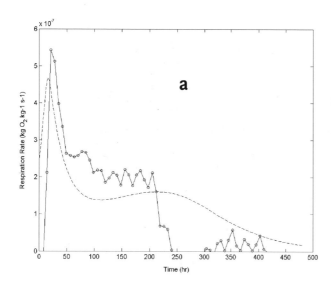

5.3H Estimated respiration rate from Dewar vessel reactors (line with circles) and modeled respiration rate at **25°C** (dashed line) from isothermal data for:

> (a) wheat straw at 100% moisture, and
> (b) rice straw at 100% moisture.

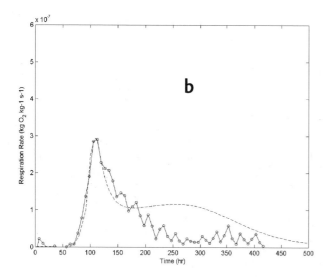

Based on these studies and experience with straw, we can make some recommendations for straw bale builders:

1) **Only bales with bulk moisture content below 25% dry basis (20% wet basis) should be used in wall systems.** This helps insure that free moisture is not being added to the system and is below the level that can initiate fungal growth.

2) **Bales showing any sign of discoloration or with any moldy scent (indicating microbial activity, active or dormant) should never be used in buildings.**

3) **If bales become wet during transport or storage, they should be discarded or allowed to dry out thoroughly before they are placed in a wall.** Once they are in the wall, their drying will be heavily retarded by the wall plaster (itself a moisture source for the first few weeks). Wet bales can be sampled to determine the depth and extent of the moisture entry.[A] If high-moisture straw is only on the bale surface, then it is possible – though by no means certain – that it will dry out readily. If moisture content is elevated deep into the bale, then the temperature should be monitored until the bale dries out, although this drying period could take weeks to months depending on conditions. **As a practical matter, if the core of the bale has been wetted, it shouldn't be used (or remain) in a building.**

FOOTNOTE

A

Moisture content can be determined with a hay moisture meter or by drying a sample in an oven at 105°C for 24 hours. Wet basis moisture content is determined by the weight loss (ie water weight) over the initial weight of the sample.

4) **Forced-air drying of wetted bale walls has sometimes been used with success, but is generally not recommended because it could accelerate heating and decomposition by providing oxygen.** Fungal and microbial growth require oxygen, which can be quickly used up in the core of a plastered bale wall, so limited growth areas will sometimes "choke" themselves and self-arrest. The success stories involve very limited volumes of wetted straw, such as a gallon or so of water below a window leak, and very fast drying – i.e., a rate of drying much faster than the rate of decay. If an entire bale or more within the wall is soaked – per note 3 – you almost surely need to open up the wall to remove and replace all wet straw.

Elevated temperature is a direct measure of decomposition activity within a bale. Decomposition gives off carbon dioxide and also gives off heat. Since bales are good thermal insulators, this heating will lead to an increase in the bale temperature, similar to the way a compost pile heats up. In our experience, wet bales in the field reach a maximum center temperature of 60-70°C [140-158°F] about seven days after becoming wet and slowly drop in temperature as activity decreases. If moisture penetrates deeper into the bale upon re-wetting, the same heating process can repeat itself. As with hay, though much less so, bales whose temperature rises above 70°C [158°F] should be handled with caution because of a risk of spontaneous combustion.

Once a bale has been identified as wet, temperature is the primary indicator of the level of decomposition activity. A compost thermometer can monitor the interior bale temperature. Temperature should be measured at the bale center because the outside of the bale will appear normal. Alternatively, a metal rod (like reinforcing bar) can be inserted into a bale for a minute or two. If the rod comes out hot to the touch, the bale has an elevated temperature and is self-heating. Again, forced-air drying has sometimes been used with success, but is generally not recommended.

Good building design to avoid moisture entry – as per sections 5.1 and 5.2 – and moisture management during construction should prevent problems with straw decomposition and microorganism growth in straw bale houses. With good practices to prevent moisture contents above 30% dry basis, straw bale structures should last a long time.

REFERENCES

Atkey, P.T., D.A. Wood (1983) "An electron microscope study of wheat straw composted as a substrate for the cultivation of the edible mushroom (Agaricus bisporus)" *Journal of Applied Bacteriology* 55:293-304.

Brinton, W.F., E. Evans, M.L. Droffner, R.B. Brinton (1995) "Standardized test for evaluation of compost self-heating" *Biocycle* 36(11): 64-68.

Carlyle, R.E., A.G. Norman (1941) "Microbial thermogenesis in the decomposition of plant materials" *Journal of Bacteriology* 41:699-724.

CSIRO (2005) Food Science Australia Fact Sheet – Water Activity Food Science Australia. North Ryde, NSW, Australia. (online at http://www.foodscience.afisc.csiro.au/water_fs.htm)

Dobie, J.B., A. Haq (1980) "Outside Storage of Baled Rice Straw" *Trans.* ASAE 23(4): 990-993.

Koenig, A., Q.H. Bari (2000) "Application of self-heating test for indirect estimation of respirometic activity of compost: Theory and practice" *Compost Science and Utilization* 8(2): 99-107.

Summers, M.D. S.L. Blunk, B.M. Jenkins (2002) "Moisture and Thermal Conditions for Degradation of Rice Straw" *ASAE Meeting Paper #026153* St.Joseph, Mich. ASAE

Summers, M.D. (2005) "The Role of Moisture in Spontaneous Combustion" PhD Dissertation. University of California, Davis.

Swift M.J., Heal O.W., Anderson J.M. (1979) "Decomposition in terrestrial ecosystems" Oxford, UK: Blackwell Scientific.

Make it HOT!

– James Brown

FIRE

with Bob Theis

6.1 Introduction

We are accustomed to building with flammable materials. For example, wood studs with air spaces around each one burn very well. With this as the cultural baseline, our building codes do not typically concern themselves with, "Does it burn?" as much as, "Can people escape *while* it's burning?"

These building codes express the fire safety of walls as a function of fire *resistance*. This means how long a conflagration can exist on one side of a wall before enough heat is transmitted through the wall to ignite materials on the other side, even if fire has not actually breached the wall. So while a wall made, say, of a single slab of steel is not going to burn under normal fire conditions, it is not fire resistive because the heat of the fire would pass so quickly through it. In the United States, the fire resistivity of a wall is expressed as a function of this time of heat transmission: a "one-hour wall" has kept a set of flame throwers heating a furnace to over 1700°F [927°C] from heating the opposite side of the wall any more than 250°F [139°C] over its initial temperature for one hour.

6.2 Bales Burn Badly

One would not generally suppose that a straw bale wall would increase a building's fire safety, since the straw is so obviously flammable. However, fire requires three things: high temperature, fuel, and oxygen; compressing the straw into a dense block dramatically decreases the oxygen's ability to feed a fire at the straw.

6

FIRE

(This is the same reason that building codes give a relatively high fire-resistance rating to "heavy timber structures"; massive blocks of wood will char on the outside but not easily burn, just like bales of straw.) After the surface of a bale or bale wall has been charred – providing that the wall of exposed bales remains intact – the worst it will generally do is smolder. Fire departments actually utilize this quality in training exercises, igniting wire-tied bales as smoke generators. This resistance to rapid combustion has been observed during a few accidental fires during construction of bale buildings, and during a lab test, called a "corner test," on unplastered bales at the Richmond Field Station of the University of California in March 1996.

The author was present for this corner test, which was meant to simulate what a burning wastebasket would do to the walls of an interior corner. When exposed to the fire source, the surfaces of the bales rapidly charred, after which there was no observable effect. This was said by the fire experts present to be comparable to how drywall performs in such a test. At the test's completion, we were asked to remove the charred bales from the test chamber to a dumpster without first subjecting the chamber to a soaking-down. When we did, we saw firsthand that when the bales fell apart, sparks inside the straw then had sufficient oxygen to develop into open flame – and dramatically did.

6.3 Laboratory Test Results

In general, once a bale wall has been plastered on both faces, the combination of incombustible plaster skins and an insulating interior that neither burns well nor melts makes a straw bale wall a very fire-resistive assembly. This has been verified in the lab tests to date:

1. **1993** Two small-scale ASTM E-119 fire tests at the SHB Agra lab in Sandia, New Mexico – one test wall with plastered faces, the other unplastered – showed bales to be very fire-resistant. The unplastered bale wall withstood the heat and flames of the furnace for 30 minutes before flames penetrated a joint between bales. The plastered bale wall was naturally much better, resisting the transmission of flame and heat for two hours.

2. **1996** A full scale ASTM E-119 fire test at the University of California Richmond Field Station easily passed the criteria to qualify as a one-hour

wall. In the opinion of the experts present at the test[A], the wall would probably have passed as a two-hour assembly. (The report was never written or made public.)

3. 2001 The Appropriate Technology Group at Vienna Technical Institute conducted an F90 test (similar to the ASTM E-119 test), which gave a plastered straw bale wall a 90 minute (1 -1/2 hour) rating.

4. 2000 As reported in *The Last Straw* (issue #31, p. 21), an eight-foot-high circle of walls of differing construction was built and fire-tested under the auspices of the Santa Fe, New Mexico Fire Department. Wall types included both plastered and unplastered straw bales, conventional wood studwalls with ½" gypsum board, and fired straw-clay blocks. A fire of paper and gasoline was ignited in the center, reaching a temperature of 2000° F [1093° C]. The unplastered bales charred but did not burn, and collapsed in 30 minutes; the studwalls burned and collapsed after 35 minutes; the straw-clay blocks and plastered straw bale walls remained essentially undamaged through the conclusion of the test at 40 minutes.

5. 2001 The Danish Fire Technical Institute tested a plastered straw bale wall with exposed studs on the fire side as a worst-case scenario, and got these results: in a 30-minute test with a 1832°F [1000° C] fire on the exposed side, the unexposed side rose just 1.8°F [1°C]. The maximum average increase permitted in order to pass that test is 144°F [80°C].

6. 2002 Bohdan Dorniak and members of AUSBALE tested individually plastered bales to the Australian standard, simulating the heat of a bushfire. Subjected to a maximum heat intensity of 29 kilowatts per square meter, none of the nine plastered bales ignited or even developed visible cracks. According to Mr. Dorniak, this qualifies them as non-combustible under the current Australian Bushfire Code AS 3959.

7. 2006 See 6.7.4.

FOOTNOTE A

personal communication with R. Brady Williamson, Spring 2004

6.4 Flame Spread and Smoke Density

The issue has sometimes been raised that bales inside a wall should conform to the code criteria for insulation, which specifies minimum surface burning characteristics based on a standard test (ASTM E84-98). According to Professor R. Brady Williamson (one of the authors of this section of the Uniform Building Code [UBC] section 707), this notion is misguided, as this part of the code is meant to address insulation installed *within* a cavity in a wall. In typical straw bale construction, the straw bale insulation *is* the wall, more like the situation in a log cabin. With no concealed draft tunnels through which fire can rise, surface burning characteristics, as measured in what is commonly called a "tunnel test," are not relevant.

In some buildings, though, people have indeed inserted bales between extra deep "studs" to construct walls. With that in mind, Katrina Hayes sponsored an ASTM E84-98 test on unplastered straw bales in 2000 at the Omega Point Laboratories. They passed the test easily; where the Uniform Building Code allows a flame spread of no more than 25, the test produced a flame spread of 10; where the code allows a smoke density of no more than 450, the bales produced a smoke density of 350.

6.5 Still, It Burns – Field Reports

The author has collected fourteen reports of fires in straw bale buildings during and after construction. These range in severity from the inconsequential flash of flames across the loose surface straw of an unplastered wall to the complete loss of a structure.

The sources of the fires break down as follows:
- One was caused by a votive candle breaking in a recess in a wall.
- One was caused by candles at a party in an unplastered bale house.
- One was caused by a fireplace with no air gap separating it from an adjacent bale wall.
- One was caused by a portable electric heater in a crawl space.
- Two were deliberate arson.
- Two were electrical short circuits.
- Six were caused by construction activity (welding, soldering, grinding).

This field data begins to indicate where the greatest fire danger resides in straw bale construction. If sorted by stage of construction and extent of damage:

- Eleven fires occurred during construction; of them,
    - six had local damage
    - five were a total loss.
- Three fires occurred after occupancy; of them,
    - two had local damage
    - one was a total loss.

However, the best single correlation with extent of damage seems to be whether the plaster was in place at the time of the fire:

- Six fires occurred after plastering; of them,
    - five had local damage
    - one was a total loss (in which the fire began in the roof framing).
- Eight fires occurred before plastering; of them,
    - two had local damage
    - six were a total loss.

The most typical pattern of fire, reported in five instances, was where a construction activity ignited loose straw on the ground, which ignited loose straw on the surface of an adjacent wall. Regardless of the source of fire, in all five instances in which a fire climbed an unplastered wall on which framing lumber stood unprotected, the framing ignited, resulting in the complete loss of the structure. In the two instances that were timed, the collapse of the roof occurred within 25 minutes of the fire's beginning.

In at least five of the reported fires, the fire smoldered in the spaces between bales and was difficult or impossible to fully extinguish with a water hose. New protocols for dealing with this new kind of fire are evidently necessary, because in most of these smoldering instances, substantial sections of intact wall were demolished simply to get at the fire in the crevices.

6.6 Fire Safety Measures

A few simple safety measures should be standard on straw bale construction projects and jobsites:

1. Maintain awareness. Make certain everyone on site, especially tradespeople, understand the flammability of exposed straw, and that extra precautions are required.

2. Remove loose straw on the ground, continuously during the bale raising, and as a cleanup two to four times a day until the walls are plastered.

3. Have pressurized water hoses ready everywhere on site. They must be within less than one minute's access to make the difference in controlling the start of a fire.

4. Stuff all cracks between bales, and between bales and framing, with clay-coated (not loose) straw to reduce its ability to smolder. Trimming the bulges at the ends of bales prior to stacking substantially reduces the amount of this stuffing required.

5. Get the initial plaster coat on the bales as soon as possible. The practice of pre-coating the bale surfaces that will remain exposed, *prior* to stacking, while not yet widely practiced, would reduce fire vulnerability tremendously.

6.7 Published Straw Bale Fire Tests

1. Transverse Load Test and Small Scale E-119 Fire Test on Uncoated Straw Bale Wall Panels and Stucco Coated Wall Panels 1993 by Bryce Simons, P.E. of SHB Agra, Inc. Available from Natural Building Resources, 119 Main Street Kingston, NM 88042; ph 505-895-5652; www.strawbalecentral.com

2. ASTM E84-98 Surface Burning Characteristics, (on) Straw Bale 2000 by Guy Haby and William E. Fitch, P.E. of Omega Point Laboratories, Inc. Available from Development Center for Appropriate Technology (DCAT) P.O. Box 27513, Tucson, AZ 85726-7513; ph 520-624-6628; www.azstarnet.com/~dcat

3. **Wall Systems of Renewable Resources** (Wandsysteme aus nachwachsenden Rohstoffen) which includes an **F90** (European fire resistivity test)) **and B2** (European flammability test) 2001 by Robert Wimmer, Hannes Hohensinner, Luise Janisch and Manfred Drack of the Gruppe Angepasste Technologie (GrAT) an der TU Wein (the Appropriate Technology Group at Vienna Technological University); posted (in German) as a PDF document at www.grat.tuwein.ac.at

4. **In July of 2006 two walls were fire-tested per ASTM standard E119** at Intertek Laboratories in San Antonio, Texas. Both walls were built with two-string wheat bales; a brief description and commentary follows, and the entire test report can be downloaded as a PDF document at www.ecobuildnetwork.org.

The ASTM full scale fire test consists of constructing test specimen walls in moveable steel frames, allowing the plaster to cure at least 28 days, moving the wall specimens up against a furnace with a ten foot by ten foot [3M x 3M] aperture, and starting the burners.

6A

Moving completed Wall 2 into position at the fire chamber

Over about an hour, the temperature is raised above 1700° F [927° C], and held there or higher for the duration of the time of the test. Immediately afterwards, the specimen is moved away from the furnace to a position where a fire hose can spray the burned surface of the wall so as to apply pressure and verify the

6B PULLING WALL FROM FIRE CHAMBER

The surge of flame was both dramatic and short-lived for both walls at this moment

6C THE HOSE TEST

6D

photo courtesy of David Eisenberg

6E

CHINKING CRACKS AND
VOIDS WITH STRAW-CLAY
ON WALL 1

*This proved to be a far
superior method of filling
voids than merely stuffing
loose straw; fire and
charring penetrated far
less in both walls where
clay was mixed with the
chinking straw.*

photo courtesy of David Eisenberg

structural stability of the specimen. The hose is mounted 20 feet [6 M] from the wall, and is of sufficient force to knock a man from his feet.

Failure of the test would be caused by too much temperature rise on the far side of the wall from the furnace, or by penetration of the hose stream through the wall specimen. **Both walls passed their respective tests easily.**

Wall Descriptions

Wall 1: One hour test / earth plaster / load-bearing

Wall 1 was built with bales laid flat for a 16 inch [406 cm] thick core, loaded with 600 pounds per linear foot [8.76 kN/M] directly on the straw before plastering, and coated with earth plaster in two applications, applied ten days apart, for an average total thickness of one inch [25 mm].

Wall 1 had no mesh, and some chopped straw in the first plaster coat. Three shrinkage cracks of up to 3/16" [5 mm] wide by 6 feet [2 M] long had appeared on the non-burn side during curing, and were patched the day before testing with earth plaster. Another much larger crack (¼ inch / 8 mm) appeared during the mounting of the wall to the test frame, again on the non-burn side. This crack was not patched, which proved to be a mistake as it admitted air into the wall cavity to feed and "invite" the expected burning and charring from the burn side through to the non-burn side.

Wall 2: Two hour test / lime-cement plaster

Wall 2 was built with bales on edge for a 14 inch [356 cm] thick core, leaving the polypropylene tie strings exposed just under the surface of the plaster. This was very deliberate, as there has been much speculation that a fire could melt the strings, and, if accompanied by a loss of the protective plaster, lead to a complete burn of the wall.

Wall 2 was coated with lime-cement plaster in two applications, applied ten days apart, for an average total thickness of 1" [25 mm], and reinforced with 17 gauge hexagonal wire mesh. Unlike the condition in most real buildings, there was very little wood in the surround to which the mesh could be stapled, and it was attached to the straw with 8 inch by 2 inch wire "robert pins" stuck into (but not through) the bale core.

Commentary

Wall 1:

Wall 1 began to develop cracks on the burn side (visible through portholes in the chamber) about 25 minutes after the burn began; the cracks increased in size and number for the duration of

6F
WALL 2 IN CONSTRUCTION

The vulnerable polypropylene strings are visible on the surface to be plastered.

photo: David Eisenberg
model: Bill Christensen
styling: Matts Myhrman
clothes: Le Mart du K

the hour test, and admitted air to the straw, increasing charring. Smoke was visible coming from various cracks on both sides through the test, and flames were coming from the burn-side cracks, but later it proved that charring of the burn-side straw averaged only 3 or 4 inches [7 to 10 cm]. Where chinking between bales was loose (i.e., only packed straw without clay) the charring penetrated several times deeper, and where the crack had formed on the far side the charring penetrated all the way through the wall. In some places the plaster on the burn-side fell away in small pieces, exposing the straw to further charring. When the wall was pulled from the fire chamber, most of the burnt plaster fell away and there was a brief burst of flame (figure 6B).

The hose test lasted for one minute, and washed away the rest of the burnt plaster and charred straw, but never penetrated to the far side. As was tentatively expected, the earth (clay) plaster had been slightly strengthened by the heat, and an outer veneer (less than a millimeter) had been partially vitrified to an even greater hardness (see figure 6G).

The fire test on Wall 1 reaffirmed what was already obvious: patch cracks in the plaster, as they can otherwise admit water, fire, or oxygen to feed fire on the far side. It was also reaffirmed that filling, or chinking, voids and cracks with a dense straw-clay mix well-packed into the bales is far superior to packing those voids only with dry straw.

6G
HARDENING AND
VITRIFICATION OF
EARTH PLASTER

The dark surface on this
sample of burnt plaster
is partially vitrified clay,
which extended the life
of the plaster and wall
under both fire and
hose testing.

Wall 2:

Wall 2 began to develop cracks on the burn-side about 20 minutes after the burn began – earlier than with wall 1. Again, the cracks increased in size and number for the duration of the hour test, admitting air to the straw and increasing flames and charring, and by the end of two hours a very large portion of the burn-side plaster was bulging away from the straw by as much as 10 inches [25 cm]. The wire mesh was clearly holding the plaster together, but as with Wall 1 smoke was visible coming from various cracks and edges through the test, and flames were coming from the burn-side cracks. There were no cracks in the non-burn side. It later proved that the charring pattern roughly matched that of wall 1.

The hose test lasted for two and a half minutes, and from the beginning was directed against unprotected charred straw. As expected, the exposed polypropylene bale strings had melted, but the straw bales – even badly charred – remained intact by virtue of being compressed together (as is typically done with walls in the field.) In other words, the test ended longstanding concerns that just such a wall might burst open without the confining strings, leading to a conflagration; if the bales are reasonably well placed and snug, they remain intact. In light of this result and that of Wall 1, we believe it reasonable to expect at least as good a fire resistance from the same type of wall with the bales laid flat.

6.8 Conclusions

Our knowledge of the fire-resistive properties of straw bale construction is ever growing – as it is with building assemblies in general – and tests and field experience have been very encouraging. Most straw bale construction to date has been low-density, single-family dwellings, which building codes typically allow to be built with essentially zero fire resistance. Within this context, fire safety concerns usually don't come up as a significant issue; the standard, as set by wood frame construction, is very low.

Fire safety concerns rise as building and population density increase. Straw bale construction has now been demonstrated to be acceptable for uses such as urban infill, row housing, and commercial, retail, and educational buildings – applications in which the additional attributes such as its excellent thermal and acoustical insulation would be of great value.

Straw bale construction has achieved its remarkable growth largely due to its aesthetic characteristics, its environmental credentials, and its excellent insulation value. In all these aspects, it compares very favorably with stud wall construction. Those of us who have worked with it for years find it, in fact, to be a far superior wall system, whose potentials are barely tapped. As its fire-resistive qualities become better known, we will see new economies realized where it can, for example, be substituted for concrete block, or remove the need for fire safety measures such as sprinklers.

The only thing I can't stand is discomfort

— Gloria Steinem

INSULATION Thermal Performance of Plastered Straw Bale Walls

with Nehemiah Stone

7.1 What is Thermal Performance?

We build shelter for many reasons: to keep the rain and critters out, to keep children in and burglars out, and to control the temperature. We want it to be warm inside in winter, cool in summer. How easy or hard it is to do that is the measure of *thermal performance*. Regardless of what is used to heat (or cool) a building – for example sun, wind, coal, gas, or wood – the ability of the building enclosure to insulate and store heat plays the dominant role in defining thermal performance.

Those who regularly work with these issues have defined a measure of how easily heat will flow through a barrier such as a wall or roof, and call it the *U-factor.* Technically, U–factor is a measure of Btu/(hr. s.f. °F), or British thermal units per hour, per square foot of material, per degree Fahrenheit of temperature difference between the two sides of the material or assembly[A]. The inverse of U–factor is the better-known *R-value,* or the measure of how well a barrier such as a wall assembly resists the flow of heat; this is the unit we see most often used and misused to represent the thermal performance of a material or building assembly. Mathematically, R = 1 / U.

The second of the three laws of thermodynamics says that heat will always flow from warmer things to cooler things. (It actually says much more and in very unsimple terms, but for our purposes this will do.) An ice cube melts because the heat in the room flows to it and raises its temperature. Leave the furnace off

FOOTNOTE

A
In most other countries, the (metric) U-factor is defined in terms of Watts per square meter per degree Kelvin [W/(m²*K)]. To convert metric (SI) U-factors to inch-pound (IP) U-factors divide by 5.678; to convert the other way, simply multiply by 5.678. To convert IP R-values to metric R-values, multiply by 0.1761.

7

INSULATION

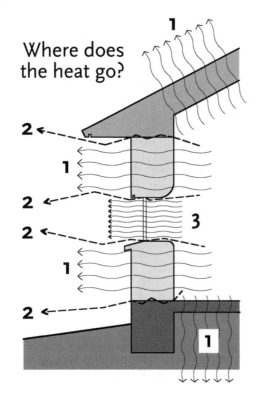

Where does the heat go?

7.1A

Heat will escape a building in three ways, *all of which are always happening, but usually some much more than others. This shows conditions in winter, when the inside is warmer; reverse the arrows for summer when the interior is cooler.*

1 Conduction
(the property measured by the R-value) is heat moving through the material or assembly, molecule to molecule.

2 Convection
is heat-bearing air or water vapor moving through gaps and air passages (both small and large) in the building enclosure.

3 Radiation
is infrared radiation emanating from the warm surfaces of the interior, primarily through windows (especially single-pane, untreated windows).

in winter and you will soon be shivering because all that heat in your house will escape to the great, cool outdoors. Heat can "travel" by any of three means: conduction, convection, and radiation. *Conduction,* which is heat energy moving laboriously from molecule to molecule through a medium, is a dominant means of heat transfer in a very tightly sealed building. Put your hand on a hot stove, and you've got conductance. It is also the means of heat flow defined by the U-factor and R-value. In a not-so-tightly sealed building (that is, most buildings), *convection* is the dominant mode of heat transfer, in which the heat energy takes a metaphorical bus ride around or between barriers via moving air (or, sometimes, water). Leaky windows, unsealed joints at fixtures, ceilings, and walls, the crack under the door — all provide easy means for heat (and water vapor) to enter or leave conditioned space. When you feel a draft in the room, that's convection. *Radiation* is heat moving via light rays, primarily in the infrared wavelengths; generally, the warmer an object is, the more it will radiate energy away. This is usually only a large factor in buildings at the windows, and then mostly with older windows not manufactured to reflect infrared radiation. If you sit in a window seat with the sun shining on you, the heat you feel is radiation. In any building, at any given time, all three heat transfer mechanisms are operating, but depending on many factors one or two will often predominate.

7.2 R-Values of Wall Systems

Defining R-value is far from simple – for straw bale walls as well as all other building assemblies. As will be discussed, many factors affect the R-value, which itself plays but a part of a building's overall thermal performance (figure 7.1A).

7.2.1 Measurement

Several ways have been used to estimate the thermal performance, or R-value, of walls:

a) Testing of walls using a hot-plate or thermal probe methodology,

b) Testing of wall assemblies in a guarded hot-box facility,

c) Monitoring of wall performance under ambient conditions,

d) Modeling of wall performance using known or assumed physical properties of the materials, and

e) Infrared thermographic imaging of *in situ* walls

Honest researchers will admit that any of these approaches provides only an estimate. Each method has its advantages and proponents, just as each has shortcomings and detractors, and all but the last method has been used at least once in trying to establish the thermal performance – i.e., R-value – of straw bale wall assemblies. By wide agreement the most definitive test was run at Oak Ridge National Laboratories[1] using state-of-the-art equipment of type (b). The researchers determined a plastered straw bale wall to have an average of R–1.45 per inch. Interestingly, they found the R-value per inch to be higher for bales laid on edge, in which the general orientation of straw fibers was perpendicular, not parallel, to the direction of heat flow. The net result was that a 24-inch-wide wall with bales laid flat has about the same net R-value as a 16-inch-wide wall with bales laid on edge.

7.2.2 Factors affecting the R-value

The actual R-value of wall systems will vary hugely with a number of factors. For straw bale walls these include the type of straw, the straw's moisture content, density and orientation of the fibers, the presence and size of other wall elements (such as windows), the type and thickness of plaster applied, and other factors. The number, size, and quality of doors and windows alone will often have the greatest effect on any wall system's "effective" R-value, in which case they matter more than the insulation value per inch of any particular material in the assembly.

Insulation manufacturers advertise the R-value of their product. It is tested and verified, and you can count on it being correct – for the *material*. However, when insulation (e.g., fiberglass batts or sprayed cellulose) is placed in a studwall *assembly*, a number of other factors affect how that assembly performs, including size, material, and spacing of the studs; sealing (or lack of it) around wall outlets and switch plates; sealing (or lack of it) at the junction of the wall and the floor; and fill of the insulation to the top of the wall cavities (Is there a gap? Does it settle with time?). Standard construction practice in almost all these categories results in R-values for the wall systems that are significantly less than the advertised R-value for the insulation. An "R-19 wall" often has a system R-value around R- 11 (California Energy Commission research, 2004). Straw bale walls, by the nature of the construction, generally do not suffer these same losses: an R-35 straw bale wall is R-35. Even after all that, the wall is only the wall; the overall performance of the building includes roofs and floors, either of which can and often do have more effect than the walls. (See Afterthought #1 at the end of this chapter regarding the use of bales as insulation in floors and roofs.)

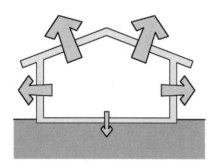

7.2A

Heat will escape (or enter, in summer) a house at different rates through the different surfaces. At the residential scale, the roof is usually by far the most important component, whereas in a high-rise structure the walls and windows govern thermal enclosure performance.

You can have perfectly built straw bale walls and still get poor thermal performance if the roof is poorly insulated or there are too many air leaks.

7.2.3 R-value is dynamic, not static

When a laboratory tests a material (or system) to determine its thermal conductance or resistance, they calculate the the amount of heat flow from one side to the other on the basis of measured surface temperatures and heat energy required on the warm side of the wall to maintain a steady heat flow. This provides the U-factor, or by conversion the R-value.

Before they can say they have a steady heat flow, there must be several temperature readings in a row, all with the same or nearly the same value. This is an important point that has significance for understanding how relevant the R-value of a system (e.g., a straw bale wall) is to the comfort or energy efficiency of a home. For most "standard" construction systems (e.g., 2x6 studs with R-19 insulation), it takes anywhere from 20 minutes to a couple of hours to reach steady state heat flow conditions. For plastered straw bale walls, it can literally take weeks. Nature, by stark contrast, rarely holds still for so long; conditions and temperatures are usually changing outside the building.

Therefore, what is being measured in the lab has a direct corollary to a straw bale building only in a climate where the temperature stays extremely cold for weeks on end, but has much less direct relevance to buildings where winter or summer temperatures vary appreciably through the 24-hour, or *diurnal,* cycle. In their analysis of the Real Goods Solar Living Center in Hopland, California, three UC Berkeley graduate students[2] determined that the thermal lag (the time it takes for a "pulse" of heat to travel through the wall) was about 12 hours. Other research has provided similar results. In most climates, at most times, the outside temperature goes through a diurnal swing (one full cycle per day), so that just about the time that heat from the inside of the building is reaching the exterior, the air temperature outside rises, and the heat loss at the surface decreases. This effect will make a building wall with a good R-value act effectively like one with a much higher R-value[A]. Both the thickness and "thermal mass" (density) of the wall act to buffer diurnal temperature swings inside, and this is the same phenomenon that makes earthen structures in many parts of the world provide a surprising level of comfort.

Furthermore, most materials will have different R-values depending on the mean temperature and on the material's age. The insulation value may more or less depend on whether it's very cold or hot outside, and on how old and/or moist the material itself is. If plastered straw bale walls show any appreciable variation due to these effects, it is as yet untested and unknown.

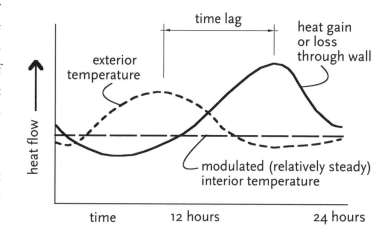

7.2B THE DIURNAL CYCLE

The rate at which heat will flow through an assembly varies with the assembly's temperature. That, and the presence of thermal mass (such as the plaster on the bales) will modulate temperature swings inside a building; heat flow is a very dynamic condition.

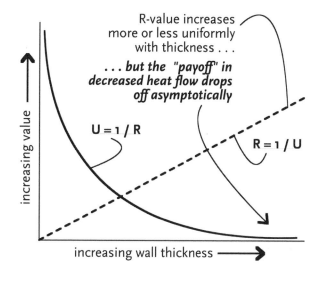

7.2C DIMINISHING RETURNS

Above R-30 or R-35, there is comparatively little to be gained by increasing the R-factor. Even in the extreme cold of the Antarctic, housing and labs for year-round scientific study are only insulated to between R-50 and R-60.

FOOT NOTE

A Note that the effect discussed in the previous paragraph argues that the straw bale wall system will actually perform much better than the laboratory tested R-value in most climates

7.2.4 More Isn't Always That Much Better

There is a point of diminishing returns in the pursuit of higher R-value wall systems. When comparing two R-values that differ by 10, there is a very significant impact on energy performance if both values are relatively low (e.g., R-9 and R-19). When comparing two R-values that are relatively high (e.g., R-33 and R-43), a difference of 10 has much less significance. An R-9 wall allows more than twice as much heat to flow through each hour than does an R-19 wall. An R-33 wall, by contrast, allows less than a third more heat to flow through compared to an R-43 wall. Add to this the previous points that most "R-19" stud walls are really only at R-11 when assessed as assemblies, and that a straw bale wall, due to the thermal lag, actually significantly outperforms its rated R-value, then the long-running debate about whether the true R-value of a straw bale wall is around R-35 or R-45 or R-55 becomes essentially pointless.

7.2.5 Straw Bales Aren't Bricks

Another of the issues associated with modeling the R-value of straw bales or straw bale wall systems is that straw bales are not homogenous. When straw is baled there are pockets of very tight straw and pockets where it's loose. Straws in one portion of the bale will appear to have fairly uniform orientation along a particular axis, whereas in other portions of the bale the straws might be oriented along some other axis or not uniformly oriented at all.

All of this applies even in the industrialized countries, where bales are produced by powerful, efficient machines to relatively precise standards. In many parts of the world, the method of production and the quality of straw bales vary greatly by every measure, from region to region and often within any one batch of bales.

The R-value of plastered straw bale walls has been carefully measured, and, after dividing by the wall thickness, is often described as "1.45 per inch" or some similar number of R per unit thickness. This is misleading in that both the bale assembly (as described above) and the plastered surfaces make for a very non-uniform package. Most plasters, being good thermal conductors, wouldn't by themselves show such a high "R per inch" value; likewise, the bales are relatively porous to air movement (convection) and so by themselves do not perform so well. But the *assembly* of materials works very well to inhibit heat flow by conduction, convection, and radiation. As with structural functioning, the sum of the parts is far less than the value of the whole.

7.3 What About Straw Bale Ceilings, Arches, and Floors?

If a plastered straw bale wall provides good thermal performance, then why not use the same sort of thing for the floor and roof? Many have now tried, and it's worth reporting on the unpromising results, preceded by a few words of relevant comment.

1) The averaged R-value of a plastered straw bale wall assembly is generally accepted to be at or near the value established at Oak Ridge National Labs – 1.45 per inch. Emphasis must be given to the qualifier *averaged,* because the number refers to a stacked assembly of bales with a relatively impermeable plaster coating worked into each side. Take away the plaster, and you are talking about something else entirely – with a considerably lower effective R-value. As discussed, a straw bale is far from homogenous, and heat-laden air can and will move through it at varying rates. The same is even more true for a layer of stacked bales, with their gaps and relatively less dense seams between individual bales. The implication here, as for walls, is that a vertical or horizontal layer of straw bales will not function well as an insulator if not thoroughly coated on both sides with some kind of plaster. Simply covering the ceiling or roof with straw may be better than no insulation at all, but carries the dangers described below.

2) Straw can't insulate, even with plaster, if it's not there. If the assembly leaves straw trapped below grade with no chance of drying, and it gets wet, it will decay and become black goo. Field investigations of straw bale floors[3] revealed that they all experienced decay to one degree or another – usually severe – without exception.

Many straw bale-insulated slab floors have been proposed and tried, typically involving a layer of gravel or concrete, covered by a layer of bales, covered by a finish floor slab of concrete or earth. Sometimes the bales are set a few inches apart to admit "structural ribs" of concrete between the upper and lower slabs, which both defeats the thermal efficiency of the assembly by creating thermal bridges, and anticipates the eventual failure of the bales due to moisture decay. When a number of such floors between one and ten years old were investigated, virtually all showed bales in fairly advanced states of decay. The same phenomenon has now been observed even with vertical bale walls that had been effectively entombed by too much concrete gunite plaster – the result was a robust structure with a virtual guarantee of extreme (and hidden) moisture degradation.

3) If the straw, whether baled or not, is unprotected by plaster it is far more susceptible to ignition by fire; it might not only burn but provide fuel that turns a mere fire into a conflagration. Or, as has more often been the case, the straw bales may burn and char a bit on the outside, then smolder for days. Usually the solution is to douse the smoldering area with water, thus exchanging a fire problem for a water problem.

4) Bales are relatively heavy. Even just the weight of plastered straw bales walls in a single-story residence can be enough to double the seismic demands on the lateral bracing system when compared with wood-framed buildings. If the structure is in a highly seismic area, then stabilizing the extra weight of bales overhead can be problematic – the heavy ceiling must support the extra weight, including vertical seismic loads, and the building system must be able to handle the considerable additional racking load imposed by the bale layer.

Given all of these conditions, it usually doesn't make a lot of sense to use bales anywhere in the building but the walls. These are the possible exceptions:

• Bale-insulated ceilings, especially in non-seismic areas, can be effective and inexpensive if they are plastered, if only minimally, so as to block convective air flow and not be a fire hazard.

• Bale-insulated floors – framed floors with bales set between joists – *might* be effective if plastered on exposed surfaces (for the same reason as ceilings). However, rising damp from the ground surface below can condense and cause moisture problems, so a bale-insulated floor must be either well-ventilated or regularly inspected or both.

• There have been notable successes with arched or vaulted structures with plaster thoroughly worked into inside and outside surfaces, and with extra precaution taken against moisture intrusion. However, there have also been plenty of failures, and, given the propensity of all plasters to crack with time, and the attendant difficulties with keeping water from leaking in through those cracks, the long-term durability of arches and vaults remains in question.

7.4 Conclusion

Tests consistently show that R-values for insulation materials used in "standard" walls are generally much higher than the R-value for the wall as an assembly of disparate materials. The same is simply not true for a tested, plastered straw bale wall assembly, in which structure, insulation, and finish are all the same package – and a generally unleaky one at that.

All tests of straw bale wall systems prior to the Oak Ridge test in 1998 had potentially significant shortcomings and are not considered particularly reliable. The test of 1998 had no identified deficiencies and is considered by most to be the definitive measure of the thermal resistance of straw bale walls. Those researchers determined the net R-value to be R-27.5 (or averaged R-1.45/inch), or R-33 for three-string (23") bale wall systems. Shaving a bit off the top just to be conservative, the California Energy Commision officially regards a plastered straw bale wall to have an R-value of 30.

A final note is a reiteration of a point made earlier: it matters little whether the final truth about the R-value of straw bales walls is R-33 or R-43 or even R-53. Above R-30, the differences in the energy performance of the overall building enclosure are minor and will usually be overshadowed by siting (solar orientation), windows, floors, doors, and ceiling/roof insulation.

7.5 How Much Does A Straw Bale Structure Save Energy and Sequester Carbon?

In the only calculation we know of to date, Kelly Lerner wrote in 2000[4]:

While carbon sequestering is a clear benefit of straw-bale construction, it pales in comparison to the potential benefits of reduced carbon dioxide emissions (due to energy efficiency) over the life of the building. Of course, these benefits only accrue in a climate which requires heating or cooling. Just some quick math and simplistic explanations (all that will fit in an email) which reflect our projects in China:

7

INSULATION

We're building new straw-bale houses which would have been new brick houses. In Heilongjiang, the new brick houses burn 5 tonnes of coal/winter. Let's say our straw-bale insulated, day-lit, passive solar model will be 75% more efficient - only use 1.25 tonnes of coal/winter - basically, families are now heating with just the fuel they need for cooking. [Editor's note: this assumption was later borne out by a survey of coal usage in the area.] That's a savings of 3.75 tonnes of coal/winter. My carbon reduction consultant tells me each tonne of coal gives off 1.3 tonnes of CO_2. Let's say (as the politicos dictate) that the effective lifetime of the house is 30 years (even though we know it will last much longer). The total, please: 3.75 tonnes of coal/winter x 1.3 tonnes of CO_2/tonne of coal x 30 years = 146 tonnes of reduced CO_2 emissions over 30 years. Of course this equation doesn't take into consideration improved air quality, higher comfort, improved health, reduced clay mining and brick manufacture, increased seismic safety, etc. etc.

ENDNOTES

1
Christian, Eisenberg, 1998

2
Carter, Jain and Hou, 1996

3
Lacinski, P, and Bergeron, M, (1998) *Serious Straw Bale* Chelsea Green Publishing Company, Brattleboro, Vermont

4
Email to strawbale listserv, describing an ongoing project that went on to win the 2005 World Habitat Award from the United Nations and the Building Social Housing Foundation in Great Britain that promotes innovative and sustainable housing solutions throughout the world.

CO2 Reductions

• *sequestration*	*3 tonnes +/-*
• *replacing bricks with straw (reduce brick firing)*	*3 tonnes*
• *reduced brick transportation*	*1 tonne*
• *reduced emissions*	*146 tonnes*
Total	*153 tonnes reduction per house*

*I don't feel sorry for myself
because I can't see.
I feel sorry for most people
because they can't hear.*

— Ray Charles

ACOUSTICS

with René Dalmeijer

8.1 Introduction

Anyone who has ever worked with straw bales knows firsthand how well they absorb sound – the simple act of trying to talk or shout with someone on the opposite side of a wall is amazingly difficult. Likewise, most everyone who has been in a straw bale building has had the sensation that interior sounds somehow seem louder; those sounds become more distinct for not being drowned out by outside background noise. Straw bale walls work very well as acoustic insulators, and there are definite reasons why.

Conventional structures depend on high mass for effective sound isolation, especially in the low frequency range. It's easy to keep out the sound of singing birds, but very difficult to impede the deep mooing of the cow in the apartment next door. But there is another way of achieving good sound isolation, which depends on a damped cavity sandwiched by two not-so-stiff membranes with sufficient mass.

8.2 Review of Tests

As recent test results clearly illustrate, a straw bale wall, especially with earth plasters, is an excellent example of this alternative way of achieving good sound isolation. A number of tests have been conducted to date, though not all are available in English:

1) In 1995 at Swarthmore College, Pennsylvania, Mas and Everbach measured the sound transmission losses (T) of a 20-inch-thick stuccoed wall of wheat and rye-grass straw bales. They reported an A-weighted Sound Transmission Class (STC) for the assembly of 59.8 dB. (*A-weighted* means the impedance is corrected to approximate human hearing sensitivity, which varies depending on frequency.) They did not elaborate on the test protocol or wall construction details such as stucco mix or thickness.

2) In 1999 in Sydney, Australia, John Glassford reported via email on some informal tests as follows:

We have just completed testing the acoustical qualities of three sound recording studios in an inner Sydney office/residential area that we built two years ago. The studio is located on the third floor of a 6-storey office block. There are five straw bale walls 450 mm (18 inches) thick which were sheeted in 10mm Gyprock on a 2x4 timber studwall. Each room has a double cavity door 450 mm deep, no windows, and a wall-mounted air conditioner.

The University of Technology Sydney kindly lent me the equipment to measure the sound levels. The tests were carried out by myself with a couple of witnesses, no cheating was allowed. The instrument was a Radio Shack Sound Level Monitor made in China under a Canadian license, does that make it Canadian? I used two weightings in the tests:

Weighting A: curve frequency of 500-10,000 Hz range
Weighting C: curve frequency of 200-18,000 Hz range

The C frequency is for musical instruments and the A is for humans. The three studios were in full operation, and three very loud bands began using the studios during the time of the recordings:

Inside Studio 2
- *background noise level*   *A 55 db with no bands playing*
- *background noise level*   *A 61 db with just air conditioning*
- *background noise level*   *C 54 db with no bands playing*
- *background noise level*   *C 61 db with just air conditioning*

Outside Studio 2
- *background noise level*   *A 58-62 db with no bands playing*
- *background noise level*   *C 63-68 db with no bands playing*

Inside Studio 2

- one very loud band playing C 114-117 db

Outside Studio 2

- three very loud bands playing A 60-62 db
- meter held 12" from walls C 71 db
- meter held ten feet from walls C 68 db

Outside Studio 3

- three very loud bands playing A 66 db
- meter under the air conditioner C 75-78 db

There was sound travel coming from the air conditioner in Studio 3 to all the other studios.

Outside street noise levels A 68-71 db
C 68-70 db

3) In 2003 Jasper van der Linden, a building engineering student at the Eindhoven (Holland) Technical University, tested the transmission loss (T) of an earth-plastered straw bale wall according to ISO 140-3 (comparable to ASTM E90 protocols). With the assistance of straw bale builders Rob Kaptein and René Dalmeijer, he found that a reasonably well-built straw bale wall without acoustic defects (like protruding post-and-beam members, or excessive windows) will have an STC in the region of 53dB and upwards (55dB with A weighting). The 2dBA increase in weighted performance (compared to the test) is mainly because a very thin (worst case) plaster thickness was applied to the test sample; normally, earth plaster finishes would be thicker. The test assembly consisted of two acoustically-separated chambers, with the test sample placed in an aperture between the chambers. The size of the aperture, as per ISO 140-3, was 1.88m² [20 ft²]. The tested straw bale wall section had the following configuration.

- Two-string (460 mm [18 inch] wide) building-quality bales laid flat, density of 120 to 130 kg/m³ [7.5 to 8.1 lb/ft³]
- Earth + straw plaster 25 mm [I inch] and 35 mm [1.4 inch] thick (intentionally asymmetrical cover)
- No reinforcing plaster netting or mesh, nor any form of pinning

8.2A
CONSTRUCTING
EARTH-PLASTERED
ACOUSTIC TEST
SAMPLES AT EINDHOVEN
UNIVERSITY

photos courtesy of René Dalmeijer

The chosen sample structure was to be as representative as possible of a normal earth-plastered straw bale wall as constructed by the experienced straw bale builder Rob Kaptein of RAMstrobouw. Rob was also responsible for manufacturing the test sample. The graph and table shown in 8.2B summarize the test result.

The 53dBA STC might seem low, but in fact it is very good – for example, conventional wall systems that include a brick cavity wall with much higher mass have a lower performance. (See the end of this chapter for comparative values of wall assemblies and the effects of various sound levels on human hearing.) Specifically interesting to note is the 2-3dB better performance at very low frequencies of the straw bale test sample when compared to brick wall systems. Nearly all wall systems, including wood stud walls, are able to sufficiently subdue high- and mid-frequency sound but not low-frequency sound. In practice, better impedance at low frequencies is typically only achieved with added mass, which is worthwhile in urban areas because it dampens the ever-present background noise. A plastered straw bale wall achieves this without need for additional mass or materials.

8.3 Recipe for Straw Bale Wall Acoustic Isolation

Besides simply adding mass, low stiffness layers with sufficient mass and acoustic de-coupling are very important for acoustic sound isolation. The relatively low stiffness of a straw bale wall with earth plasters is ideal. The fact that the cavity between the two plaster shells is filled with straw provides excellent acoustic damping.

To achieve a truly sound-isolated space, it is essential to fill all cavities and voids (such as course and head joints between bales, and spaces between bales and framing) with a light straw clay or blown insulation. It is also essential to avoid any direct mechanical connection between the inner and outer plaster shells, as such a connection will seriously degrade sound-damping performance. Contrary to what you might expect, loosely packed bales will perform better than very tightly packed bales. Extra thick (>35mm) [1.5 inches] earth plaster specifically improves low-frequency performance. Cement and lime plasters perform almost as well, but earth plaster with lots of straw is the best due to its lower modulus of elasticity

8.2B
EARTH-PLASTERED ACOUSTIC TEST
RESULTS AT EINDHOVEN UNIVERSITY

Expressing the STC in one number (e.g., 53dBA) is a simplification. In actual fact, giving the performance at each of various frequencies is much more meaningful. Generally this is done either at one octave intervals or at one-third octave intervals (1/3 oct), the latter giving even more detailed information. The table at right shows both measurements (not A-weighted). The dip at around 250Hz is believed to be due to the transition between the mass and damped cavity modes of operation of the test sample, something very much like what was seen in some, but not all, other straw bale tests.

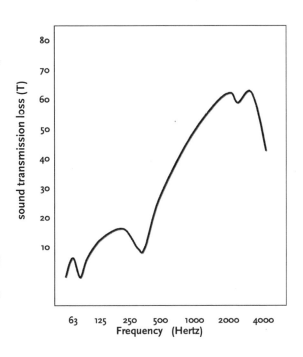

Freq.	R 1/3 oct.	R 1 octave
Hz.	dB	dB
50	29.6	
63	33.5	30.9
80	30.5	
100	34.7	
125	37.4	36.4
160	37.8	
200	38.1	
250	34.8	36.1
315	36.1	
400	43	
500	47.8	46.2
630	52.4	
800	56.8	
1000	59.7	59.1
1250	62.9	
1600	66.4	
2000	68.2	67
2500	66.6	
3150	68	
4000	60.9	59.2
5000	55.8	

(stiffness) and its less reflective surface. Applying significantly asymmetrical plaster thicknesses helps to avoid coincident reverberation of the inner and outer plaster layers. The thicker plaster layer should be on the sound source side of the wall. Pay a lot of attention to all openings and edge details; these are the weak points. An air leak of only one square millimeter will seriously degrade performance. Door openings and windows are literally acoustic holes in the wall; these need special detailing and attention to even remotely approach the acoustical performance of the surrounding walls. Even double doors generally show poor performance compared to the wall. The gaskets and seals in the doors should be double or even triple, but even then there is the problem that over time the seals will degrade and leaks will occur. If you need extreme sound isolation, the type of door you would want is more like a steel watertight door in a ship with multiple closing bolts and tightening clamps.

To sum up, a straw bale wall is an excellent sound barrier, so the wall is not the acoustical problem; the connections between the wall and all other elements incorporated into or surrounding it are. In other words, it is the same issue as with structural, thermal, fire, and moisture performance: details and connections matter as much or more than the wall assembly.

8.4 Room Acoustics

Here are some simple rules of thumb depending on the type of acoustics you want, from very lively to very well damped. Soft acoustic instruments require a "live" (reflective) room. Loud amplified sound needs a "dead" (absorbtive) room. The single most important parameter is the reverberation time and level. The harder the surfaces, the livelier the sound. A bathroom is lively; hence your drive to sing even if you can't. The opposite is standing on top of a snow-covered hilltop – virtually no sound reflects back to your voice. The bigger and harder the room, the longer the reverberation time: think of the sound in a cathedral. Next to consider are the relative dimensions: an oblong box (like Concertgebouw Amsterdam) approaches the ideal. Preferably the relative dimensions are approximately 2 to 3 to 5; this ratio will avoid the formation of dominant harmonic resonance and standing waves. The exact ratios needed for a given acoustical requirement depend on the size and acoustic reflectivity. Some prefer rooms without parallel surfaces, which completely avoid resonance (standing waves). If you finish a room with earth plaster on straw bale walls, with wooden flooring and a well-pitched ceiling, you will have quite acceptable acoustics for musical performances. If it's too "live", you can always add some damping afterwards with soft furnishings or hanging curtains. A bigger audience also helps.

Good acoustic isolation is clearly one of straw bale construction's merits. It should be seriously considered for purposes where sound isolation is of importance. It would be hard to find a more affordable option for sound studios, quiet houses in noisy neighborhoods, or noisy workshops in residential surroundings.

8.5 Sound Transmission Class Examples

STC	What can be heard
25	Normal speech can be understood quite easily and distinctly through wall
30	Loud speech can be understood fairly well, normal speech heard but not understood
35	Loud speech audible but not intelligible
40	Onset of "privacy"
42	Loud speech audible as a murmur

STC	
45	Loud speech not audible; 90% of statistical population not annoyed.
50	Very loud sounds such as musical instruments or a stereo can be faintly heard; 99% of population not annoyed.
60+	Superior soundproofing; most sounds inaudible

STC	Partition type
33	Single layer of $\frac{1}{2}''$ drywall on each side, wood studs, no insulation (typical interior wall)
45	Double layer of $\frac{1}{2}''$ drywall on each side, wood studs, batt insulation in wall
46	Single layer of $\frac{1}{2}''$ drywall, glued to 6″ lightweight concrete block wall, painted both sides
48	8" fully grouted concrete block
54	Single layer of $\frac{1}{2}''$ drywall, glued to 8″ dense concrete block wall, painted both sides
55	Double layer of $\frac{1}{2}''$ drywall on each side, on staggered wood stud wall, batt insulation in wall
55 +/-	**Straw bale wall with one inch +/- of plaster both sides**
59	Double layer of $\frac{1}{2}''$ drywall on each side, on wood stud wall, resilient channels on one side, batt insulation
63	Double layer of $\frac{1}{2}''$ drywall on each side, on double wood/metal stud walls (spaced 1" apart), double batt insulation
72	8″ concrete block wall, painted, with $\frac{1}{2}''$ drywall on independent steel stud walls, each side, insulation in cavities

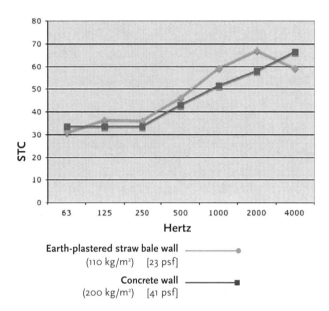

Earth-plastered straw bale wall
(110 kg/m²) [23 psf]

Concrete wall
(200 kg/m²) [41 psf]

8.5A
COMPARISON OF PLASTERED STRAW BALE
WALL TO **100 MM [4 INCH]** CONCRETE

"You get out of this House!"
said the fish in the pot.
"But I like to be here. Oh I like it a lot!"
said the Cat in the Hat
to the fish in the pot.

– Dr. Seuss, *The Cat in the Hat*

INSECTS AND OTHER UNINVITED GUESTS

9.1 Introduction

People naturally wonder how inviting and accommodating straw bale buildings are to the various critters that like to come share our warm, protected spaces. As it turns out, not very. A miscellany of field reports over the years suggests that a plastered straw bale wall is substantially less appealing as food or habitat than is an open pile of bales or a wood studwall.

Despite the lack of formal or controlled experiments, a modest wealth of experience has emerged, largely through very active Internet-based straw bale discussion groups. Given the thousands of straw bale buildings now in existence around the world, and the ability and willingness of builders and owners to pass along problem reports, the following somewhat comprehensive list is remarkably short. In other words, we haven't heard many complaints about vermin, but here we pass along several anecdotes representative of those few complaints.

9.2 Insects

In general, insect problems in bales seem to be linked to moist bales, especially those that were wetted in the field, and to construction detailing that fails to separate the plaster from the ground. Also, "trash" straw – bales from the bottom layer of a stack – will be more likely to harbor bugs, as will straw with a high grain content (food to insects and mice). In most cases, the insect problems seem to disappear after one hatching and the subsequent drying out of the bale wall.

9

In *The Last Straw,* entomologist Linda Wiener reported[1]

> *The typical case involves people who have moved into a new straw bale house who start finding thousands of small insects coating walls, floors, countertops, and other surfaces … I have identified a species of book louse [psocids], and several different species of beetles [Lathridiidae and Cryptophagidae]. I've also found some stem-boring wasps which live inside the stem of growing plants. Aside from the wasp, these insects are small, typically less than 3 millimeters [⅛ inch], and all feed on fungi and molds. Since these fungi and molds grow only on damp straw, I'm rather certain that the straw bales in structures that have insect problems all became wet either in the fields or at the construction sites. If the bales are wet when sealed into the walls, the fungi will prosper (at least for a while) and the insects will multiply. Since these insects are so tiny, they can get through small cracks and crevices, electrical outlets, and any other openings into the structure … the situation [can be] truly nightmarish for a while, but then the problem is self-limiting.*

What Dr. Wiener predicts in theory is confirmed by field experience – in North America, in Israel, in Australia, all over – as described in the following culled anecdotes. We would add to her list of potential invaders an unidentified species of a small moth (according to an unidentified report from North America) and a microscopic itch mite, noteworthy for its painful bite (according to a report from Israel in the same referenced journal.) In both cases, the problem went away as the walls dried out.

Summarizing her knowledge of insect problems, Catherine Wanek reported[2]

> *It's probably no surprise to anyone, but we have concluded that a bug problem is really a moisture problem. Solve the moisture issue, and the bugs – beetles, mites, whatever – don't have suitable habitat.*

> *One story: Some friends of friends in our region – southwest New Mexico at about 6,000 feet [1830 M] in altitude – reported getting thousands of annoying (not biting) bugs coming from their straw bale walls. They had first appeared in spring (April), went away during the winter, then came back the next spring. When we went to check it out, we smelled mold in one of the bedrooms on the north side, where the worst problem was.*

While their stem-wall was minimal, we couldn't find any cracks in the stucco, or other definitive explanations for moisture, until Pete asked "Of course your roof is vented, right?" Wrong. While these were partly owner/builders, they HAD worked with a contractor who had done foundation and roof. This "professional" had not vented their metal roof.

The homeowners had exacerbated the problem by keeping dozens (more than a hundred) house plants, in the theory that they brought oxygen and would help clean up their indoor air. Of course the moisture they expired made its way up to the roof, where it condensed and then ran down onto the top of the bales and soaked in.... The north side seemed to be the worst, which is consistent with the idea that sun on the south side helped dry out the walls. Also, there are more windows on the south, hence fewer bales. In the winter, the cold conditions did not provide a nurturing environment, but with the advent of spring, the tiny straw bugs were fruitful and multiplied.

Fortunately we could see a fairly easy way for them to add soffits and venting to their roof, and recommended that, which they did. About a year later (this spring) they called back with questions about potential moisture in the walls coming up from the ground. Pete went over with the moisture meter, and found the walls were within accepted tolerances. He reported that the family no longer had bugs coming from the walls, and while there was visible evidence of moisture in the walls – a small amount of discolored wall inside and out on the north side – they appeared to have dried out.

9.2.1 Termites

Although we know of no reports of termite damage elsewhere, straw bale construction is vulnerable in the North American Sonoran desert to the termite *Gnathamitermes perplexus*. *Gnathamitermes* is present throughout the American desert southwest wherever creosote bush is found, as well as the lower Gulf coast of Texas and the coast of California south of Los Angeles. Apparently, *Gnathamitermes* only likes earth-plastered structures, so cement-based plasters may be an advantage in their habitat. Bill Steen reported[3]

The lower Sonoran desert has more termites than almost anywhere in the world. We have had extensive experience with termites with the [straw bale] buildings in Tucson and Mexico over the years, and I'm not sure we have all the answers, but here are some ideas.

First of all, the biggest cause for termites in earth plasters is taking the plaster to the ground, or having the plaster in contact with something that is directly in contact with the ground. It will cause problems with termites, ants, and all other types of soil-in-habiting creatures including things like scorpions. With that in mind, I can say that wherever we have made a clean separation between the plaster and the ground we have not had problems . . . For all the walls we have torn apart and inspections done we have never found them eating the straw in the bales. But they do love straw encased in mud – it provides more moisture, which they love.

Matts Myhrmann reported[4]

In the way of background information, my interest in the question of termites and straw bale construction is a narrow one. It is based on three related things.

The first is the fact (arguable?) that virtually all termites commonly found in North America are specifically wood eaters and need the protection of the wood as they utilize the cellulose it provides. Experience to date with this type of termite suggests that, when confronted with straw in a bale that could meet their need for cellulose but does not simultaneously provide the sort of protection they require, they ignore the straw and look elsewhere for wood to attack.

The second is my commitment to using earthen plasters whenever possible.

The third is the realization (through direct experience and conversation with Bill and Athena Steen) that one termite common in Southern Arizona poses problems in regard to the use of earthen plasters. The termite is apparently Gnathamitermes perplexus, *although the closely related* G. tubiformans *probably poses the same problem. Although this termite appears not to do significant damage to an unplastered bale sitting on the ground, the application of mud plaster to a bale creates a "zone of mixing", where the straws on the surface of the bale become surrounded by earth. If, as is now commonly done, chopped straw is incorporated into the earth plaster during mixing, the complete, applied layer of plaster constitutes a zone of mixing. For G. perplexus, a very attractive situation has been created, where it can eat the straw while protected by the earthen plaster. In the natural environment, it must expend energy creating earthen tubes around, or earthen shields over, the dried grass stems and small twigs that it normally eats.*

When this termite eats chopped straw that has been added to the plaster, the plaster is weakened and is often disfigured by tubes or shields that are constructed on the outer, visible surface of the plaster. Perhaps of greater significance, however, is the likelihood that when the termites eat the straw in the zone of mixing created by pushing the first layer of earth plaster into the bale, the physical bond between the plaster and the bale is seriously compromised. Any assumptions about the positive effect of this bond on the structural performance of the wall are thrown into question. The diminished attachment of the plaster to the bale wall also has implications for the functional longevity of the plaster layer itself, whether or not it is contributing significantly to the structural performance of the complete wall system.

Catherine Wanek reported[5]

Andre de Bouter reported that during their six-month trip to India, in conversations with farmers, they learned that termites would infest wet straw in the field, but would not eat dry straw. Andre and Coralie designed their SB foundation detailing to thwart termites, anyway.

To repeat and summarize, insect infestations are generally the result of building with bad (i.e., previously-wetted) bales, of allowing moisture to collect in the straw wall core, and/or of running plaster to the ground – which is bad practice with *any* type of construction. Here, an ounce of prevention is worth twenty pounds of cure, as there is very little that can be done to eliminate an infestation other than to dry out the wall – not always easy to do – and keep it dry. Those who have tried chemical methods, both conventional and "natural", to eliminate pests have quickly found that there is just no effective way to get liquid or powdered insecticides into the wall where the insects live and breed. Happily, it appears that if there is an infestation, it will go away when the moisture supporting it does.

9.3 Other Uninvited Guests

A pile of bales, in the field or in a barn, will quickly become habitat to all manner of creatures. Innumerable spiders and insects, as well as rats and mice, fit easily into the crevices between bales where they make their homes, and are often followed by snakes, skunks, possums, raccoons, and other creatures further up the food chain. Birds and squirrels will nest if they can, and cows and goats will stop to graze and poke around for seed heads if given the chance. In other words, leave a pile of bales somewhere and you will eventually have, as time goes by, a small ecosystem of increasing complexity.

By stark contrast, a stacked wall of bales sealed in plaster has almost none of the same allure. We know of no instances of mice or larger creatures infesting a finished bale wall, though there have been cases in which mice inhabited pockets within unfinished bales. They simply can't move around easily, and the straw is too tough for them to bother chewing with so little carbohydrate benefit. (They *will* chew through most rigid insulations, given the chance, and make a home in structural insulated panels and similar types of construction. And, as is well known, mice and rats travel at will throughout a wood-framed house, having been provided with a convenient network of interconnected passageways.)

The most famous, and presumably intrusive, infestation problem happened to a builder in Arizona many years ago. He stacked the bale walls and left them unplastered for a few months to settle, i.e., self-compress. He didn't notice the hole in the fence between his property and the neighbor's field, where cows were grazing. Nature took its course, and the cows wandered over and ate a fair portion of his walls. Thankfully, there were no reports of mass panic or loss of life.

9.4 Summary

Use dry bales, keep them dry, plaster them as soon as possible, and keep the plaster away from the ground. The cows and other creatures will stay away. Do not panic.

ENDNOTES

1
The Last Straw issue #31, Fall, 2000, p. 17

2
excerpted from email communications to the author and others 7/20/04

3
excerpted from email communication to Carolyn Roberts (copied to GSBN listserv) 11/2002

4
excerpted from email communication to the author and others 1/2002

5
excerpted from email communications to the author and others 1/21/01

God is in the details.
— Anonymous

The Devil is in the details.
— Anonymous

*The mistakes are all out there,
just waiting to be made.*
— Chessmaster
Savielly Grigorievitch Tartakower

DETAILS AND DESIGN

10.1 Introduction to the Design Checklist

You may have turned directly to this section in the expectation of seeing dozens of pictures showing you exactly how to put together your straw bale building. You will note that they are not here, or at least not many.

This is in part due to the laziness of the authors, yes, but much more importantly it is because we *can't* tell you how to design and detail your straw bale building, any more than we can tell you how to dress, eat, speak, or dance for joy; we are definitely pro-choice. Successful building design – and the details that turn good design to reality – require knowledge, experience, and attention to a great many factors that in total will be unique for each project. In the preceding chapters we presented practical information (and some details) about plastered straw bale structures and how they behave in various conditions. Using all that, you can and must think through for yourself both the overall design, and each annoying-but-crucial detail of your particular project. We can't do that for you, but, with an understanding of the basic principles and building truths conveyed in these chapters, you can certainly do it for yourself.

In the pages that follow we have added a few basic rules that have emerged in the twenty years of the straw bale revival, things you should always or never do. We can also point you, here, to detail books published elsewhere. In particular, the California Straw Building Association (CASBA) is at work on a detail book as this one goes to print; you can access CASBA's work via their website, www. strawbuilding.org. Everything, however, requires your own intelligent scrutiny, and your recognition of the fact that straw bale construction is still very much a developing technology; things change, and they will keep changing.

The following list of questions, interspersed with the rules, will help you to think through your details, choice of plaster and other materials, and architectural detailing.

10.2 Seismicity

If you are in an area of low seismic risk, jump and click your heels, because your life (as a builder, anyway) is thus a lot easier. If you don't know, ask a local engineer, building official, architect, or geologist. If you are in an area of medium-to-high risk, make a sad face and then get over it, or move.

There are two ways to think about earthquakes in designing and building. First, the obvious one: a really big earthquake can collapse buildings large and small, and you don't want your building to collapse in The Big One. That means everything has to be tied together really well, and be consciously and intelligently designed to yield, crush, or rattle a bit in a way of your choosing. Read chapter 4, *Structure*, again, keeping in mind the caveat that although seismic engineering (and our understanding of straw bale structures) has evolved considerably, it is still imperfect and incomplete. Err on the conservative side, because this is about protecting life.

The other, parallel way to think about earthquakes is to keep in mind that where Big Ones occur (typically every one to three hundred years), lots of little and medium ones also occur, and far more frequently. The worst visible damage they do is crack an occasional window, shake books off of shelves, and give everyone something to talk about for a few days. Most of those earthquakes are so small that you won't feel them – but your building will. Flashing, nails, glue, and sealants all will. The more brittle anything is, the more likely it is to be cracked or broken by a shaker. Keep that in mind as you design anything crucial to moisture control (especially windows), because a bad detail may work loose over time, admit water, and let rot get started within the wall.

Basic guidelines for buildings in seismically active areas: Besides the obvious need to have a carefully designed system of walls or braces to hold the entire structure up (see chapter 4, *Structure*), fasten other items – such as kitchen cabinets and anything big enough and/or high enough overhead to hurt you if it falls – very securely to something solid and firm. See also part 10.6 about structure in general.

10.3 Building Codes

Here in California, we have very detailed and exacting codes that are often enforced with breathtaking zeal and ignorance. In other places, there are, technically, building codes in force, but no one will be watching what you do. In many places, you're entirely on your own. (See chapter 11, *Codes and Standards*.)

If you're in a place with enforced codes or regulations, get to know them, at least roughly, as they will sometimes be very clear about how you detail things, and can also be a very useful resource. Even better, get to know your local building official, ask for his or her advice at the outset of your project, and make him or her your ally, not adversary. Buy her a copy of this book! What could be more fantastic? One way or another, allow for some extra time to figure out details for yourself, and to discuss design criteria with the building official. This usually takes more time than people expect, and if the building official is difficult, a *lot* more time, so be prepared and patient.

10.4 Climate

This is the big one, really, because by "climate" we mostly mean moisture risk. This can be broken down into many specific questions you should answer in order to detail your building well:

10.4a Exterior Moisture Exposure

1. What is your local climate? What is the microclimate at your site? The micro-micro climate at any particular wall? In most areas rainstorms come from some predominant direction, but nearby hills and buildings will affect the strength and direction of wind at your site; you had better know which wall will get the worst of the rain and weather.

2. Is the wet season long or short? Do you experience severe storms with blowing rain or hail? Does the sun usually come out right away and start drying things out? In a wet place like Oregon or Denmark, where it can rain mildly for months and there will be virtually no external drying of walls, all parts of the building should aggressively shed water. In a desert location like Arizona, where the rain comes in short, intense, and windy storms but is followed by sunny weather (drying time), the demands on water management systems are less severe.

3. How tall are your walls? The taller the wall, the greater must be the roof overhang to protect it. If the weather includes heavy rain with strong winds, such as along seacoasts, an overhang must be huge – essentially, a veranda all around – or a rainscreen must be built over the bale wall. (See figure 10.B)

10.4b Interior Climate (Moisture Exposure)

1. How much cooking will be done in the building, and is the cooking area adequately ventilated? Are there excessive moisture loads from bathing facilities (shower or laundry rooms), and are those rooms adequately ventilated? If you will not be ventilating moisture from the interior, either by opening a window or by mechanical fans, then the vapor-laden air will try very, very hard to escape through any crack it can find in the interior plaster, rush into the straw bale wall core, condense, and very likely start becoming a problem. If you have high interior moisture loads, seal the interior walls very well, and ventilate!

2. Is the building air conditioned during the summer? Are any rooms in the building kept especially cold? Cooling or refrigeration will dry out the air, tending to "pull" moister air in from the outside. Again, seal all the joints and cracks against air passage, but in this case on the outside. Control air flow!

3. What is the expected cleaning schedule? Will the floor be wet-mopped? Are there potential sources of flooding, such as water heaters or second-story plumbing fixtures, whose failure would dump a lot of water into the house? Floors get wet. Allow for it, and give the base of walls a means of drying out quickly if wetted.

10.4c Basic Guidelines for Moisture Control

• **Worry over the horizontal exposed surfaces;** in any kind of construction, these are the hardest to seal against water entry. This applies not only to windowsills, but to surfaces above the bale wall such as – if you are so foolish as to design these features in – bathroom floors or parapet roofs.

Unless you like mold and lawsuits, we urge you to avoid parapet roofs and other zero-overhang styles such as "Santa Fe" entirely. We know that limits your architectural options, but wouldn't you rather not have to worry about water so much?

- **Shed water away from the exterior of the building wherever you can:** overhanging roofs, overhanging windowsills, head flashing for doors and windows (see figure 5.2.1D)
- **Then allow for the fact that water will get in anyway;** give it a means to drain and dry out.
- **Caulks and sealants are very nice for filling cracks, but should never be your primary means of keeping water out,** *especially* if they are exposed to sun (i.e., ultraviolet light).

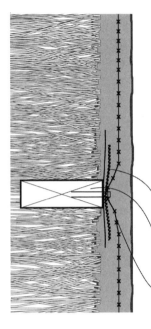

In order to protect both the wood and any metal fasteners in the wood, all wood in contact with plaster or concrete should be:

1) Non-ammonia-based pressure-treated, or
2) Any pressure-treated lumber with stainless steel staples, or
3) Untreated lumber bolted over a plastic (or other) capillary break from the foundation, and with a capillary break such as Grade D paper separating it from the plaster.

Diamond lath reinforcing over grade D paper or other vapor-permeable separation

Any and all wood members within bale wall

Mesh and staples if and as needed for structural loads

10A
Any wood framing embedded in a straw bale wall must be prepared to receive plaster, especially where there will be weather exposure.

- **Use vapor-permeable plasters** unless you have a *really* good reason not to.
- **Be very cautious about applying waterproof membranes;** all too often, they end up trapping water against the straw (or wood, or sheetrock) rather than keeping it out.
- **Apply siloxane, silane, or a topical sealant of the same class;** these are inexpensive, relatively non-toxic ways to make the plaster shed liquid water without trapping vapor, and they don't affect appearance.
- **See chapter 5, *Moisture,* and read it three or four more times.**

10.5 Use and Durability

What is the building's use? How many people will be using the building? Of what ages? Is the building public or private? In short, is high plaster durability required because of anticipated abrasion, physical abuse, or defacement? You can get a much harder and more durable earth plaster – if you know what you're doing – than most people think, but high usage areas generally call for a hard skin plaster (see chapter 3, *Plaster and Reinforcing*). Doors and windows obviously need to be sturdier when used more often, as do, especially, the joints between the frame openings and the surrounding straw.

Baseboards can be useful for protecting plaster from foot traffic and other abuse,

If a wall has particularly heavy exposure to wind-driven rain . . .

. . . then you need an extra level of protection from water infiltration.

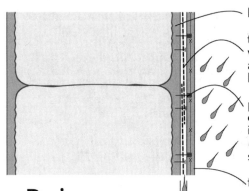

base coat of plaster on bales

two layers of overlapping vapor-permeable building paper attached with concrete nails while base plaster is stiff but not dry

plaster mesh attached with concrete nails and spacers immediately after building paper (tie to far side of wall in seismically-active areas)

finish plaster coat with siloxane coating

1. Drainscreen
relatively easy to build, but less effective than a full rainscreen

(no actual air gap between plaster layers -- shown this way for clarity)

same as above, except ---

pressure-treated vertical wood spacer boards attached to stiff plaster; the gaps between these boards provide drainage plenums, and must have protected and screened openings at the top and bottom to let water drain through

2. Rainscreen
more work to build, but very effective at protecting the straw

10B DRAINSCREENS AND RAINSCREENS

Any wall with appreciable exposure to wind-driven rain must at least have a siloxane coating, or an owner willing to replaster it on a regular basis. If the driven rain intensity is particularly heavy, use a detail like one of the above to shed the water in two layers outside the bales.

but they generally shouldn't be sealed, as that would just as likely trap water as keep it out. (The wall plaster should be sealed against air movement, as emphasized throughout this book, but a baseboard is really for protection against mechanical abrasion – not a dam to hold back a floor flood.)

10.5a Basic Guidelines for Mechanical Durability

Think about the size, speed, and hardness of the various objects and life forms that will, conceivably, be bouncing, scraping, and rocketing around your building. Protect your walls, and especially the joints – base of wall, door and window surrounds, electrical outlets and fixtures – from their abuse. You can't design against the impact of a fuel-laden 767 crashing into your wall without forty or fifty feet of reinforced concrete, but you can do a reasonable job of, say, allowing for a group of ten-year-old boys having an indoor skateboard party on a rainy day.

10.6 Structural Requirements

If this is a load-bearing structure, that is, with no structural frame to keep weight off the bale walls, then the walls, and especially plasters, must be designed to carry anticipated loads (see chapter 4, *Structure*). Think about a path by which the weight of the floors and roof above can get down to the ground through the plaster skins. What is the required compressive strength of the plaster? Have good bearing surfaces been detailed at the top and bottom of the wall? It is always a good idea to have the plaster bear on something firm at the base of the wall, whether it is a load-bearing structure or not; a standard light-gauge metal plaster stop nailed to a wooden sill plate doesn't qualify.

What are the vertical dead and live loads? The seismic and wind loads? Will the plasters be part of the lateral

At the top of the wall . . .

*. . . a **lot** of things are happening. The roof must be held down against uplift from wind (hurricane-force winds can and do lift entire roofs from houses), and the floor or roof must attach to the wall both to support and be supported by it. Forces can occur from wind or earthquake in any direction -- up and down, side-to-side, and perpendicular to the page (parallel to the wall); the connections must allow for all of that.*

The roof above should overhang the wall (see section 5.2.1) to deflect rain, and the joint with the ceiling must be sealed against air movement, both for thermal performance and to prevent moisture transport into the roof or wall.

Finally, the roof-bearing assembly (whether a let-in beam as part of a post-and-beam structure, or a true bearing assembly for the wall), should be one that can be adjusted to allow for the irregularities in the bale assembly, and be pre-tensioned as needed to stiffen the bales before plastering (see section 4.1).

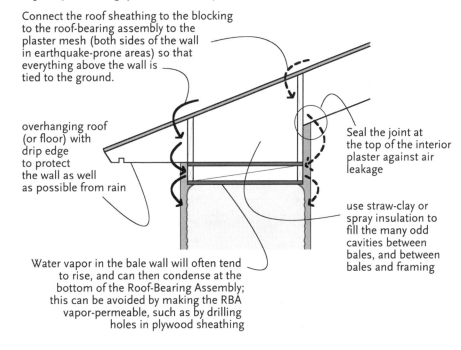

Connect the roof sheathing to the blocking to the roof-bearing assembly to the plaster mesh (both sides of the wall in earthquake-prone areas) so that everything above the wall is tied to the ground.

overhanging roof (or floor) with drip edge to protect the wall as well as possible from rain

Seal the joint at the top of the interior plaster against air leakage

use straw-clay or spray insulation to fill the many odd cavities between bales, and between bales and framing

Water vapor in the bale wall will often tend to rise, and can then condense at the bottom of the Roof-Bearing Assembly; this can be avoided by making the RBA vapor-permeable, such as by drilling holes in plywood sheathing

10C THE TOP OF THE WALL

Again, there are dozens of ways to effect the transition from the top of a straw bale wall to the floor or roof above, depending on climate, structural needs, aesthetics, available materials, and other factors. Even so, some basic concepts always hold true.

At the bottom of the wall . . .

Structural and moisture considerations predominate. There must be connections to tie the wall and building down under wind and seismic loads, joints must be sealed against water infiltration, especially rain splash and snowmelt on the outside, and the bales must have a capillary break from the foundation or floor.

1) No earthquakes? Lucky you . . .

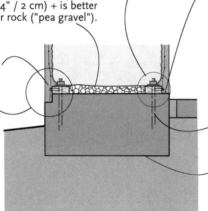

Setting the bales on a bed of gravel provides a capillary break, but the top of concrete should be still be coated with a waterproofing membrane

Round rock is better than sharp rock. Larger rock (3/4" / 2 cm) + is better than smaller rock ("pea gravel").

Mesh and staples may or may not be necessary -- see chapter 4, *Structure*

The outer plaster should sit on a shelf in the edge of the foundation below the sill plates, and have a capillary break from the concrete such as metal or asphaltic flashing.

Sill plates should either be pressure-treated, or bolted over a capillary break from the foundation. (See detail 10A)

The inner plaster must be firmly-supported, and the inner edge of the foundation should be insulated so as not to transmit cold (or heat, in summer) to the interior.

Anchor bolt and sill plate sizes and spacing will be dictated by structural requirements.

Foundation design is dictated by local codes, customs, soil and climate, but either the foundation or the interior slab must support the edge of the interior plaster.

2) Got earthquakes? See chapter 4 . . .

10D THE BOTTOM OF THE WALL

Just as at the top, there are dozens of ways to effect the transition from the bottom of a straw bale wall to the floor or foundation below, depending on climate, structural needs, aesthetics, available materials, and other factors. Again, some basic concepts always hold true.

load-resisting structure? If so, what strength and re-inforcement are required? If the plaster is part of the structural system, what field quality controls are in place to ensure good construction?

Basic guidelines for structural effectiveness and durability

At the very least, a straw bale wall must be able to remain in place and structurally intact in a high wind, and must hold onto the roof somehow so it won't blow away. That's pretty easy to do. At the other extreme, the wall must be able to re-main in place and intact under violent, simulta-neous three-dimensional seismic shaking, which is a bit more difficult. You can do it, but it takes a **lot** more care during design as well as construction. Structural engineers can be very, very handy here. Your local building of-ficial, in such cases, will very likely vigorously en-courage you to hire one.

10.7 Materials

What local materials – especially straw bales – are available, and what is their quality? At the very beginning of design, find out the size of the bales you will acquire, or make onsite, and then let the bale module (especially height) dictate the building dimensions and location of openings. This gives you a means of minimizing the very labor-intensive task of cutting partial bales to fit odd wall dimensions.

How much preparation will the materials require, and who will do it? Especially, who will specify and formulate the plaster? How much time (if any) will be needed for plaster formulation, creating samples, and testing? Is time for experimentation built into the construction schedule? With plaster design, follow the lead of the concrete industry, which requires preconstruction testing of any mix that doesn't have a history of use in the area; this is just common sense.

A few comments about windows . . .

There are more window details, both good and bad, than stars in the sky, and the ones that suit your project best will depend on available materials, aesthetics, rain exposure, and other conditions. That said, here are some basic rules --

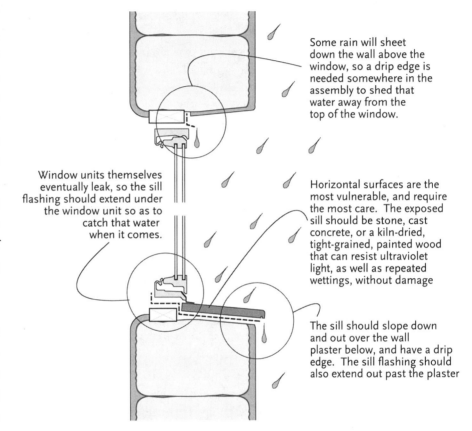

Some rain will sheet down the wall above the window, so a drip edge is needed somewhere in the assembly to shed that water away from the top of the window.

Window units themselves eventually leak, so the sill flashing should extend under the window unit so as to catch that water when it comes.

Horizontal surfaces are the most vulnerable, and require the most care. The exposed sill should be stone, cast concrete, or a kiln-dried, tight-grained, painted wood that can resist ultraviolet light, as well as repeated wettings, without damage

The sill should slope down and out over the wall plaster below, and have a drip edge. The sill flashing should also extend out past the plaster

10E Windows

"All windows fail, eventually" said a man who has investigated hundreds of moisture failures. Allow for that, and for the fact that water is smarter than you are, and will find a way into the wall eventually. Make it as hard as possible for water to get in, and as easy as possible for the water that gets in, anyway, to dry out.

David Eisenberg on window detailing   [from an email March 7, 2006]

The issue of good moisture detailing for windows is, in my view, one of the most important and most often neglected aspects of straw bale design and construction. When you talk with the people who look at moisture failures in buildings for a living, this is often cited as the most common or one of the most common areas of moisture damage and failure.

It is a more important issue to get right in bale walls because they are susceptible to moisture damage. The fact that it is so often a problem in conventional construction should make us even more vigilant and diligent. And this is important: good design and detailing should never rely on caulking as the only method of preventing moisture from getting into the walls around windows.

Here is my ideal scenario - what I would like people thinking about as they design their detailing for openings in bale structures. There should be flashing all around the opening that is, in essence "shingled" - overlapped starting from the bottom, so that any leaks are directed onto (not behind) the next piece of flashing, and eventually, out of the wall. There are a number of products available with which to do this and this is one place where I think the judicious use of synthetic materials makes a great deal of sense. This flashing should not just be applied over the surface of the plaster, but should start, ideally, behind it so that the plaster is actually part of the shingling system.

I'm a big proponent of having a sill pan (which can be made of hard or soft waterproof material - could be the same material as the rest of the flashing), which extends underneath the window and a bit beyond each side of it, is turned up at the back and sides (so that water can't run off the back or ends into the wall), preferably slopes to the outside, extends beyond the exterior finish surface, and has a drip edge.

The less weather exposed the window, the less critical this detailing is. But if the wall above the window is going to see rain, ideally we would have a piece of flashing that extends above the top of the buck and up behind the plaster. I know this is a challenge, especially if you are cutting an opening into the wall after plastering. But if the top of the buck had even a small strip of wood nailed to the top and set back so that it was behind the inside surface of the exterior plaster, the flashing could be attached to the top of this strip and extend out and down the face of the top of the buck. It should be long enough to be able to overlap over the top of the window as well as the top of the side flashing. Then, moisture that got to the inside face of the stucco above the window, and moisture that leaked behind the trim at the top of the window would not be able to end up inside the wall or sitting on top of the window buck or the top of the window.

It is important to note that caulking, even the best caulking, is only going to reliably last a few years. If it is all that you are depending on to keep moisture out, and it is hidden by trim or in places you rarely or ever inspect and maintain, you have designed in a problem rather than designing it out. It's much easier to think these things through before you build and if it's too hard to visualize this, build a mock-up, a model, of what you're thinking about building and work out the details at full scale where you can try different things and even test them . . .

When I was building, I used to try to think like water—how could I get in and how could I get out. Use great care in your efforts to keep water out, and, knowing that you will not be able to achieve this completely, take as great an amount of care making sure that the water that does get in can get out. Of course I also used to think that you "only had to be smarter than water" to do this and it turns out that, like many others, I had woefully underestimated the IQ of water...and similarly overestimated my own...

10.8 Environmental Considerations

What are the environmental performance goals for this project? What is the anticipated lifespan of this building? You may have never thought about that, or simply not care, but the ecosystems from which you get your materials, water, and energy do. A building made to last two hundred years is ten times as good, from an environmental perspective, as one built to last just twenty. No one deliberately designs a poor building, but inattention to moisture, structure, and durability detailing can leave you with just that.

10.9 Labor and Construction Methods

Will you have a professional contractor run the job, or is it to be owner-built? We are entirely in favor of enabling people to build their own homes, but it would be monstrously naïve to imagine that without any construction experience you could run and complete the job without a fair number of mistakes both large and small – even the best professional builders make them on most jobs. If you will build it yourself, allow a lot of extra time, and/or hire experienced help when and where you need it. If you expect your building to perform to the current standards of the industrialized world – no leaks or settlement, no cracked glass, sticking doors, or moldy smells; safety against fire, hurricane, and earthquake; warm in winter and cool in summer – then you'd better do your homework. Building a serviceable shelter to last for five years is fairly easy; building a modern home that meets modern expectations just isn't. If you only want a simple hut in the woods, great! Go build it! But if you're building a big, luxurious straw bale house, or a police station, or a winery, or you simply want to do a good job and build something that will last, then you need more than common sense. Welcome to the very complicated world of modern construction.

Again, some special notes about plaster and plastering: Who will be mixing, applying, and curing the plaster? Are skilled plasterers available in the area? Is there someone with a plaster pump? What other sources of labor are available (work parties, family members, etc.)? If the owner will be plastering, does he/she/you have the time and ability to develop the necessary skills and complete the project? Are there large uninterrupted wall surfaces or lots of detail around many window and door openings? (Complicated details = time = cost.) Who is responsible for installing lath, mesh reinforcement, and flashing related to plasters?

10.10 Construction Scheduling

Be absolutely fanatical about protecting the straw bales from moisture of every sort, from the day they are baled until the day they are covered by a roof and plastered. What time of year do you anticipate plastering? What will the weather conditions be? Don't try to apply any type of plaster if you can't keep it above 40°F [5°C] for at least the first week. If the project is delayed for any reason and the conditions are not conducive to plastering, is there a contingency plan? These are the types of concerns that often drive people to use a post-and-beam system; the frame and roof can be installed before the bales even arrive onsite, hugely diminishing the risk of getting the bales wetted by untimely rains.

10.11 Financial Considerations

We hope this book has proven useful, but remember that straw bale construction is relatively new to most of the people who will be involved with your project, and the "right way" to do things is still very much evolving. Figure out your costs in as much detail as possible, add a little for contingency, and then double the whole thing – that's a realistic project budget. No, we are not kidding. We might prove to be *wrong* – wouldn't that be nice? – but we've seen plenty of projects cost well over twice what the owner had anticipated. This is often true of "regular" construction, and is even more so with straw bale buildings for the reasons stated. Don't kid yourself; plan for things to take longer, go wrong, get wet, cost more. Welcome again to the very complicated world of modern construction!

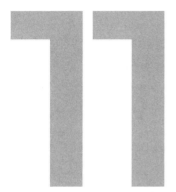

sw: *"I thought you weren't supposed to do this."*

bm: *"Well, it's more of a guideline than a rule."*

– Bill Murray to Sigourney Weaver in *Ghostbusters*

BUILDING CODES AND STANDARDS

by Martin Hammer

11.1 The Status of Straw Bale Codes and Permitting Worldwide

11.1A
THE FIRST EVER PERMITTED STRAW BALE BUILDING (1989).

Clark Sanders' meditation hall and retreat in Kortright, NY. Load-bearing, finished with gunite.

photo courtesy of Catherine Wanek

In 1989 Clark Sanders obtained the first-ever straw bale building permit in the rural town of Kortright, New York. Clark's permit, for a straw bale meditation hall and retreat facility, was issued over the building inspector's dining-room table. Clark describes the inspector's initial reaction upon hearing the building was to be constructed with straw bales: "He was shaking his head no, in disbelief, but his eyes were sparkling." That reaction, at that modest yet historic event, exemplifies but one of the many responses people have since encountered when seeking building permits for straw bale buildings.

Generally, reasonable ways have been found to resolve issues surrounding straw bale buildings and building codes. At times, however, this has required great effort by straw bale proponents, and in some instances has led to unnecessary restrictions by cautious building officials. Other factors have further hindered acceptance, as when insurance and finance companies are nervous about building methods that are not in the building codes, and have at times refused to insure or finance straw bale buildings.

Although there are many advocates of establishing and maintaining straw bale building codes, others would rather not have straw bale construction in the building codes at all. They argue that such a code is premature, and that the absence of a straw bale code leaves them unfettered in developing new methods and applications. Thus, the question lingers: What is the proper place for straw bale construction relative to building codes? The debate continues as straw bale construction passes through its adolescent stage.

What follows is a look at the worldwide status of straw bale codes and permitting. It begins with an overview of the various code-related situations a proposed straw bale building may encounter. That is followed by a broad look at how straw bale buildings are permitted in over twenty countries and regions throughout the world. Finally, the question of where straw bale codes and permitting might or should go from here is explored.

11.1.1 A General View

With respect to building codes, straw bale buildings fit into one of the following situations, listed from the least restrictive to the most:

- **No building code** (or an extant code is not enforced) When there is no building code in place for a particular location, the straw bale designer or builder is on his or her own, free to make his or her own successes or mistakes.

- **Building is exempt from building permit** Some buildings are exempt from needing a building permit because of size, use, or other exemption. This is the case in the United States for accessory buildings (typically limited to "storage sheds, playhouses and similar uses") that don't exceed 120 sq. ft. (or 10 sq.m. in many other countries) and sometimes for agricultural buildings or other non-habitable buildings. However, the model code in the United States (the *International Building Code,* or IBC) also stipulates, "Exemptions . . shall not be deemed to grant authorization for any work … in violation of the provisions of this code…" The practical reality is that without plan checks and inspections there is great freedom to build these exempt buildings as one chooses.

- **Building code with general mandate regarding straw bale construction** Some jurisdictions have adopted provisions that relate specifically to straw bale construction. For example, the State of Nevada mandated in 1995 that, "A local governing body shall permit the use of straw in the construction of a structure…" But mandates are general, providing no specifics about construction.

- **Building code with "Alternative Materials, Design, and Methods" section** If a building code is in effect, then straw bale buildings, when permitted, typically do so through the window of an *Alternative Materials, Design, and Methods* section. Here the onus is on the applicant to demonstrate equivalency with the performance requirements of the Code such as structural and fire safety, ventilation and sanitation, etc.

- **Building code plus informal "Straw Bale Guidelines"** Some jurisdictions have straw bale guidelines that have not been legally adopted but are still utilized informally. These guidelines are sometimes created for or by that jurisdiction for that purpose; other times they are a code or guidelines borrowed from another jurisdiction, from a book, or from other documents. Currently, the "California Straw Bale Code", HS18944, is actually a set of statewide legislative guidelines which have been formally adopted as code in very few jurisdictions (cities or counties), but are utilized informally in most jurisdictions within the state.

- **"Straw Bale Code"** In the United States, two states, at least ten counties, and at least six cities have officially adopted a straw bale code. Two other countries, Belarus and Germany, have also adopted straw bale codes. Permitted straw bale structures in these jurisdictions must comply with that code or would need to demonstrate equivalency through the *Alternative Materials and Methods* sections of the applicable building code.

- **Straw bale construction prohibited** On rare occasions a jurisdiction has been known to prohibit straw bale construction – not necessarily by official decree, but in practice because of the stated position of one or more building officials. Sometimes it has been temporary until sufficient evidence was presented to convince officials to change their minds.

Regardless of which of the above situations is applicable, all other codes usually apply (e.g., electrical, plumbing, and mechanical codes, with straw bale codes sometimes superseding or modifying aspects of the electrical or plumbing codes.) Water supply or septic systems also typically require permits and inspections, even where no building code is in effect.

11.1.2 A Worldwide Survey of Straw Bale Codes and Permitting

The first straw bale codes were created in the United States, where straw bale building was born in Nebraska over one hundred years ago, and where its recent rebirth took root in the Southwest in the 1980s and 1990s. Those first codes have spread in a limited manner to other parts of the U.S., and have generally not kept pace with the development of straw bale construction technology and best practice.

Outside of the United States there are only two officially-adopted straw bale codes (Belarus and Germany; see below), and both are rather limited. However, the work being done with straw bale building in those countries and throughout the rest of the world is extensive, and equals or surpasses that of the United States in quantity, variety, and innovation.

The following is a broad, though by no means comprehensive, survey of the status and nature of codes and permitting for straw bale buildings around the world. Included are countries of particular interest because of their manner or status of permitting and/or the extent of straw bale building activity there.

Australia

Straw bale buildings in Australia are approved in accordance with the Building Code of Australia. Straw bale construction can be classified as an "Alternative So-lution," which either complies with "Performance Requirements" (through test results and examples of built work, by an engineer's statement, or by an architect detailing critical aspects of the construction, such as waterproofing) or is shown to be equivalent to "deemed to satisfy" provisions of the Code, usually by draw-ings and compliance with Fire Safety, Health and Amenity, and Safe Movement and Access.

Belarus

In 1999 Belarus adopted "Compressed Straw Construction Bales (Heat Insulating) – Technical Conditions." This was the first straw bale code outside the United States. After beginning and succeeding for two years as "Experimental," the Belarusian straw bale code has achieved "Technical Condition" status, the next level of acceptance in the National Building Code for a new material or method of construction. After five to six years of more widespread and successful use, the highest code level is achieved with a "State Standard." A State Standard for Straw Bale Construction is expected to be established in 2006

11.1B
Straw bale infill
residence near Minsk,
Belarus (2002)

photo courtesy of Evgeny Shirokov

or 2007. This Standard might also become the Straw Bale Construction Standard for the former Soviet Union countries of Russia, Ukraine, Moldova, and Latvia. Evgeny Shirokov, Chairman of the Belarusian Division of the International Academy of Ecology and the leading proponent of straw bale building in Belarus, describes the current Technical Code as requirements for the quality, moisture content, and density of bales. It allows the use of straw bales for insulating infill only. (An English translation of the document is available by contacting Martin Hammer at *mfhammer@pacbell.net*.)

Canada

Straw bale buildings are having little difficulty being approved on a case-by-case basis in Canada. Each province adopts the National Building Code of Canada (NBCC) with amendments as necessary. The Provincial Code is then enforced at the local level. Straw bale buildings are approved through Section 2.5 of the Code, which allows alternate materials, appliances, systems, and equipment, and also allows Structural Equivalents. Equivalency for alternate materials must be demonstrated to the building official's satisfaction with documented "past performance, tests or evaluations," and, in the case of structural equivalents, with ". . a loading test, or studies of model analogs." Structural equivalents must be designed by "a person especially qualified in the specific methods applied," – in other words, an engineer.

Various documents, including the Arizona, New Mexico, and California straw bale tests and codes, and the numerous research reports on straw bale housing by the Canada Mortgage and Housing Corporation (CMHC) have been used to demonstrate equivalency. In practice, if an engineer stamps a straw bale building design, it is usually accepted at face value. However, approval is entirely at the local building official's discretion. Occasionally an official has denied approval, and in some instances appeal to the highest provincial level has been necessary to obtain approval. A few years ago the Ontario Straw Bale Coalition took steps towards creating a straw bale code for Canada, but the effort was abandoned due to lack of funding for testing. To date the NBCC has been prescriptive, but the 2005 NBCC was rewritten in "objective based" (performance-based) terms. Provincial adoption of this code could occur by the end of 2006. Presumably this would make it even easier to obtain approval for straw bale buildings.

Central America

Straw bale buildings have been built in Nicaragua, Costa Rica, and other Central American countries. Most, if not all, have been built in areas where there are no building codes or they are not readily enforced. In the less-industrialized regions rectangular bales are uncommon, and in tropical areas there is a strong preference for building with non-cellulosic materials that won't mold, such as masonry and concrete (see section 2.2.2: *Plastic and other Baled Materials*).

China

Hundreds of straw bale homes have been constructed in China over the last eight years, largely due to the efforts of American architect/builder Kelly Lerner. There is no straw bale code in China, but all straw bale structures there have been built with government approval. Kelly now reports that, during the Spring or Summer of 2006, the Department of Rural Construction in the Province of Hei Long Jiang will make blueprints available of five straw bale home designs that are winners of a recent design competition. Any local contractor or citizen who can pay for the land and construction may use them to build a home. These designs amount to government-sanctioned prescriptive straw bale prototypes. If successful, they could be a step towards a straw bale code.

Czech Republic

There are two known permitted straw bale buildings in the Czech Republic. Both are timber frame houses with straw bale infill, of which one is two-story. Typically, the local "Building Office" requires all proposed buildings (even a garden shed or an addition) to have drawings, a "technical report" by an authorized engineer or architect, a "fire safety report" by an authorized fire specialist, and statements from government departments regarding utilities, etc.

All materials used must have been tested and must have received an "agreement protocol," but there currently is no such certification for straw bales. Straw bales are not products of an authorized enterprise and their quality can't easily be standardized, so an agreement protocol may be difficult to achieve. However, for the current permitted buildings, well-known specialists were involved and the local authorities did not object. Also, there are now hopes of obtaining permission for a load-bearing straw bale building soon.

11.1C
FIRST STRAW BALE BUILDING WITH FULL "BUILDING PERMISSION" IN THE CZECH REPUBLIC (2002) IN MLADA BOLESLAV.

Exterior bales are insulation and finish.

photo courtesy of Petr Suske / SEA Architects

Denmark

In January of 2004, the Danish Building and Urban Research Institute published *BY og BYG Resultater 033 – Halmhuse.* This is the result of a straw bale test program overseen by civil engineer Jørgen Munch-Andersen, and is a compilation of those tests, other test references, and the resulting design guidelines. The document is over 60 pages, mostly in Danish, with 8 pages in English (sections on thermal performance and moisture). It is extensive and is filled with text, graphs, tables, photographs, and drawings documenting the testing and design guidelines.

Straw bale builder and advocate Lars Keller says, *"The Resultater 033 is not a Building Code per se, but being published by the one and only Institute in Denmark publishing these things, it is a very powerful thing to bring to your building inspector."* People in other Scandinavian countries such as Norway have utilized the Danish document in seeking approval for their straw bale buildings.

France

All building materials are allowed, as French legislation clearly states it is illegal to refuse a building permit on the grounds of a chosen material. Owner-builders of straw bale buildings appreciate this attitude, but among professional builders there is demand for a straw bale DTU (French building code), to make it easier to obtain insurance coverage. Some do not obtain the normal professional insurance for straw bale buildings, which some say is obligatory, and some say is not.

11.1D
KRACHT RESIDENCE,
WESTERLINDE, GERMANY
(2006)

*with straw bale wall
assembly that is
approved by the new
German Straw Bale
Code (adopted 2/06)
(split-image of finished/
unfinished building)*

photo courtesy of Stefan Kracht

Certain builders argue they should be insured when building with straw bales because they are insured when building with traditional materials that have no DTU, like stone or wattle-and-daub. There is recent word from one builder that an insurance company is willing to insure her straw bale work, and an effort currently underway to develop a straw bale DTU.

Germany

In February of 2006 Germany adopted a limited Straw Bale Code, only the second government-adopted straw bale code outside the United States. Although it only allows straw bales as insulating infill in a restrictive application, it has satisfied broader acceptance criteria in the process and constitutes a first step towards more general acceptance by the code body, the *Deutsches Institut für Bautechnik* (German Institute of Building Technology).

Prior to the recent code adoption, straw bale structures had been permitted only on a case-by-case basis. In this way building officials have approved at least 31 straw bale structures to date, based on test reports and certificates that establish material properties such as thermal conductivity, fire resistance, and flammability. These reports and certificates were also used as supporting evidence for the new code.

Greece

Greek citizens are very interested in straw bale building as word and practice spreads. Greek building officials are open to relatively new building systems, such as structural insulated panels (SIPs) and foam blocks with plaster finish; however, they are very resistant to the use of straw bales. This is largely due to the fact that property values (used for permit fee and tax purposes) are determined from the accepted euro value of the tradeswork used to construct each building. Straw bale construction has no such established value, so instead of determining one, building officials say that straw bales cannot be used for building.

As a consequence, what is done is either to build without government knowledge, or to present drawings for the permit showing the walls of the building made with conventional materials, such as concrete frame with hollow clay tile infill, for which straw bales are then substituted. This ploy works only in rural locations where permitted buildings are not inspected. In these cases, receipts are saved from the construction of the project (including borrowed receipts for the straw bale "hollow clay tile" walls), shown to the building official, and he or she approves the building. This is far from ideal, of course, and what is needed is for the unreasonable policy to be corrected.

11.1E
STRAW BALE RESIDENCE WITH CANE VAULT (2001), ISLAND OF RHODES, GREECE

photo courtesy of Chris Stafford

Ireland

The situation in Ireland is similar to that in the United Kingdom (see below). The Irish Building Regulations are guidelines, and while very similar to those of the UK, the architect or designer tends to carry most of the responsibility for ensuring that a building complies with the regulations. Also, inspections during construction can be relatively informal. There is apparently little difficulty gaining approval for straw bale buildings, whether load-bearing or infill.

Italy

There are only two known permitted straw bale buildings in Italy, both infill, but many more are planned. Builders are also preparing to seek approval for load-bearing straw bale, but Italian building codes are very rigid, and this may prove difficult.

Japan

The Japanese Building Code only mentions wood, masonry, steel, and concrete construction, although in 2002 it was changed to a performance-based code. Thus, if straw bale construction is shown to meet the structural performance criteria, it can be and has been used. Tea rooms, azumayas (garden rest places), and stockrooms less than 10 square meters do not need approval and can be freely built with straw bales or any other material.

Mexico

Most if not all straw bale buildings in Mexico have been constructed in areas where permits are not necessary. This includes Bill and Athena Steen's extensive work in Ciudad Obregon (see *www.caneloproject.com/pages/mexico.html*). In the suburban surrounds of Oaxaca, straw bale structures have been built without permits, under the loose assumption that they are not necessary because adobe construction there does not require a permit.

11.1F
STRAW BALE ARTIST'S
STUDIO (2003).
OAXACA, MEXICO

photo courtesy of Martin Hammer

Mongolia

As many as 50 straw bale homes and over a dozen straw bale health clinics have been constructed in Mongolia, most of them with government approval. In 1998 Kelly Lerner reported the beginning of work on a national straw bale code for Mongolia (see *The Last Straw* #24). She now reports this has not yet come to fruition, citing a difficult bureaucracy as much of the reason.

The Netherlands

In general there has been little trouble receiving building permission for straw bale buildings in the Netherlands. Most councils are supportive or even enthusiastic about ecological building projects. The difference between receiving permission or not depends mostly on whether or not the project is well documented. The straw bale codes from the United States are a good reference, but they are not fully enforced as long as one explains why departures from these codes have been made. Bruce King's book *Buildings of Earth and Straw* (1996) is another important supporting document, as is Catherine Wanek's video, *Building With Straw*, Volume 3, *Straw Bale Code Testing*.

New Zealand

Both the Building Research Association of New Zealand (BRANZ) and the Building Industry Authority (BIA) have issued advisory bulletins on straw bale construction (BRANZ *Bulletin #398*, March 2000; and *BIA News #125*, June 2002). Both are based largely on the work of pioneering architect Graeme North. North also wrote an article in BRANZ Build Magazine – Nov/Dec 1998, entitled "Guidelines for Strawbale Building in New Zealand." All three are used informally as straw bale guidelines in New Zealand. The BIA News document deals almost exclusively with moisture issues.

Russia/Siberia

There is no formal acceptance of straw bale construction, but some university professors and environmental non-profit organizations are advocating that straw bales be put on the National Building Materials List. (See also **Belarus**.)

Saudi Arabia

A farmhouse, library, mosque and gatekeeper house were designed by architects in Saudi Arabia, and then adapted to straw bale construction by Washington architect Chris Stafford. The designs were engineered and submitted to local officials as an informational courtesy, not for technical review and approval. Two years after his last construction review trip to Saudi Arabia, Chris designed two straw bale and natural material additions to the library/mosque project, a 450 square meter ladies' library and a 200-seat auditorium. These were approved in a similar way.

11.1G
STRAW BALE LIBRARY AND MOSQUE (2002), AL-GHAT, SAUDI ARABIA

photo courtesy of Chris Stafford

South Africa

There are three methods of permit approval in South Africa. One is through the South African Bureau of Standards (SABS) 0400 National Building Regulations (NBR). These regulations do not include straw bale construction, but they allow approval of indigenous materials if they are "deemed to satisfy" the conditions of the NBR. With the appointment of a structural engineer (who carries the structural liability) one can easily obtain building plan approval. More than 30 straw bale structures have been approved in this way, in almost all South African provinces. A second method, used for alternate or new building systems and known as an Agrément Certificate, is used with patented systems. As it involves extensive and expensive lab testing, it is not practical for generic types of construction like straw bale. The third method, known as "Rational Design," requires an engineer to demonstrate compliance with the National Building Regulations using tests or other codes or standards. This method requires extensive research and in-depth understanding of the SABS. Apparently no one has attempted this route for straw bale buildings.

New straw bale residences financed by banks are faced with another obstacle. Banks require new homes to be registered with The National Home Builders' Registration Council (NHBRC), a regulating body recently established to protect banks and consumers against construction defects for the first five years. However, the NHBRC has no provision for straw bale construction in its manual. It will not allow straw bale construction without an Agreement Certificate or an approved

Rational Design, and then only on a project-by-project basis. The NHBRC is also getting builders to register with them; once registered, builders must register any new home they build even if it is owner-financed. Should one need to sell one's house within the first five years of its construction, banks will not finance its purchase unless it carries an NHBRC certificate.

Because NHBRC regulations apply only to new homes, there is a loophole: building a starter house with conventional materials through sign-off and then doing the straw bale work as an alteration to an approved conventional home. There is one other possibility for large residential projects, where developer-managed loans obviate the need for NHRBC compliance and are sometimes made available to buyers. This has not yet been done for straw bale buildings, but has been with homes built with adobe.

As a result of all of these difficulties, almost all straw bale residences are currently owner-financed, and they are increasingly owner-built as well. There are a number of non-residential straw bale buildings in South Africa, including a game lodge, a meditation hall, and crèches. Because they are not encumbered by the NHBRC, non-residential straw bale buildings are often more easily realized than straw bale houses, but difficulties with financing and insurance (especially for fire during construction) have been reported.

**11.1H
BRODIE HOUSE,
SCARBOROUGH –
CAPE TOWN, SOUTH AFRICA**

photo courtesy of Andy Horn

South America

Relatively little straw bale construction has been documented in South America, although straw bale buildings have been constructed in Chile, Argentina, Uruguay, Peru, and probably other countries. As in Central America there is a strong preference for building with non-cellulosic materials that won't mold (see section 2.2.2: *Plastic and other Baled Materials*). Also, there is little demand for insulation for heating or cooling purposes, even in the higher elevations where heating is needed. The straw bale buildings to date have apparently been built without permits.

Spain

There are three known permitted straw bale residences in Spain. Two are load-bearing and one is post-and-beam. Residences must be designed and stamped by an architect and a "technical architect." To obtain a permit a project must first be approved by the area's *Colegio de Profesionales* (Board of Professionals). If the project is approved (some boards will not approve straw bale construction), the municipal government will usually issue a permit. At least 60 other straw bale residences have been constructed without permits in rural areas where permits are not required or codes are not rigorously enforced. At least as many agricultural and non-habitable straw bale buildings have been built with local permission, but such buildings do not require approval from the Board of Professionals.

11.1J
NITZKIN STRAW BALE RESIDENCE (2002), PALLARS JUSSA, LEIDA, SPAIN

photo courtesy of Rikki Nitzkin

A 1999 national law requires that new houses be insured against construction defects for ten years after construction, but most insurance companies will not insure straw bale structures. The few that do are more apt to insure post-and-beam structures. The law was revised in 2002 to exclude houses built for the owner's use, and the house can be sold without insurance if the new owner accepts in writing that it is uninsured. Still, all lenders require insurance, and those with "in-house" insurance do not insure straw bale buildings. Thus, straw bale houses in Spain tend to be owner-financed and owner-occupied, and are usually located where permits are not necessary. This may change, however, as more and more lenders and insurance companies are proving receptive to straw bale construction.

United Kingdom

In the United Kingdom, each Local Authority Building Control Department administers the National Building Regulations, which are guidelines for good building practice rather than a prescriptive code. This provides the opportunity to persuade the local building inspector to allow a type of design that is not included in the regulations. There is no mention of straw bale construction in the regulations, even though straw bale buildings have been built in the UK with full permission for over ten years. Nor is there any mention of *cob* (molded earth construction), though cob buildings have been built on those islands – and lasted – for hundreds of years.

In the last few years a change in the law has allowed competition within the Building Control system, and the Local Authority in which the building is located is no longer required to approve the design. This has resulted in the emergence of private companies authorized to give design approval and conduct site inspections to fulfill the obligations of the National Building Regulations. For the purposes of straw bale building and other sustainable types of construction, the leading company is JHAI Ltd, founded by Jon Hollely, who has been involved with straw bale construction in the UK from its beginnings. Another result from the change in the law is that national building contractors who build identical houses in many parts of the country can now work with a Local Authority of their choice who is able to approve all their buildings, regardless of location. Builders have now used this system to gain approvals for straw bale buildings, both load-bearing and infill, first locally and then throughout the country.

United States

With straw bale building originating and then being reborn in the United States, codes and permitting have had an earlier start than in the rest of the world. Still, only a relatively small number of jurisdictions within the United States have a true straw bale code, with the first one (Tucson/Pima County, Arizona) being adopted in January of 1996. In those jurisdictions, if a straw bale building complies with the straw bale code, then obtaining approval is no more difficult than with a conventional building that complies with the conventional building code.

A comprehensive Table of U.S. Straw Bale Codes, Guidelines, and Mandates follows in section 11.2. It reveals much about the way these straw bale codes are related, and allows easy reference to how each code stands on important issues such as which occupancies it applies to, whether load-bearing bale walls are allowed, and whether an engineer or architect is required.

Most U.S. straw bale codes were derived from the Tucson/Pima County, Arizona code, "Appendix Chapter 72 Straw-Bale Structures." That code was groundbreaking, and has served the cause of straw bale building well. However, the Tucson/Pima Code, its descendents, and the few unrelated U.S. straw bale codes inevitably contain flaws. These flaws have become evident over the last ten years as the practice and understanding of straw bale construction has evolved. They relate generally to requirements that are either too restrictive or not restrictive enough, or to issues that are simply not addressed. Certain requirements such as pinning and moisture barriers have proved problematic because with few exceptions they are unnecessary and/or detrimental.

In recent years, the most substantial movement forward with straw bale codes in the United States has occurred in California. The issues of pinning

11.1K
PRESENTATION CENTER STRAW BALE DINING HALL AND WELCOMING FACILITY, LOS GATOS, CALIFORNIA (2005)

Design and photo courtesy of Dan Smith & Associates, Architects

and moisture barriers were addressed in revisions to the voluntary California guidelines in 2002. Subsequently a draft Straw Bale Code has been developed by this author and others at the request of the California Department of Housing and Community Development (HCD). Although in places it borrows and extends historical straw bale code language, it is largely a new document, especially in the areas of structure and finishes. It is currently being considered for inclusion as an appendix to the 2007 California Building Code. If adopted by HCD, it would apply only to occupancies under HCD's jurisdiction, but would do so across the State, and could eventually be broadened to include other occupancies. It might also travel across state borders in the same way that the Tucson/Pima County code did. The latest draft of that document (as of the time of this book's publication) is included here as section 11.3. **(That portion of this book (section 11.3) is not encumbered by the copyright protection on the rest of the book, and may be used and reproduced as the reader wishes, but only with the clear understanding that it is very much a work in progress. Further amendments will surely change it before it becomes an official building code.)**

In New Mexico, preliminary discussions began in April of 2006 with the Construction Industries Division to allow load-bearing straw bale construction – currently prohibited – through a limited number of Experimental Permits. There is also discussion about changing the State Standards for Baled Straw Construction to explicitly allow load-bearing construction. The New Mexico code was developed parallel to the Tucson/Pima County code in the 1990s, so it, too, was groundbreaking, but it has to date been famously conservative for not allowing load-bearing construction.

In areas where there is no straw bale code, or if a design goes outside the limits of a straw bale code, the following factors are reported to have an effect on the ease or difficulty of permitting straw bale buildings:

- Approval is easier to obtain in rural areas than in urban areas.
- Residential approval (especially single-family) is easier than commercial, institutional, or other occupancies.
- Approval is easier in jurisdictions with a previously-permitted straw bale building, assuming the first ones were successful.
- Straw bale buildings designed and stamped by a licensed architect or engineer are more easily approved than those that are not.
- Treating the building official(s) as an ally, not an adversary, makes approval easier.
- Talking to the building official(s) to understand concerns at the very beginning of a project, before design begins, makes approval easier.
- Providing supporting documents to the building official(s) makes approval easier.

Supporting documents used to help obtain approval can take many forms. They can include testing results from organizations such as EBNet[A] or DCAT[B], various universities, straw bale organizations, or private individuals. They can also include articles from *The Last Straw*, straw bale videos, straw bale books, or other publications (ICC[C] *Building Standards* issue Sept.-Oct. 1998, contains an article specifically on straw bale construction). Straw bale organizations have sometimes created a collection of documents, such as the CASBA[D]'s *Building Officials' Guide to Straw-bale Construction*. Some professionals have assembled their own package of documents to present to building officials.

11.1.3 Where Do Straw Bale Codes Go from Here?

To codify or not to codify? This is the perplexing Shakespearean question for many straw bale designers and builders. Building codes are a double-edged sword for any material or method of construction because they allow and legitimize everything that is codified, but they also tend to restrict practice to *only* that which is codified. Codes also tend to create inertia and stifle innovation, both because of the industry's innate resistance to change, and because of the effort and costs required to bring a new material or method into the codes. For these reasons most

FOOTNOTES

A
Ecological Building Network
www.ecobuildnetwork.org

B
Development Center for Appropriate Technology
www.dcat.net/

C
International Code Council
www.iccsafe.org/

D
California Straw Building Association
www.strawbuilding.org

codes worldwide are routinely updated every two to four years in order to accommodate our ever-evolving understanding of good building practice, and of the materials and techniques with which we build.

A strong argument can be made against a straw bale code simply because straw bale construction is still in a formative stage. Any straw bale code will enshrine – and many already have – methods, materials, or systems of building with bales that we now know to be unnecessary or even detrimental. Furthermore, codification tends to impede further exploration of new uses and methods, or to restrict the clarification of both minimum and best practice.

There is substance to arguments against codification, but our belief is that the benefits of a well-written straw bale code far outweigh any detriments. Although most people report that obtaining permission to build a straw bale building is not especially difficult, whether there's a code, a guideline, or nothing at all (especially after the first straw bale structure has been completed in a jurisdiction), one still hears of the occasional permitting horror story or long drawn-out battle. Also, there are straw bale buildings that we may or may not know about that have been built poorly due to lack of enforced minimum standards – that is, for lack of a code.

In Mongolia, for example, a fire started because of bare copper electrical wire laid in loose straw insulation in an attic (See *The Last Straw* #44, page 35). This gained much media attention and an undeserved regional bad name for straw bale that has been difficult to reverse. Such an event would be unlikely to occur with an enforced straw bale code that addressed such an issue. In addition, a government-adopted code goes a long way towards satisfying the insurance and finance industries, both of which justifiably require their own assurances of the efficacy and safety of straw bale construction. Codes also establish credibility in the eyes of building officials and members of the general public, and they demand and focus testing, scrutiny, and understanding in the course of their own development.

Creating a well-written code is no easy task, however. It requires extensive knowledge, broad experience, foresight, wisdom, skill, and more. No single person has all of that, and thus it requires thorough peer review from as many perspectives as possible. It is a document of both singular vision and broad consensus. It can be either or both prescriptive and performance-based wherever appropriate. It should clearly allow for alternatives that are not in its own language, and allow performance paths to minimize obstacles to innovation and best practice. It should be user-friendly for designers, engineers, building officials, builders, owners, and occupants. Most of all, it should friendly to straw bale building itself.

Because building codes fit within the structure of governmental authority, they have historically been created and/or adopted at the national, state/provincial, or local governmental level. And, although there are recognized international standards (e.g., ISO[E] and ASTM[F] standards), and various code organizations are aware of and sometimes borrow from each other, building codes have rarely been fully utilized across national borders. To a large extent this is reflective of the fact that construction itself is very much a product of local culture and locally-available materials. But, as building professionals, materials, labor, and products move across national boundaries with increasing regularity, that is changing. The development and publication of the Eurocodes will be complete in 2006, for example, and their adoption throughout Europe will occur from 2007 to 2010. They are also being promoted for use worldwide. The content of the Eurocodes is primarily structural, with some content relating to fire.

In the United States, the three longstanding regional code organizations were consolidated over the past decade into the International Code Council (ICC), which publishes the International Building Code (IBC) along with its entire series of 'I' Codes. The use of "International" in the name seems to some presumptuous, but was in fact born out of requests from abroad during the development of the I-codes, and they are thus intended to have applicability beyond the United States. There is a memorandum of understanding between the ICC and Mexico regarding their proposed use of the International Residential Code. This year Saudi Arabia will begin using the IBC (90% intact) as well as the International Fire and Mechanical Codes. The ICC has offices in Argentina (where Spanish translations are being made) and Puerto Rico, and chapters in Canada and Kenya.

The relevant point here is that getting straw bale construction into model codes like the IBC or the Eurocodes could pay large dividends in terms of broad adoption, use, and acceptance. In addition, the major model codes tend to reflect and encourage the increasing use of "modern" (meaning fossil fuel-based) industrial-

FOOTNOTES

E
International Organizatin for Standardization

F
American Society for Testing and Materials

ized building materials and systems, so it is especially important that more environmentally-friendly materials and systems such as straw bales make their way into these codes.

There are three avenues by which to establish acceptance of straw bale construction (or any other building material, method, or system) by the ICC Codes:

- **ICC Evaluation Report** An Evaluation Report is used as evidence of minimum compliance with the Code (e.g., to submit to one or more jurisdictions). ICC Evaluation Services establishes acceptance criteria that meet ICC standards. Where no ICC standard exists, one must be created through public hearings. Testing that complies with those criteria is conducted, and the applicant pays for the testing and the report. The report only evaluates what is tested, so this route is very limited and/or extremely expensive. As such, it is not an appropriate path for straw bale construction.

- **Reference Standard** A Reference Standard is created through a peer review process under the auspices of a recognized standards organization, such as ASTM or ISO. It can then be adopted by reference into a code.

- **Code Change Proposal** A Code Change Proposal can be made by any individual or organization. Proposals are accepted every 18 months. This period relates to the three-year interval of the ICC Code editions as well as the publication of supplements halfway in between. Proposals are evaluated by committees via a public hearing process at which the proponent testifies, as well as others in favor or opposed.

The effort to obtain incorporation into the IBC or other international codes is enormous in terms of time, effort, and funding. Yet it is clearly the appropriate goal for straw bale construction, and for construction using other natural building materials and methods. That said, it is extremely important that any such code be done "right" – with insight regarding the implications in the field, and the code's applicability to all combinations of climate, seismic risk, and available material and technology throughout the world. It should allow for all legitimate applications, while assuring a minimum standard of safety and longevity. Supportive testing should be conducted to meet the highest testing standards. This is a tall order, but should certainly be the goal. Otherwise there will continue to be unnecessary duplication of effort, lack of uniformity where it is needed, and confusion or conflict. Parallel to such broad efforts, straw bale codes should continue trying to gain footholds where they can, and where local or regional need demands them.

11.2 Table of Straw Bale Building Codes, Guidelines, and Mandates in the United States

As adopted by state, county, or city governments in order of adoption date. Current through June, 2006.

Jurisdiction	Dated Adopted	Code, Guidelines, or Mandate	Derived[1] from Tuscon/ Pima County Code?	Applies to which occupancies	Load-bearing allowed?	Pinning required?	Engineer[2] or Architect[2] required?
New Mexico – Strawbale Construction Experimental Permits	12/17/93	Mandate[3]	NA	R-3, U	No	unstated	Yes
Utah – Grand County – Straw Bale Construction Policy of Requirements	4/94	Guidelines[4]	No[5]	R-3, U[6]	No	No	Yes
Nevada - AB171/NRS278.580 - Straw Bale Guidelines 1995	1995	Mandate[7]	NA	unstated	unstated	unstated	unstated
California - Guidelines for Straw-Bale Structures (SB332/HS18944)	10/15/95 (rev. 4/02)[8]	Guidelines or Code[9]	Yes	All	Yes	No[10]	No[11]
California – Napa County[12] – Chapter 15.06 – Guidelines for Use of Baled Rice Straw (Buildings and Construction)	1/1/96	Code	Yes	All	Yes	Yes	No
Arizona – Tucson / Pima County – Appendix Chapter 72 Straw-Bale Structures	1/2/96	Code	-	All	Yes[13]	Yes	No
New Mexico – 14NMAC11.9 – Standards for Non-loadbearing Baled Straw Construction	1/19/96 10/15/97	Guidelines, Code[14]	No[15]	R-3, U	No[16]	Yes	Yes
Texas – Austin – Chapter 36 – Straw Bale Construction	8/21/97	Code	Yes	All	Yes[13]	Yes	No

Jurisdiction	Dated Adopted	Code, Guidelines, or Mandate	Derived[1] from Tuscon/ Pima County Code?	Applies to which occupancies	Load-bearing allowed?	Pinning required?	Engineer[2] or Architect[2] required?
Colorado – **Cortez** – Load Bearing & Non-Load Bearing Combined Prescriptive Standard for Straw Bale Construction	1/13/98	Code	Yes	All	Yes[13]	Yes	No
Colorado – **Boulder** – Chapter 98 – Baled Straw Structures	3/98	Code	Yes	R-3, U / All[17]		Yes	No[17]
Arizona – **Maricopa County** – Straw-Bale Structures	2/17/99	Code	Yes	All	Yes13	Yes	No
Oregon – State Residential Code Appendix[18] M – Straw-Bale Structures	4/1/00 (rev. 4/01)[19]	Code	Yes[20]	R-3[21], U	Yes	Yes[22]	No
Nebraska – **McCook** – Chapter 9-201 Straw-Bale Structures	1/11/03	Code	Yes[23]	R-3, U / All[17]	Yes	Yes	No[17]
Arizona – **Yavapai County** – PB-11 Straw Bale Building Code for Yavapai County	8/26/04	Code	Yes	All	Yes	Yes	No
Arizona – **Cochise County** – Resolution 04-117	12/04	Mandate[24]	NA	All	unstated	unstated	unstated
Colorado – **Paonia** – Ordinance 2005-11	9/13/05	Code	No	R-3, U	No	Yes	Yes
PROPOSED STRAW BALE CODES – NOT ADOPTED TO DATE:							
Pennsylvania – **Easton** – Strawbale Ordinance Amendment[25]	-	(Code)	No	R, U	No	Yes[26]	No
Arizona – **Cochise County** – Straw Bale Structures[27]	-	(Code)	Yes[28]	R-3, U / All	Yes[13]	Yes[30]	No
California – Appendix L - Strawbale Construction[31]		(Code)	No	R[32]	Yes	No	No

11

BUILDING CODES AND STANDARDS

FOOTNOTES

1   Directly or indirectly.

2   Licensed to practice in that State.

3   Construction Industries Commission approves issue of up to 20 Experimental Permits (10 were issued) for "straw bale construction residences." This is in addition to 6 permits C.I.C. granted in 1991, and the permit for Virginia Carabelli's residence, widely and long considered to be the first permitted straw bale building anywhere. The first permitted straw bale building is now known to be Clark Sanders' meditation hall/retreat in Kortright, New York in 1989.

4   An eight-point list of requirements, including an administrative requirement that a notarized letter release the County of responsibility for the experimental portions of the project.

5   Written by County Building Official Jeff Whitney and Roger Evans who was ICBO President at the time.

6   Although not explicitly restricted to single-family residences, County Building Official Jeff Whitney indicates the County would have "real heartburn with other occupancies."

7   Stating - "A local governing body shall permit the use of straw in the construction of a structure..., to the extent the local climate allows."

8   Revisions include no pinning and no moisture barrier required if designed by an architect or engineer.

9   The Guidelines are voluntary, and must be adopted at the local level to be utilized or enforced as part of the local Code. They are commonly modified in the local adoption process. In practice, the Guidelines are also used informally by many jurisdictions without being officially adopted.

10   If designed by an architect or engineer.

11   Required if no pinning is used, or if no moisture barrier is installed between bales and plaster.

12   By adopting the voluntary California Guidelines with an effective date of 1/1/96, Napa County, CA became the first jurisdiction anywhere to have a Straw Bale Building Code. It did so one day ahead of Tucson/Pima County, AZ, whose language it was based on. Numerous other Counties, Cities and Townships in California have since adopted the Guidelines into their local Building Code, often with modifications.

13   R-3 and U occupancies only.

14   Approved on 1/19/96 by the Construction Industries Commission, but was not adopted into the NM State Code until 10/15/97 by the Construction Industries Division. Between those dates, the C.I.D. modified the Code Draft to require stucco mesh in cement plasters, and attempted to require moisture barriers on bale walls, which they were persuaded not to do. Also between those dates, and as early as 1994, the Draft was used as a guideline for the straw bale buildings with experimental permits.

15   Although communication and sharing occurred between straw bale advocates in Arizona and New Mexico, both Codes were largely created in parallel. Different attitudes from respective State building officials, as well as different regional ways of building, were factors. This includes the differences between the commonly available 2-string bale in NM, versus the commonly available 3-string bale in AZ.

16 In April 2006 the Straw Bale Construction Association in NM approached the C.I.C. with a request for "experimental" load-bearing permits, and to consider incorporating load-bearing into the Code. These requests are being considered at press time.

17 Is limited to R-3 or U, one story, max. roof span of 32', unless structural design is by an architect or engineer.

18 Although it is an Appendix, it is mandatory for all jurisdictions in the State, as is the entire Oregon Building Code.

19 Revised to apply to one-family dwellings only (two-family removed). Also removed acceptance of 1-hour fire-resistive rating for plastered straw balewalls.

20 Base primarily on the Tucson/Pima County Code, but also the New Mexico Code and the California Guidelines.

21 Revised in 2001 to apply to one-family dwellings only (two-family removed). Other occupancies are allowed and have been permitted under Sec. 104.11

22 Reduced to one prescriptive method of pinning.

23 McCook used Boulder, Colorado's Straw Bale Code (which was derived from Tucson/Pima) as its basis, partly because of similarity in climate.

24 Board of Supervisors - "Whereas, the Board encourages the use of appropriate alternative construction methods, such as strawbale and rammed earth; the Building Official has the authority to approve alternative construction standards..., and...has acceptable guidelines for alternative construction standards that will be made available..., so that the adoption of these Codes will not unduly restrict the use of these alternative building methods;"

25 Proposed as an Ordinance Amendment for a Habitat for Humanity project of 10 strawbale units. Before adoption of the Amendment, it was decided that the Habitat units would not be built with straw bales, so the proposed Strawbale Ordinance is on indefinite hold.

26 Pinning with bamboo or wood dowels only (no steel pins).

27 Steve Kemble proposed this Straw Bale Code to the County. Adoption was recommended, but because it was not written by a National Code Agency, adoption was legally possible only if the largest City in the County, Sierra Vista, agreed to adopt the code. Sierra Vista refused. Resolution 04-117 was adopted instead. See footnote 24.

28 With numerous changes, and the addition of alternative tie-downs, roof-bearing assemblies, and methods of pinning.

29 Non-loadbearing only.

30 Allows/prescribes external pinning in addition to internal pinning methods.

31 Requested by the Dept. of Housing and Community Development for all occupancies in their purview. Would replace the California Guidelines for those occupancies only. Non-binding: this is in review process at time of publication of this book – see section 11.3 for text.

32 Includes R-1, R-2, R-3, R-4, and U occupancies and any use or occupancy secondary and appurtenant to those occupancies.

11.3 Draft Straw Bale Code for Inclusion in the California Building Code

Note: *This document is being developed at the request of the California Department of Housing and Community De-velopment. It is proposed as an Appendix to the 2007 California Building Code (CBC), which is an amended version of the 2006 International Building Code (IBC). Chapters and sections of the 2007 CBC (and 2006 IBC) are referred to in this proposed Appendix.* **This is a draft document, having not yet been through all of the requisite reviews and approvals involved in becoming part of the CBC. It is likely to undergo modification before and if adopted.**

APPENDIX L

STRAW BALE CONSTRUCTION 4/26/06

SECTION L101
GENERAL

L101.1 Scope. This appendix shall govern the use of baled straw as a building material, and shall apply to Group R occupancies, Group U occupancies and other occupancies when secondary and appurtenant to Group R or Group U occupancies. Unless stated otherwise in this appendix, all other provisions in this code shall apply to structures using baled straw as a building material.

L101.2 General. Within the provisions of this appendix, straw bales may be used as a structural or non-structural material. Structural uses include elements designed to support gravity loads, and elements designed to resist in-plane wind and seismic loads. Non-structural uses include, but are not limited to, infill walls, insulation, landscape walls, and benches.

L101.3 Alternatives. Alternatives to the provisions in this appendix may be used where the building of-ficial finds the proposed design complies with the intent of this appendix and this code.

SECTION L102
DEFINITIONS

L102.1 General. The following words and terms shall, for the purposes of this appendix, have the meanings shown herein. Refer to Chapter 2 for general definitions.

L102.2 Definitions

Bale. Equivalent to "straw bale" for the purposes of this appendix.

Flake. A slab of straw removed from an untied bale. In particular, an intact slab (3-5" thick) (76-127mm) as created by the baling machine.

Laid Flat. Stacking bales so the sides with the largest area are horizontal, and the longest dimension of this area is parallel with the wall plane.

Laid On-edge. Stacking bales so the sides with the largest area are vertical and the longest dimension of this area is horizontal and parallel with the wall plane.

Loadbearing. A strawbale wall or other element which bears the gravity loads (dead and live) of the roof and/or floor above. (compare with "Structural")

Mesh. An openwork fabric of linked strands of metal, plastic, or natural fiber, embedded in plaster to provide tensile reinforcement and/or bonding. (also sometimes lath)

Moisture Barrier. A continuous barrier capable of stopping the passage of water.

Non-Loadbearing. (see non-structural)

Non-Structural. A strawbale wall or other element which supports only its own weight, and may resist out-of-plane lateral loads.

Pins. Metal rod, wood dowel, or bamboo, driven into, or secured on the surface of stacked bales for purposes of connection or stability.

Plaster. Gypsum, lime, lime-cement, or cement plasters, as defined by this code and Section L106 of this appendix, or clay plaster and earth-cement plaster as defined in Section L106.9 and L106.10.

Running Bond. The placement of straw bales such that the head joints in successive courses are offset at least one quarter the bale length.

Skin. The compilation of plaster and reinforcing, if any, on the surface of stacked bales.

Structural. A strawbale wall or other element.which supports gravity loads (dead and live) and/or resists in-plane lateral loads.

Stack Bond. The placement of straw bales such that head joints in successive courses are vertically aligned.

Straw. The dry stems of cereal grains left after the seed heads have been substantially removed.

Straw Bale. A rectangular compressed block of straw, bound by polypropylene strings or baling wire.

Strawbale. The adjective form of straw bale.

Straw-clay. A mix of loose straw and clay binder.

Three-String Bale. A straw bale bound by three strings or wires. Typically with approximate dimensions of 15" x 23" x 42 to 48" long. (380mm x 584mm x 1066 to 1219mm)

Truth Window. An area of a strawbale wall left without its finish, to allow view of the straw otherwise concealed by its finish.

Two-String Bale. A straw bale bound by two strings or wires. Typically with approximate dimensions of 16" or 14"" x 18" x 36 to 45" long (406mm or 356mm x 457mm x 914 to 1143mm)

Vapor-Permeable Membrane. A material or covering having a permeance rating of 5 perms or greater, when tested in accordance with the dessicant method using Procedure A of ASTM E 96. A vapor-permeable material permits the passage of moisture vapor. (This definition is shown for convenience and is identical to that shown in Chapter 2)

Vapor Retarder. A vapor-resistant material, membrane or covering such as foil, plastic sheeting or insulation facing having a permeance rating of 1 perm or less, when tested in accordance with the dessicant method using Procedure A of ASTM E 96. Vapor retarders limit the amount of moisture vapor that passes through a material or wall assembly. (This definition is shown for convenience and is identical to that shown in Chapter 2)

SECTION L103
BALES

L103.1 Shape. Bales shall be rectangular in shape. However, the use of non-rectangular bales, such as circular bales, is not precluded.

L103.2 Size. Bales used within a continuous wall shall be of consistent height and width to ensure even distribution of loads within the wall system.

L103.3 Ties. Bales shall be bound with ties of polypropylene string or baling wire. Bales with broken or loose ties shall be firmly retied.

L103.4 Moisture content. The moisture content of bales, at the time of procurement, and at the time of application of the first coat of plaster or installation of an other weather protective finish, shall not exceed 20 percent of the total weight of the bale. The moisture content of bales shall be determined by use of a moisture meter designed for use with baled straw or hay, equipped with a probe of sufficient length to reach the center of the bale, or by other acceptable means. At least ten bales, and not less than 5 percent, randomly selected from the bales to be used, may be tested to determine if all of the bales for the building are of acceptable moisture content.

L103.5 Density. Bales shall have a minimum dry density of 6.0 pounds per cubic foot (92 kg/cubic meter). The dry density shall be determined by reducing the actual bale weight by the weight of the moisture content in pounds (kg), and dividing by the volume of the bale in cubic feet (cubic meters). At least five bales, and not less than 2 percent, randomly selected from the bales to be used, may be tested to determine if all of the bales for the building are of acceptable density.

L103.6 Partial bales. Custom-made partial bales shall be firmly retied, and where possible use the same number of ties as the standard size bales.

L103.7 Types of straw. Bales of various types of straw, including wheat, rice, rye, barley, oat, and similar grain plants, shall be acceptable if they meet the minimum requirements of this Section for density, shape, moisture content, and ties. Bales of hay and other grasses containing seed shall not be used as a building material.

L103.8 Protection of bales prior to installation. Bales shall be stored in such a manner as to protect them from weather and other sources of moisture damage.

L103.9 Unacceptable bales. Bales which show signs of damage due to moisture, including but not limited to mold or fungus growth, or associated discoloration, even if they are of an acceptable moisture content and density, shall not be used.

SECTION L104
MOISTURE

L104.1 General. All weather-exposed bale walls, other weather-exposed bale elements, and bale walls enclosing showers or steam rooms, shall be protected from water damage.

L104.2 Moisture content of bales. (See L103.4)

L104.3 Moisture barriers and vapor retarders. Plastered bale walls may be constructed without any membrane barrier between straw and plaster, in order to facilitate transpiration of moisture from the bales, and to secure a structural bond between straw and plaster, except as allowed or required elsewhere in this appendix. No vapor retarder shall be used on bale walls, nor shall any other material be used which has a vapor permeance rating of less than 5 perms, except as permitted elsewhere in this appendix, or as demonstrated to be necessary by an architect or engineer.

L104.4 Horizontal surfaces. Bale walls and other bale elements shall have a moisture barrier at all horizontal surfaces exposed to the weather. This moisture barrier shall be of a material and installation that will prevent water from entering the wall system or other bale element. These horizontal surfaces include, but are not limited to, exterior window sills, sills at exterior niches, bale vaults and arches, tops of landscape walls, and weather-exposed benches. The finish material at all "horizontal" surfaces shall be sloped a minimum of 1"/ft.(8%) and shall drain away from all bale walls or elements. If the moisture barrier is below the finish material, it shall be sloped a minimum of 1"/ft. (8%) and shall drain beyond the outside vertical surface of the bale's vertical finish wherever practicable.

L104.5 Parapets – prohibited. Parapets made of straw bales are prohibited.

L104.6 Bale/Concrete separation. There shall be a moisture barrier and a capillary break between bales and supporting concrete. The moisture barrier may be any durable sheet or liquid applied membrane that is impervious to water. The capillary break may be gravel or other material that prevents the wicking of moisture across that material and into the bale. Where bales abut a concrete or masonry wall that retains earth, there shall be a moisture barrier between that wall and the bales.

L104.7 Separation of plaster and earth. Exterior plaster skins applied to straw bales shall be separated from the earth a minimum of 6" (152mm).

L104.8 Moisture barrier at plaster support. Where supported by the foundation at its bottom edge, there shall be a moisture barrier between the exterior plaster skin and the foundation.

L104.9 Shower walls, steam rooms. Bale walls enclosing showers, bathtub/shower combinations, or steam rooms shall be protected by a moisture barrier and may be protected by a vapor retarder.

L104.10 Paints and sealers. No paint, sealer, or other finish with a permeance of less than 5 perms shall be applied to plasters or other finish covering a bale wall or other bale element, unless demonstrated to be necessary by an architect or engineer.

SECTION L105
STRUCTURE

L105.1 Scope. Buildings constructed with straw bales shall comply with this Section, and with all other structural provisions of this code unless stated otherwise in this appendix.

L105.2 General. Strawbale buildings may use any type of structural system allowed by this code and this appendix.

L105.3 Foundations. Foundations for strawbale walls and other straw bale elements may be of any foundation type permitted by this code. Such foundations shall comply with Chapter 18, and shall be designed to allow design loads from the skins, bales, and any structural framing at the base of the wall to pass into the ground.

L105.4 Alternate foundations. Alternate foundations and foundation systems may be used, if designed by an architect or engineer.

L105.5 Wall height. Structural and non-structural strawbale walls shall be limited by a 6:1 ratio of stacked bale height to bale width, unless otherwise shown by an architect or engineer to adequately resist buckling from gravity loads and out of plane seismic and wind loads. Walls may exceed this height limitation by having a structural element restraining the wall horizontally, at or below the height limitation, as designed by an architect or engineer.

L105.6 Configuration of bales. Bales may be laid flat or on-edge as limited in height by L105.5. Bales in walls with reinforced plasters may be in a running or stack bond. Bales in walls with unreinforced plaster shall be in a running bond only.

L105.7 Pre-compression of strawbale walls.
    L105.7.1 When not required:
        a) For non-structural walls.
        b) For walls designed or allowed to resist lateral forces only.
        c) For walls bearing gravity roof loads, when the full dead load of the roof is imposed and remains on the wall for at least 28 days before plastering. No design snow load greater than 20 psf (80kg/sq.m) is allowed. No floor loads may be supported by walls which are not pre-compressed.
    L105.7.2 When required. All walls bearing gravity loads, which are not described in L105.6.1, shall be pre-compressed to a force equal to or greater than the design loads on the wall.

L105.8 Voids and stuffing. Voids in the field of structural strawbale walls shall be limited to 6" (152mm) in width, and shall be firmly stuffed with flakes of straw or with straw-clay, before the application of plaster.

L105.9 Plaster skins.
    L105.9.1 General. Plaster skins on structural walls may be of any type allowed by Section L106, except gypsum plaster, and shall also be limited by Table L105-A, and Table L105-B.
    L105.9.2 Straightness. On structural walls, plaster skins shall be straight, as a function of the bale wall surface they are applied to, as follows:
        a) Across the face of a bale – Straw bulges shall not protrude more than ¾" (19mm) across 2' (610mm) of its height or length.
        b) Across the face of a bale wall – Straw bulges shall not protrude from the vertical plane of a bale wall more than 2½" (64mm) over 8' (2438mm).
        c) Offset of bales – The vertical face of adjacent bales may not be offset more than ¾" (19mm)

L105.9.3 Plaster and membranes. Structural bale walls shall have no membrane between straw and plaster, or shall have sufficient attachment through the bale wall from one plaster skin to the other, as designed by an architect or engineer. See also L106.5 and L106.6

L105.10 Transfer of loads into plaster skins. When plastered strawbale walls are used to bear gravity and/or lateral loads, such loads shall be transferred into the plaster skins by direct bearing or by other adequate transfer mechanism.

L105.11 Support of plaster skins.
L105.11.1 For structural walls. Plaster skins for structural strawbale walls shall be continuously supported along their bottom edge to allow a load path into the foundation system. Acceptable supports include, but are not limited to: concrete or masonry footing, concrete slab, wood-framed floor adequately blocked, wood beam, or steel angle adequately anchored. A conventional metal or plastic weep screed is not an acceptable support.
L105.11.2 For non-structural walls. Plaster skins for non-structural walls need not be supported along their bottom edge.

TABLE L105-A
ALLOWABLE GRAVITY LOADS (POUNDS PER FOOT) FOR PLASTERED STRAWBALE WALLS

WALL PLASTER[a]		SILL PLATES[bc]	ANCHOR[c] BOLTS (or other sill fastening)	MESH[d]	STAPLES[efg]	ALLOWABLE BEARING CAPACITY[h]
A	clay[i]	c	c	none required[j]	none required[j]	300
B	soil-cement[k]	c	c	d	e,f,g	800
C	lime	c	c	d	e,f,g	450
D	cement-lime	c	c	d	e,f,g	800
E	portland cement[l]	c	c	d	e,f,g	800

For SI: 1 inch=25.4mm, 1 pound per foot = 14.5939 N/m.

a   Plasters shall conform with L106.9 through L106.14 for makeup and thickness, with L105.9.2 for straightness, and with L105.11 for support of plaster skins.
b   Sill plates shall support and be flush with each face of the bale wall.
c   For walls supporting gravity loads only (or for non-structural walls), use sill plates and fastening as required for framed walls in 2308.2 and 2308.3. See Table L105-B for requirements for shear walls and braced panel walls.
d   May be any metal mesh allowed by this code, and must be installed throughout the plaster with minimum 4" laps. Fasten with staples per footnote e.
e   Staples shall be at maximum spacing of 2" o.c., to roof or floor bearing assembly, or as shown necessary to transfer loads into the plaster skins per L105.10, and at a maximum spacing of 4" o.c. to sill plates.
f   Staples shall be gun staples (stainless steel or electro-galvanized, 16 gauge with 1 1/4" legs, 7/16" crown) or manually driven staples (galvanized 15 gauge with 7/8" legs, 3/16" inner spread and rounded shoulder). Other staples may be used as designed by an architect or engineer.
g   Staples shall be firmly driven, diagonally across mesh intersections at spacing indicated.For walls with a different plaster on each side, use the lower value.
h   For walls with a different plaster on each side, use the lower value.
i   Mimimum 1 1/2" thickness. Building official may require a compression test to demonstrate a minimum 100 psi compressive strength.
j   Except as necessary to transfer roof or floor loads into the plaster skins per L105.10.
k   Minimum 1 1/2" thickness. Building official may require a compression test to demonstrate a minimum 1000 psi compressive strength.
l   Containing lime as described in L106.14.

TABLE L105-B

ALLOWABLE SHEAR (POUNDS PER FOOT) FOR PLASTERED STRAWBALE WALLS

WALL	PLASTER[a] (both sides)	SILL PLATES[b]	ANCHOR[c] BOLTS (on center)	MESH[d]	STAPLES[efg] (on center)	ALLOWABLE SHEAR[hi]
A1	clay[j]	2x4	2'-8"	none	none	100
A2	clay[j]	2x4	2'-8"	3"x3" knotted hemp	3"	120
A3	clay[j]	4x4	2'-0"	2"x2" high-density polypropylene	2"	180
B	soil-cement[l]	4x4	2'-0"	2"x2" 14 ga[k]	2"	300
C1	lime	2x4	2'-8"	17ga.woven wire	4"	200
C2	lime	4x4	2'-0"	2"x2" 14 ga[k]	2"	250
D1	cement-lime	4x4	2'-8"	17ga.woven wire	2"	400
D2	cement-lime	4x4	2'-0"	2"x2" 14 ga[k]	2"	450
E1	portland cement[m]	4x4	2'-8"	17ga.woven wire	2"	400
E2	portland cement[m]	4x4	2'-0"	2"x2" 14 ga[k]	2"	600

For SI: 1 inch=25.4mm, 1 pound per foot = 14.5939 N/m

a   Plasters shall conform with L106.9 through L106.14 for makeup and thickness, with L105.9.2 for straightness, and with L105.11 for support of plaster skins.
b   Sill plates shall be Douglas fir-larch or southern pine and shall be ammonia-free preservative-treated if in contact with concrete or masonry slabs or foundation walls. Multiply allowable shear value by .82 for other species with specific gravity of .42 or greater, or by .65 for all other species.
c   Anchor bolts shall be 5/8" diameter with 2"x2"x3/16" washers, with minimum 7" embedment in concrete foundation. Anchor bolts or other fasteners into framed floors shall be designed by an architect or engineer.
d   Mesh shall run continuous vertically from sill plate to top plate, roof or floor beam, or roof or floor bearing assembly, or shall lap a minimum 12". Horizontal laps shall be minimum 4". Steel mesh shall be galvanized.
e   Staples shall be gun staples (stainless steel or electro-galvanized, 16 gauge with 1 1/4" legs, 7/16" crown) or manually driven staples (galvanized 15 gauge with 7/8" legs, 3/16" inner spread and rounded shoulder). Other staples may be used as designed by an architect or engineer.
f   Staples at spacing indicated to boundary conditions including sill plate, and top plate, roof or floor beam, or roof or floor bearing assembly, and any vertical boundary framing.
g   Staples shall be firmly driven, diagonally across mesh intersections at spacing indicated.
h   Values shown are for aspect ratios of 1:1 or smaller. Reduce values shown to 50% for the limit of a 2:1 aspect ratio. Linear interpolation is allowed for ratios between 1:1 and 2:1. The full value shown may be used for aspect ratios greater than 1:1, if an additional band of mesh is installed at the base of the wall to a height where the remainder of the wall has an aspect ratio of 1:1 or less, and the second mesh is fastened to the sill plate with the required stapling, and the sill bolt spacing is decreased with linear interpolation between1:1 and 2:1.
i   For walls with a plaster type A on one side and any other plaster type on the other side, the architect or engineer must show transfer of the design lateral load into the stiffer type B, C, D, or E plaster only, and 50% of the allowable shear value shown for that wall type shall be used.
j   Minimum 1 1/2" thickness. Building official may require a compression test to demonstrate a minimum 100 psi compressive strength.
k   16 gauge mesh may be used with a reduction to .85 of the allowable shear values shown.
l   Minimum 1 1/2" thickness. Building official may require a compression test to demonstrate a minimum 1000psi compressive strength.
m   Containing lime as described in L106.14.

L105.14 Resistance to out-of-plane lateral loads. Plastered strawbale walls are capable of withstanding out-of-plane design loads prescribed in this code with the following limitations:

1. Walls with reinforced plasters shall be limited by a 6:1 ratio of stacked bale height to bale width per L105.5.
2. Walls with unreinforced plasters shall be limited by a 4:1 ratio of stacked bale height to bale width.
3. Walls with unreinforced plasters or no plaster, and with internal or external pins, shall be limited by a 6:1 ratio of stacked bale height to bale width. Pins may be ½" (13mm) diameter steel, wood or bamboo. Internal pins shall be installed vertically at a maximum 2' (61mm) spacing into the bales from top course to bottom course, with the bottom course being connected to its support similarly with pins or other approved means. Pins may be continuous or may overlap through one bale course. External pins shall have full lateral bearing on the sill plate and the roof or floor bearing member, and shall be tightly tied through the wall to an opposing pin with polypropylene string at 30" maximum spacing.

L105.15 Prescriptive design using structural strawbale walls.

L105.15.1 General. Plastered strawbale walls may be used structurally, without design by an architect or engineer, as described in this subsection. Such walls shall also comply with L105.5 through L105.11, and 105.14 of this Section and shall comply with other Sections of this appendix as applicable.

L105.15.2 Load and other limitations. As described in 2308.2 - 3 through 7, and 2308.2.2.

L105.15.3 Gravity load bearing walls. Limited to wall types B, C, D, and E in Table L105-A. Type A walls may be used if they are demonstrated to support design loads no greater than the allowable load.

L105.15.4 Braced panels. Strawbale shear walls may be used as braced panels per the requirements and limitations in 2308.9.3 Bracing, and per 2308.12 Additional requirements for conventional construction in Seismic Design Category D or E. Strawbale shear wall types B, C, D, and E, shown in Table L105-B, may be used in situations where braced wall panel types 2., 3., 4., 6., and 7. are allowed. Strawbale shear wall type A may be use in situations where braced wall panel types 1. and 5. are allowed.

L105.16 Connection of framed walls to strawbale walls. Framed walls perpendicular to, or at an angle to a straw bale wall assembly, need only be fastened to the bottom and top wood members of the strawbale wall per framing connections permissible in this code. Where such connection is not possible, the abutting stud shall be connected to alternating straw bale courses with a 1/2" (1.25cm) diameter steel, wood, or bamboo dowel with minimum 8" (20cm) penetration.

L105.17 Alternate Performance Design Criteria. When plastered strawbale walls or other elements are engineered, they may use the model of restrained, thin shell, reinforced concrete, as in the American Concrete Institute's ACI-318 Manual. This model may be used for all reinforced plasters, including those without cement. Such design and analysis shall be made in accordance with the following:

a) General. Strawbale structural systems and elements shall be designed using engineering principles, fundamental engineering behavior, and principles of mechanics.

b) Rationality. Strawbale structural elements shall be designed based on a rational analysis in accordance with established principles of mechanics. These elements shall provide a complete load path capable of transferring all loads and forces from their point of origin to the load-resisting elements based on a rational connection of components.

c) System Characteristics. Strength, stiffness and toughness (ductility) characteristics, of the bales and their skins, shall be considered in the design of the system.

SECTION L106
FINISHES

L106.1 General. Finishes applied to strawbale walls may be of any type permitted by this code, and shall comply with this Section and the provisions of Chapter 14 and Chapter 25 unless stated otherwise in this Section.

L106.2 Purpose, and where required. Strawbale walls and other strawbale elements shall be finished so as to provide mechanical and fire protection of the bales, restrict the passage of air through the bales, and to protect them from weather.
  Exception: Truth windows are allowed, but shall be protected from weather.

L106.3 Vapor retarders. No vapor retarder may be used on a bale wall, nor shall any other material be used which has a vapor permeance rating of less than 5 perms, except as permitted elsewhere in this appendix, or as demonstrated to be necessary by an architect or engineer.

L106.4 Plaster. Plaster applied to bales may be of any type described in this section.

L106.5 Plaster and membranes. Plaster may be applied directly to strawbale walls and other strawbale elements, in order to facilitate transpiration of moisture from the bales, and to secure a mechanical bond between the skin and the bales, except where a membrane is allowed or required elsewhere in this appendix. Structural bale walls shall have no membrane between straw and plaster, or shall have sufficient attachment through the bale wall from one plaster skin to the other, as designed by an architect or engineer.

L106.6 Lath and mesh for plaster. In strawbale construction the surface of the straw bales functions as lath, and no other lath or mesh is necessary, except as required for tensile strength of the plaster and/or wall assembly in particular structural applications (see Section L105). Straw bales laid flat or on-edge provide a sufficient mechanical bonding surface between plaster and straw.

L106.7 Plaster on non-structural walls. Plaster on walls that do not carry gravity loads, and are not designed to resist in-plane lateral forces, may be any plaster as described in this Section.

L106.8 Plaster on structural walls. Plaster on structural walls shall comply with L105.9 through L105.11. Plaster on walls that carry gravity loads shall comply with Table L105-A. Plaster on walls designed to resist in-plane lateral forces, shall comply with Table L105-B.

L106.9 Clay plaster. (Also known commonly as earth or earthen plaster)
  L106.9.1 General. Clay plaster is any plaster whose binder is comprised primarily of clay. Clay plasters may also contain sand or other inert granular material, and may contain reinforcing fibers. Acceptable reinforcing fibers include, but are not limited to, chopped straw, hemp fiber, nylon fiber, and animal hair.
  L106.9.2 Mesh. Clay plaster may have no mesh, or may use a natural fiber mesh, corrosion-resistant metal mesh, or high-density polypropylene mesh.
  L106.9.3 Thickness. Clay plaster shall be a minimum 1" (25mm) thick, unless required to be thicker for structure or fire-resistance, as described elsewhere in this appendix.
  L106.9.4 Rain-exposed. Clay plaster, where exposed to rain, shall be finished with lime plaster, or other erosion resistant finish.
  L106.9.5 Prohibited finish coat. Cement plaster and cement-lime plaster are prohibited as a finish coat over clay plasters

L106.9.6 Additives. Additives may be used to increase the plaster's workability, durability, strength, or water resistance.

L106.9.7 Separation of wood and clay plaster. No separation or moisture barrier is required between untreated wood and clay plaster.

L106.10 Earth-cement plaster. (Also known commonly as soil-cement, stabilized earth, or pise')

L106.10.1 General. Earth-cement plaster is comprised of earth (free of organic matter) and Portland cement, and may include sand or other inert granular material, and may contain reinforcing fibers.

L106.10.2 Mesh. Earth-cement plaster shall use any corrosion-resistant metal mesh permitted by this code, and as described in Section L105 if used on a structural wall.

L106.10.3 Thickness. Earth-cement plaster shall be a minimum of 1½" (38mm) thick.

L106.11 Gypsum plaster.

L106.11.1 General. Gypsum plaster shall comply with Section 2511 of this code.

LL06.11.2 Restriction of use. Gypsum plaster is limited to use on interior surfaces, and on non-structural walls, except as a finish coat over an allowed structural plaster.

L106.12 Lime plaster.

L106.12.1 General. Lime plaster is any plaster whose binder is comprised primarily of calcium hydroxide (CaOH). This includes Type N or Type S hydrated lime, natural hydraulic lime, or quicklime. Lime plasters shall comply with ASTM Standards C5 and C206. The plaster may be applied in 2 coats, provided that the combined thickness is at least 7/8" (22mm), and each coat is no greater than 5/8" (16mm).

L106.13 Cement-lime plaster.

L106.13.1 General. Cement-lime plaster shall comply with Section 2508 of the 1997 UBC, except that the plaster may be applied in 2 coats, provided that the combined thickness is at least 7/8" (22mm), and each coat is no greater than 5/8" (16mm).

L106.14 Portland cement plaster.

L106.14.1 General. Portland cement plaster shall comply with Section 2512 of this code, except that the amount of lime in all plaster coats shall be a minimum of 1 part lime per 6 parts cement so as to allow a minimum acceptable vapor permeability. The plaster may be applied in 2 coats, provided that the combined thickness is at least 7/8" (22mm), and each coat is no greater than 5/8" (16mm). The combined thickness of all plaster coats shall be no more than 1½" (38m).

L106.15 Alternate plasters. Plasters, or variations, which do not fit in any other category described in this Section, may be allowed if such plasters are demonstrated to be appropriate for the particular application.

L106.16 Finishes over plaster. Other finishes, as permitted elsewhere in this code, may be applied over the plaster, except as prohibited in L106.17.

L106.17 Prohibited plasters and finishes. Any plaster or finish with a cumulative perm rating of <5 perms is prohibited on straw bale walls or other bale elements, unless demonstrated to be necessary by an architect or engineer.

L106.18 Separation of wood and plaster. Where wood framing or wood sheathing occur in strawbale walls, such wood surfaces shall be separated from any plaster finish with No. 15 asphalt felt, grade 'D' paper, or other approved material per Section 1404.2 of this code, unless the wood is preservative-treated or naturally durable.

Exception: Clay plasters. See L106.9.7

SECTION L107
FIRE-RESISTANCE

L107.1 Fire-resistance rating.

L107.2.1 Rating with plaster finish. Plastered strawbale walls have a 1-hour fire-resistance rating, provided the components of the wall fit within the following parameters:

a)   Bales may be laid flat or on-edge.
b)   The bale wall must have a minimum unplastered thickness of 12" (304mm).
c)   Bales may be installed in a running bond or stack bond, but vertical joints in a stack bond, and continuous vertical gaps at any posts within both types of wall, must be fire-stopped with straw-clay, or equivalent.
d)   The wall must be finished on both sides and exposed ends with a plaster of any type allowed by this appendix, and clay plasters must be a minimum 1 ½" (38mm) thick, and a minimum of 2 layers.

L107.2.2 Rating with other finishes. Strawbale walls covered with finish materials other than, or in addition to plaster, shall be deemed to have the equivalent fire resistive rating as wood-frame construction covered with the same finish materials.

L107.3 Permitted in types of construction. Strawbale walls with a 1-hour fire-resistance rating per Section L107.2 are permitted wherever combustible 1-hour walls are allowed by Chapter 6. Such walls and unrated strawbale walls with any finish allowed by this code are permitted wherever combustible no-hour walls are allowed by Chapter 6.

L107.4 Openings in rated walls. Openings and penetrations in any strawbale wall rated and required to be rated for a particular fire-resistance rating and for a particular application, shall satisfy the same requirements for openings and penetrations in walls with the same fire-resistance rating and application as stated elsewhere in this code.

L107.5 Clearance to fireplaces and chimneys. Strawbale surfaces adjacent to fireplaces or chimneys shall have a minimum 1/4" (6mm) thick plaster coat of any type permitted by this appendix, and shall maintain the specified clearances to the plaster finish as required to combustibles in Sections 2111, 2112, and 2113, or as required by manufacturers of prefabricated fireplaces and chimneys, or as required to combustibles elsewhere in this code.

SECTION L108
ELECTRICAL

L108.1 Scope. Wiring and other elements of the electrical system, within or on bale walls, shall comply with all Sections of this code which govern electrical systems and with the California Electrical Code, unless otherwise stated in this Section.

L108.2 Wiring. Type NM or UF cable may be used, or wiring may be run in metallic or non-metallic conduit. Wiring which is unprotected by conduit shall be installed a minimum of 2" (50mm) from the face of the bale, except as necessary to enter or exit a junction box. The wiring shall be pushed into joints between bales, or into the bale itself, or the bales may be channeled to receive the wire.

L108.3 Wiring attachment. Where not held securely between bales or within a bale, and not attached via staples to a wood member, wiring on straw bale walls shall be attached with minimum 17 ga. wire in a 'U' configuration, with minimum 8" (203mm) long legs, as needed to comply with minimum attachment requirements specified elsewhere in this code and in the California Electrical Code.

L108.4 Attachment of electrical boxes. Electrical boxes on bale walls shall be securely fastened to non-bale structural elements, or to wooden stakes driven a minimum of 12" (304mm) into the bales, or shall be secured by the combination of wire mesh and plaster, or by an acceptable equivalent method.

L108.5 Attachment of service and subpanels. Electrical service and subpanels on bale walls shall be securely fastened to wood structural members, or to other wood members which have been adequately fastened to the straw bales.

TOOLS AND RESOURCES

If we were to list all the straw bale construction resources currently available – books, videos, DVDs, websites, Internet listservs, people, tools, and straw bale organizations worldwide – we would be adding ten more pages of fine type here. We would, in other words, be replicating the annually-updated *Resource Guide* published by The Green Prairie Foundation for Sustainability, publishers of the quarterly journal *The Last Straw (TLS)*. We think it better just to direct your attention their way, both to subscribe to *The Last Straw,* and to explore their website as much as you like:

photo courtesy of Dan Smith & Associates

The Last Straw Journal
The Green Prairie Foundation for Sustainability
PO Box 22706
Lincoln, Nebraska 68542-2706
USA
(402) 483-5135
www.thelaststraw.org

About Green Building Press
the art and science of building well

The term "green building" has entered the popular lexicon recently, though not in any well-defined way. Like beauty, its significance is in the eye of the beholder. For some, the term requires articulating in detail the philosophy and goals of "sustainable" or "regenerative" design, and there is already a vigorous and healthy public discourse on what those terms might connote. For others, green building means healthy, non-toxic building interiors that don't poison their occupants, or a vigorous switch away from fossil-fuel dependence to energy-efficiency and renewable energy sources, or even the radical notion that the shape, materials, and electromagnetic fields of buildings have effects, rarely quantifiable, on the physical, emotional and spiritual well-being of occupants – effects that deserve more than a little scrutiny. There are also those who measure the effects of buildings on their immediate environs as a benchmark of greenness – heat island effects in cities (where most humans now live), urban runoff effects on waterways, and the effects of the construction industry, in its immense scale and variety, on the planet-wide ecosystem that is unmetaphorically our life support system.

All of the above deserves serious attention, but it is not material for Green Building Press – though, to one degree or another, all such discussions form the intellectual corpus that underlies and overarches our work. There is theory and there is practice; we are about practice – we seek to put useful tools and information in the hands of those who design and construct buildings. We seek to specifically identify where our regular ways of building are in fact harmful or just don't work, and then specifically describe viable improvements. Others have written passionately, extensively, and articulately on the need to save at least a few patches of wild forest from the axe; we write of alternatives – there are many! – to using wood in buildings. Others may write the obscure but necessary academic papers on, say, variations on chloride-ion permeability of early-age concrete mixes containing varying amounts of fly ash; we write about improving concrete for the builder who has to pour 1600 cubic yards of foundation in the next three weeks or face ruinous financial penalties. That builder may not even know what chloride-ion permeability is; what matters is getting a lot of mud into the forms without breaking the pumps, losing strength, or creating excessive void pockets. It is, to the best of our ability, to that person that we address our work, as well as to the engineers and architects straightjacketed by the "standard of care" and overwhelmingly compelled by legal, cultural, and psychological forces to keep doing what everyone else is doing.

We – the builders, architects, and engineers who write for Green Building Press – see ways to improve the way we build, and we seek to bring those to your attention in the simplest and easiest-to-use ways we can. Just as we cannot live without causing harm, from the worms and insects we step on to the cows and cabbages we eat, we cannot build without causing harm. But we can look for ways to cause the *least* harm in our work, and even to build in a manner that regenerates life and landscapes; this is what we mean by "improve." We see this simply as good business. If nothing else, we seek to respect our descendants and the world they will inherit. Recognize and learn from our mistakes, then correct and move forward; that is the art and science of building well.

We invite and welcome your comments:

www.greenbuildingpress.com

Also from Green Building Press:
Making Better Concrete
*Guidelines to Using Fly Ash for
Higher Quality, Eco-Friendly Structures*

*The country is ruined: yet
mountains and rivers remain.
It's spring in the walled town,
the grass growing wild.*

– Tu Fu (712–770)